Postcard History Series

West Central Georgia
in Vintage Postcards

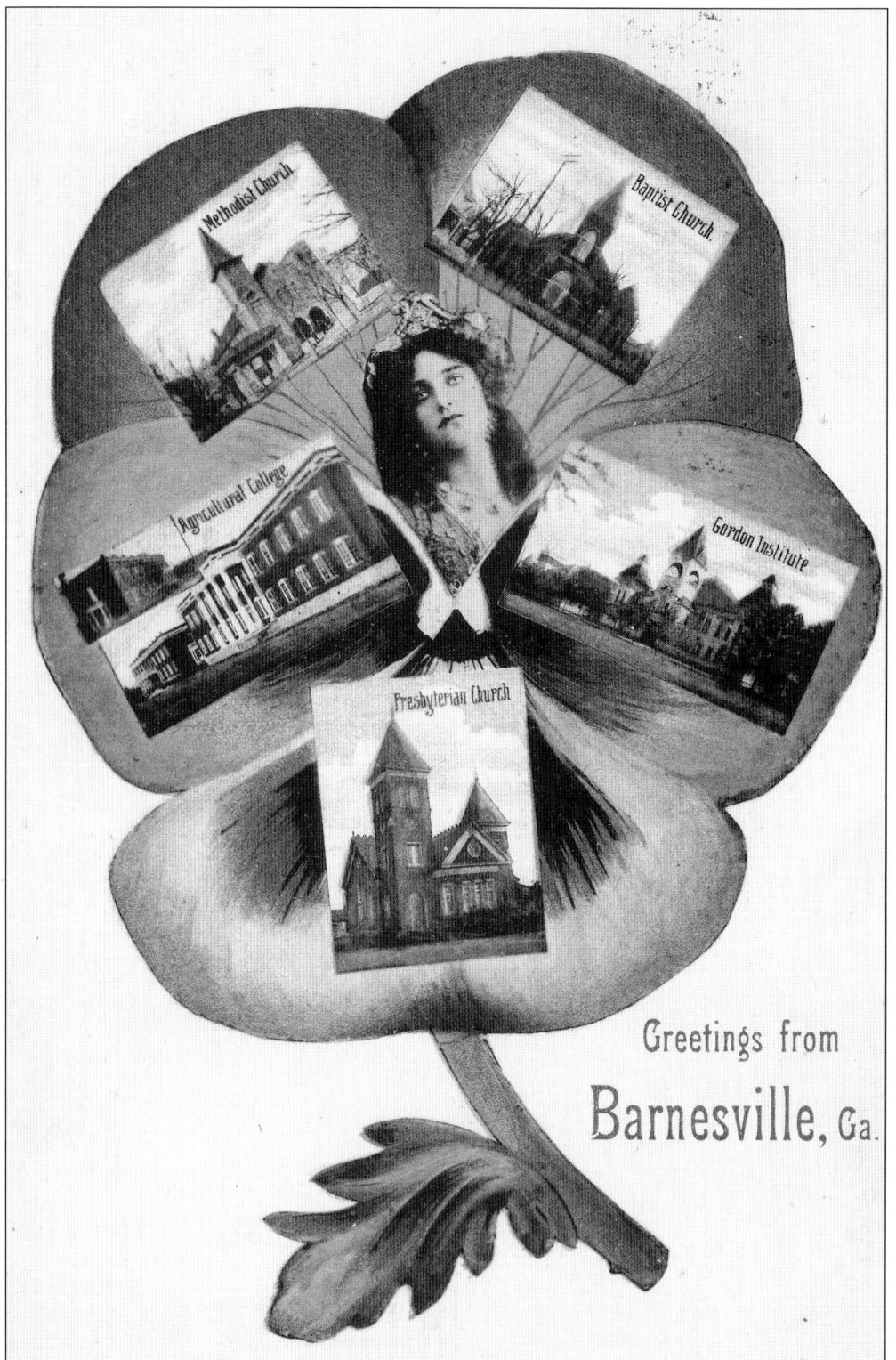

POSTCARD HISTORY SERIES

West Central Georgia
in Vintage Postcards

Gary L. Doster

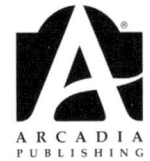

ARCADIA
PUBLISHING

Copyright © 1998 by Gary L. Doster
ISBN 978-0-7385-6895-9

Published by Arcadia Publishing
Charleston SC, Chicago IL, Portsmouth NH, San Francisco CA

Printed in the United States of America

Library of Congress Catalog Card Number: 98-88057

For all general information contact Arcadia Publishing at:
Telephone 843-853-2070
Fax 843-853-0044
E-Mail sales@arcadiapublishing.com
For customer service and orders:
Toll-Free 1-888-313-2665

Visit us on the Internet at www.arcadiapublishing.com

For Faye Thomas Doster
The Best Person I Have Ever Known

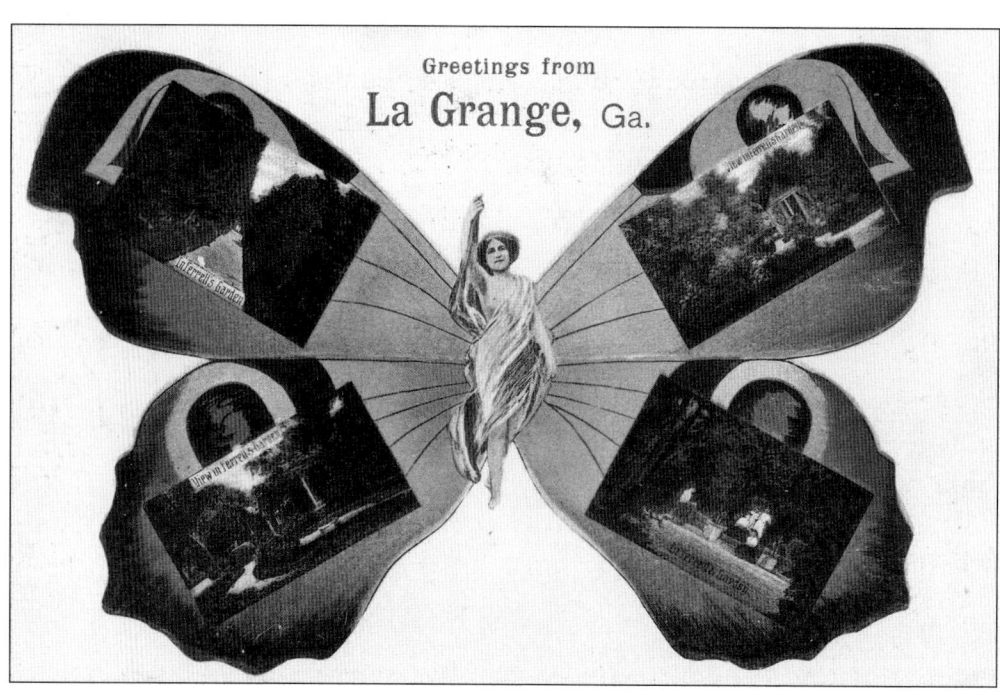

Contents

Acknowledgments		6
Introduction		7
1.	Columbus and Environs	9
2.	Macon and Environs	23
3.	Butts County	37
4.	Clayton, Coweta, Heard, and Henry Counties	57
5.	Crawford, Houston, Macon, Peach, Schley, Talbot, and Taylor Counties	67
6.	Harris, Merriwether, and Troup Counties	83
7.	Lamar, Pike, Upson, Monroe, and Spalding Counties	105
Bibliography		127
Index		128

Acknowledgments

For help in various ways, including advice, information, and post cards, I wish to thank the following people:

Carl Anderson
Jim Dunn
Nell Dunn
Jerald Ledbetter
Ernest Malcom
Dan Marshall
Bill Moffat
Edwin Oldham
Hershel Reeves
Gordon Sanford
Bill Wheless
Charlotte Marshall
George Marshall
Gordon Sanford
Sue Fan Tate
Jeff West

Introduction

We are indeed fortunate that post cards* were invented and were so popular during the first several years of this century. In the clamor to satisfy the almost overwhelming demand for more and more post cards by the public, literally thousands of scenes were photographed that were never captured on film for any other reason. Over time, many of the homes, depots, courthouses, stores, and other buildings so pictured have disappeared and these early post card views are the only images that remain. Two particularly interesting facts that were discovered while selecting and compiling the cards for these books concerned Georgia's Confederate monuments. A great many monuments were unveiled or dedicated on Confederate Memorial Day, April 26, and few of them remain on their original sites. The ladies of the United Daughters of the Confederacy and the old veterans themselves usually selected some prominent spot in the middle of town, almost always at the intersection of two main streets. Invariably, as automobile use increased over years, the monuments became traffic hazards and were moved to another part of town. Consequently, many of these post card views are the only pictures of them in their original locations.

Also of great interest are the views showing the intrusion of the automobile onto the scene. It is fun to note that the earlier post card views, those before 1907 or 1908, usually have horse- or mule-drawn wagons, buggies, or carriages in the street scenes (a few even show mule-powered streetcars!). Then, from that time to about 1912 or 1914, these views will typically show a mix of the animal-drawn vehicles and early automobiles. After this time, a wagon or buggy is only rarely seen, and the number of automobiles on the streets increased rapidly.

The collecting frenzy that swept the world began in Europe in the 1890s,

---

*Throughout the book, I have chosen to use the older spelling of the word, i.e. "post card" versus "postcard."

crept into this country before the turn of the century, and erupted a few years later. Many of the better quality post cards were produced in Europe, particularly Germany. Some of the post card factories in Germany were the size of cotton mills in this country, and they employed hundreds of people. For example, one German plant in 1909 had 112 cylinder printing presses and employed 1,500 workers. During the peak years of the post card collecting fad, more than a million people in Germany were employed in the post card business. In the three-year period from 1907 to 1909, more than 85,000 tons of post cards were imported into the United States from Germany.

In the Images of America book series published by Arcadia, the major effort has been to render pictorial books on individual towns or counties. And these are wonderful. Those of us who have an interest in preserving whatever we can of our past are hungry for books like this and they serve a valuable purpose. However, there are hundreds of smaller communities across every state that offer only a limited number of views of life of yesteryear that also are striking and important. Some medium-sized towns may have a handful of good views that show what their community and its people looked like nearly one hundred years ago. Many of the very small towns may have only one or two representative views. All of these are important, but none of them can support a book alone. Hence, this series of six volumes was conceived to provide a vehicle whereby a collection of early Georgia post cards from numerous small communities could be exhibited.

It is important to note here that this set of books is not intended to be any sort of scholarly work. It is merely an attempt to provide access to a selection of early views of Georgia that are not available in any other form, most of which have not been reprinted since their original publication. Many of the captions we provide in these books are no more than the caption printed on the cards when they were produced. Some additions have been made to some cards when the author had knowledge of some facts regarding the view in question. Other information came from the few reference books listed in the bibliography. To have researched each view and provided a comprehensive caption for each would have taken a lifetime of research, and then would still have been incomplete.

The author is a lifelong Georgian and has collected all manner of Georgiana for most of his life. Some of his other collecting interests are obsolete currency from the Colonial period through the War between the States, early letters and other documents, slave bills of sale and other items pertaining to slavery, Confederate letters and documents, old photographs, trade tokens, and Native-American relics.

One
COLUMBUS AND ENVIRONS

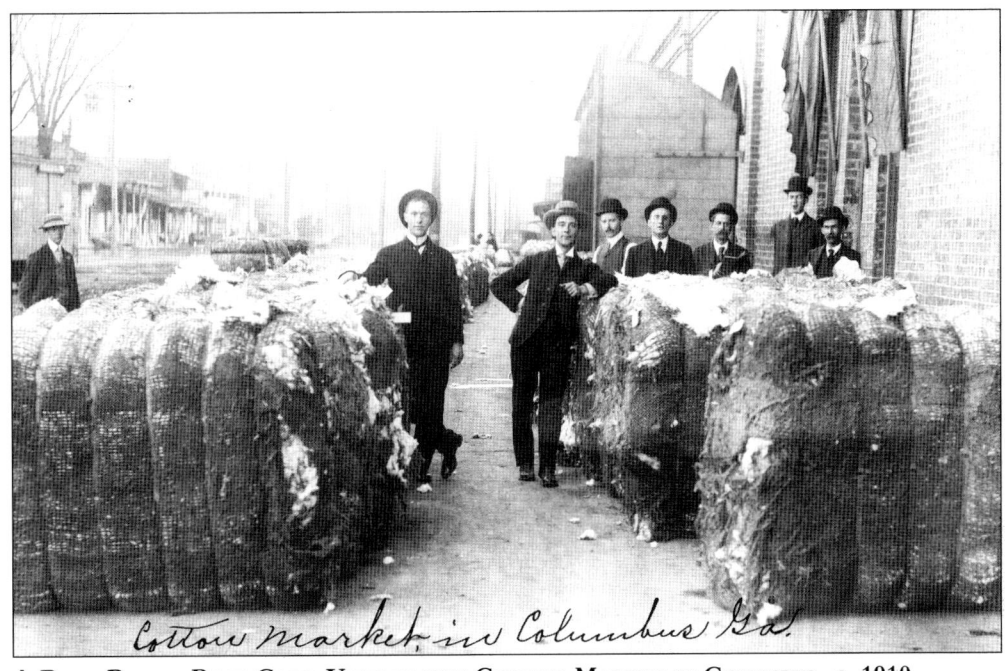

A REAL-PHOTO POST CARD VIEW OF THE COTTON MARKET IN COLUMBUS, C. 1910.

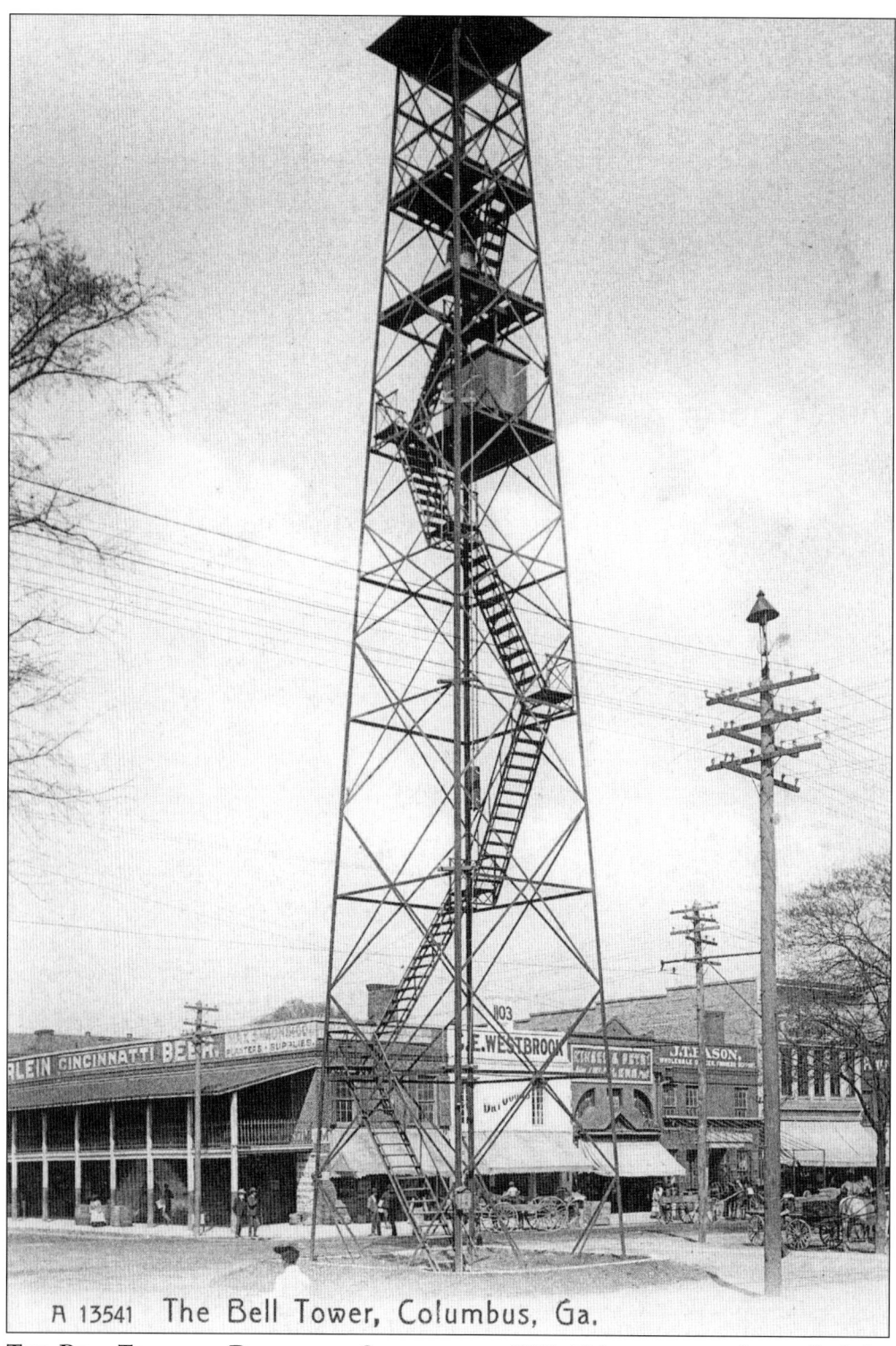

THE BELL TOWER IN DOWNTOWN COLUMBUS, C. 1905. This tower must have afforded a magnificent view of the surrounding countryside for anyone with the nerve to climb to the top.

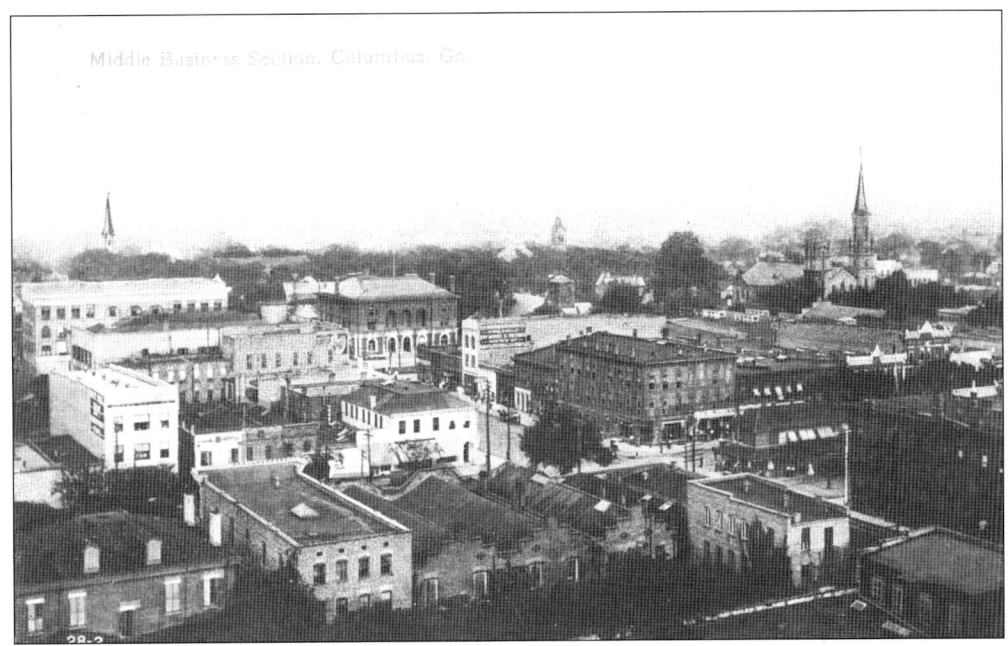

A Bird's-eye View of the Middle Business Section of Columbus.

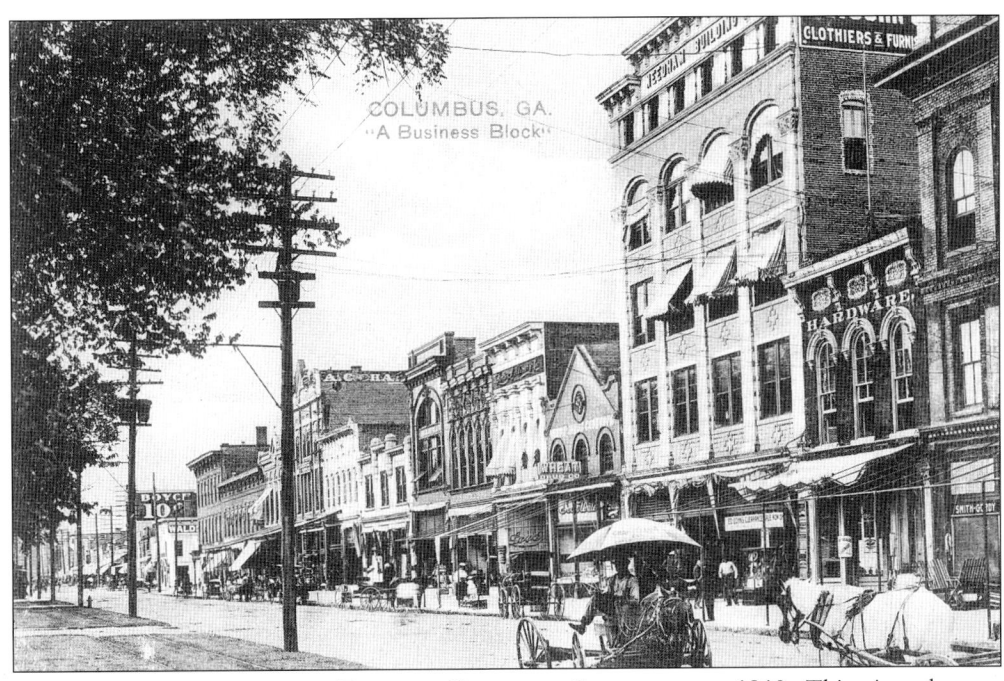

A Street-level View of a Business Block in Columbus, c. 1910. This view shows a modern-looking, progressive town.

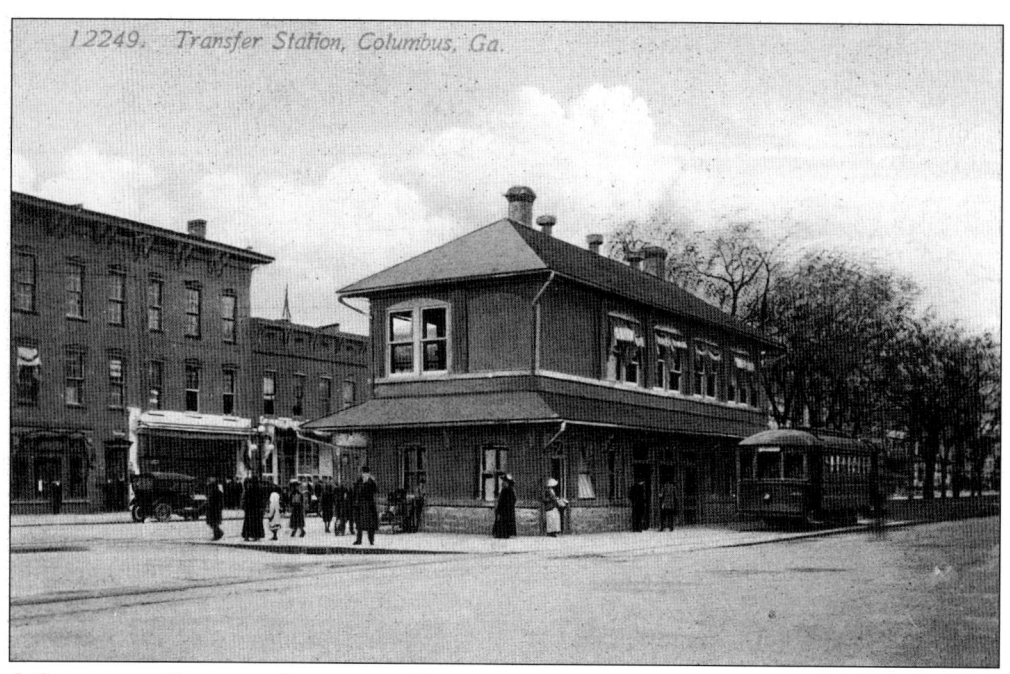

A STREETCAR TRANSFER STATION IN COLUMBUS.

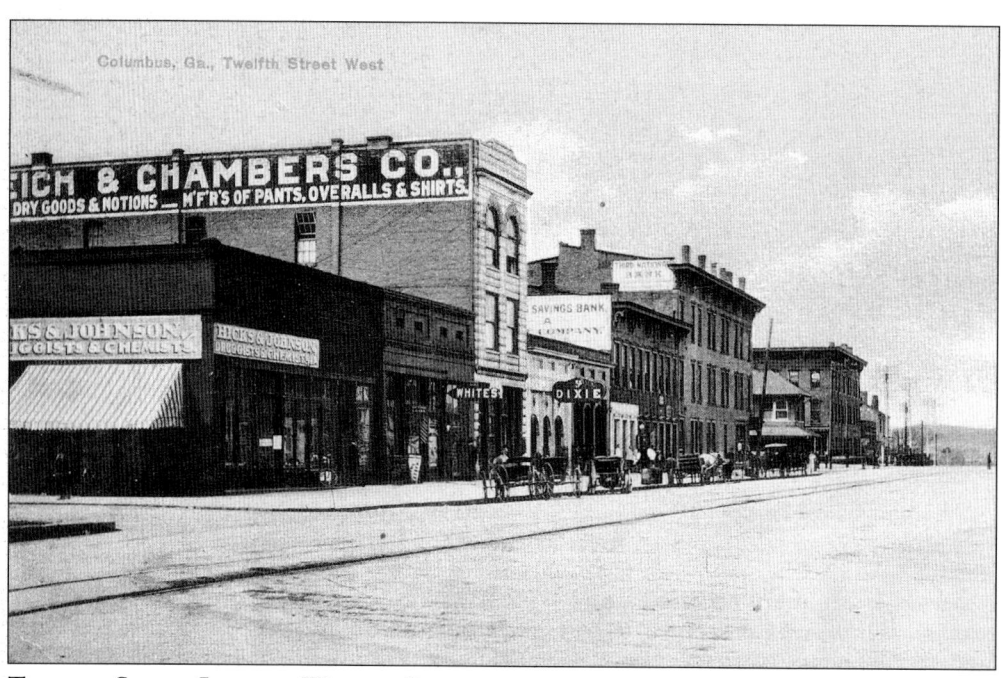

TWELFTH STREET LOOKING WEST IN COLUMBUS.

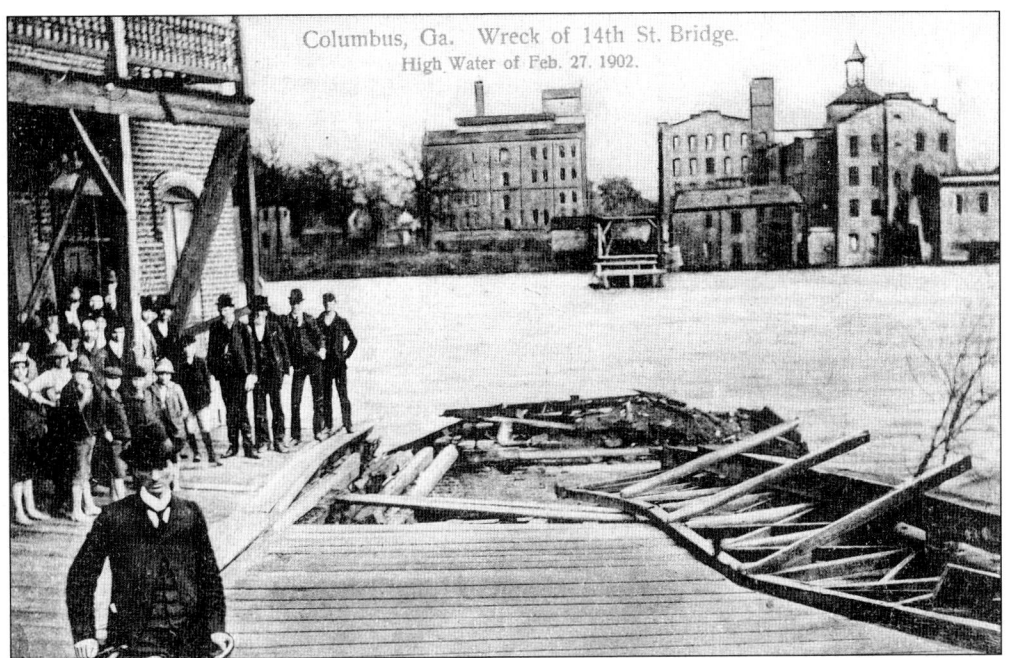

An Exciting View of the Remains of the Fourteenth Street Bridge, which Crossed the Chattahoochee River in Columbus after It Was Destroyed by High Water February 27, 1902.

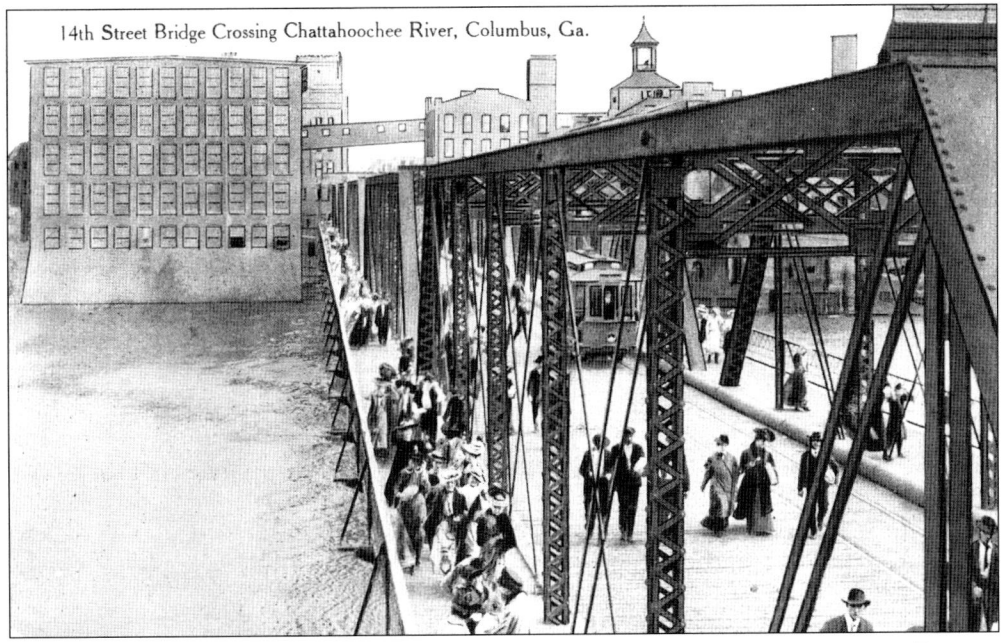

The New Steel Fourteenth Street Bridge That Replaced the Old Wooden Bridge. In additions to pedestrians, automobiles crossed the bridge and here can be seen a city streetcar. A sign over each end of the new bridge warned: "$5.00 fine for going faster that a walk. Pedestrians and vehicles."

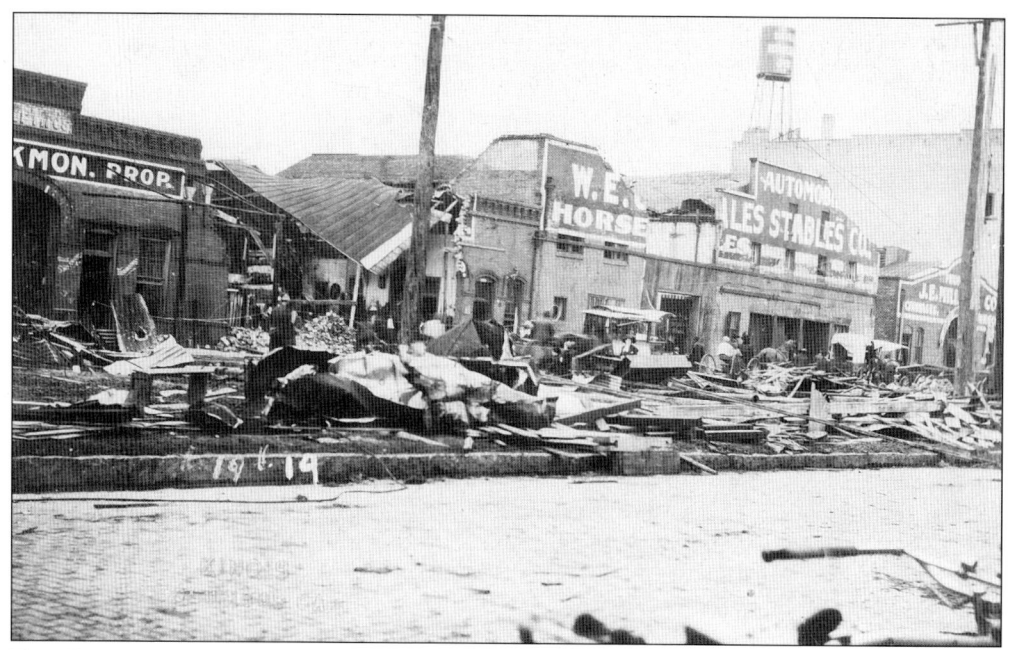

THE RESULTS OF A TORNADO IN COLUMBUS IN 1913. The writer identified the area as "from 13th Street to 12th—from Perry house to post office on east side."

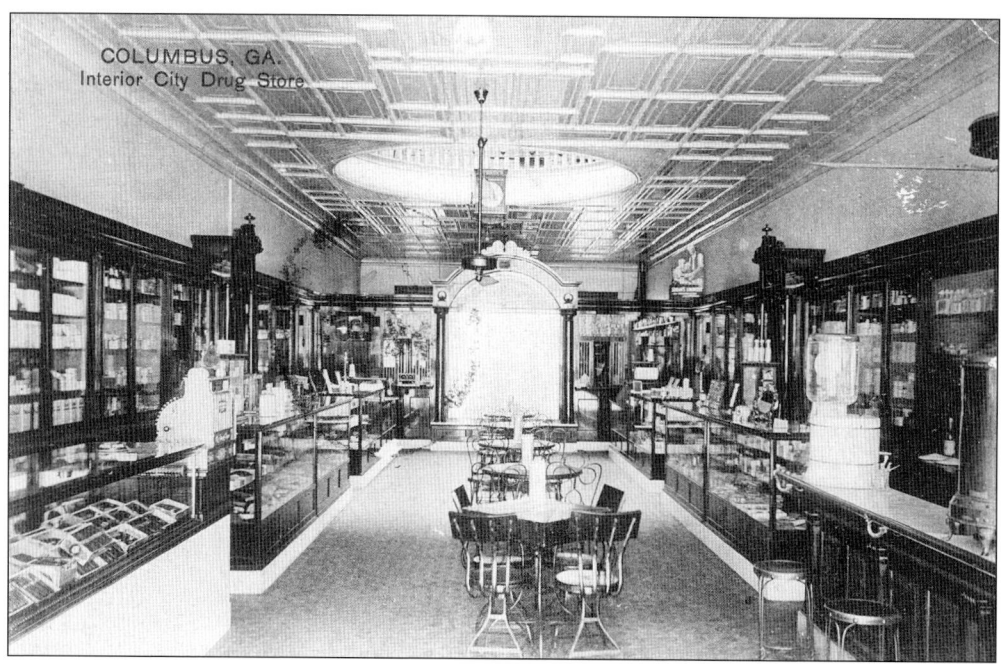

THE INTERIOR OF THE CITY DRUG STORE AT 1142 BROAD STREET IN COLUMBUS IN 1910. The store was operated by two people named "Morgan and Meadows."

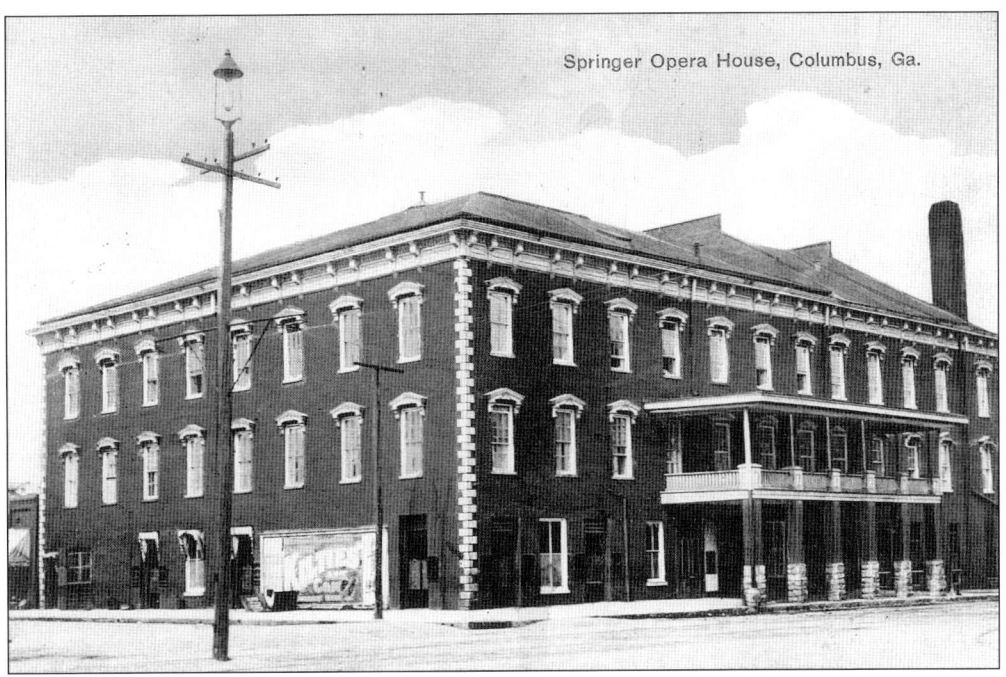

THE SPRINGER OPERA HOUSE IN COLUMBUS. The card was mailed to Lithonia, Georgia, on July 28, 1909. The message reads: "Does this remind you in any way of the Colonial? I will tell you this one thing, it is a great deal larger than the Colonial, and far better looking. Jessie B."

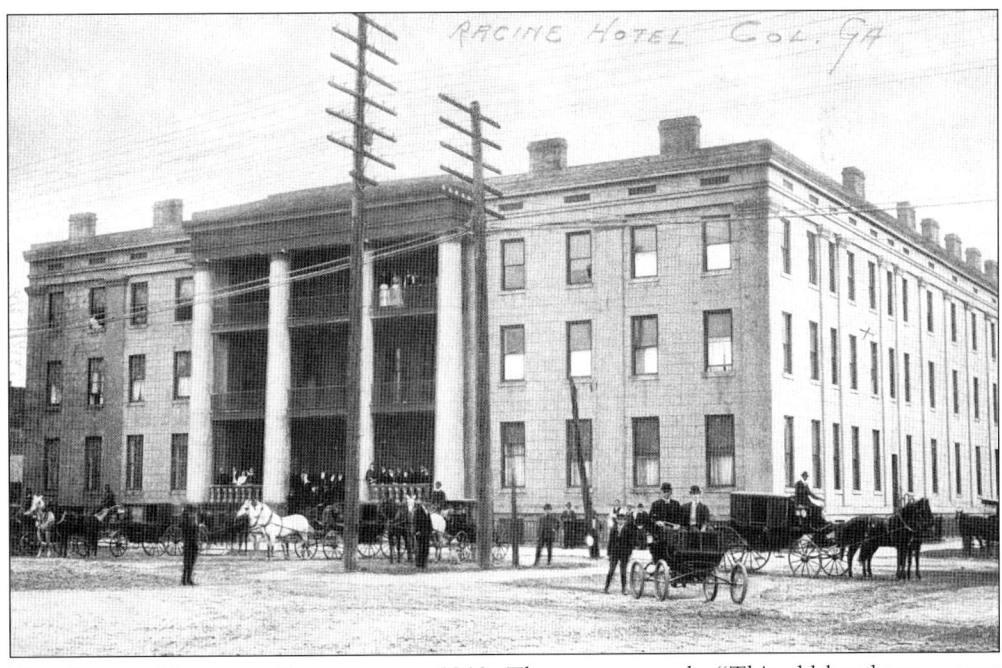

THE RACINE HOTEL IN COLUMBUS, c. 1910. The message reads: "This old hotel was a great resort for rich planters and slave owners before the war."

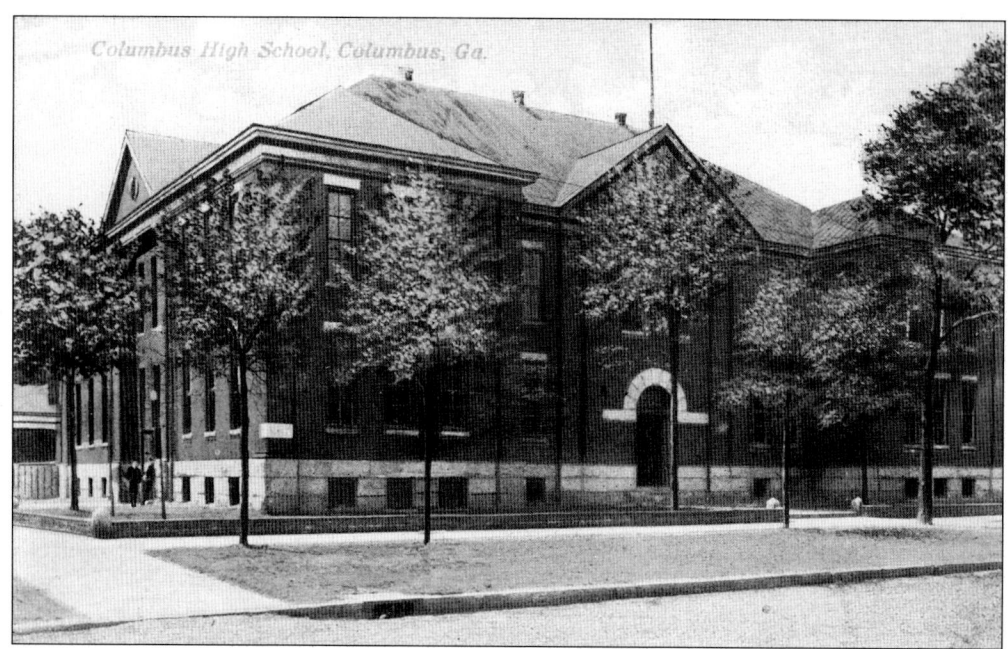

Columbus High School.

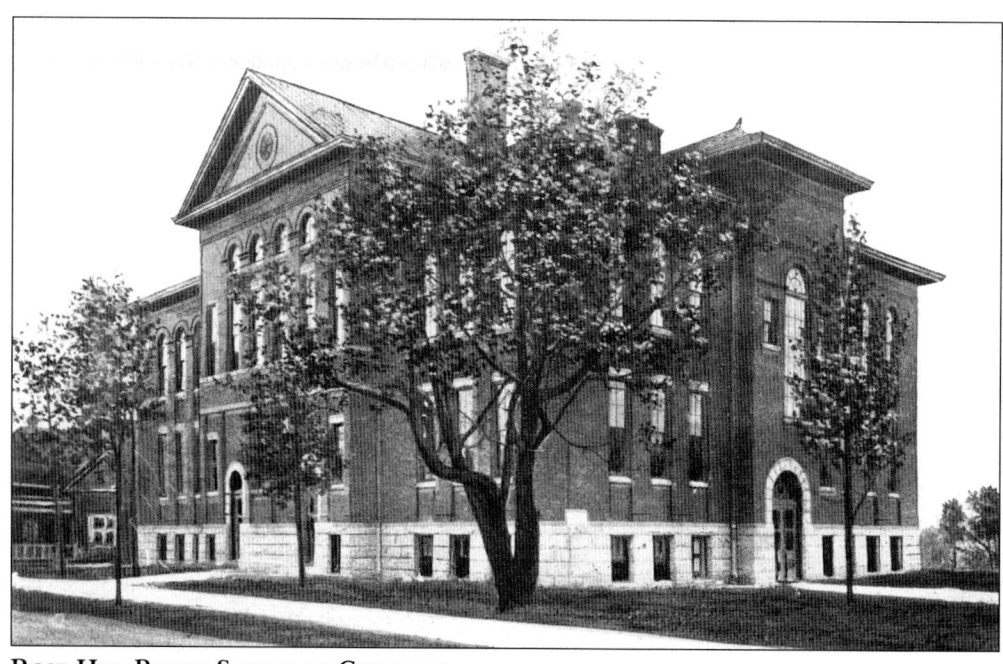

Rose Hill Public School in Columbus.

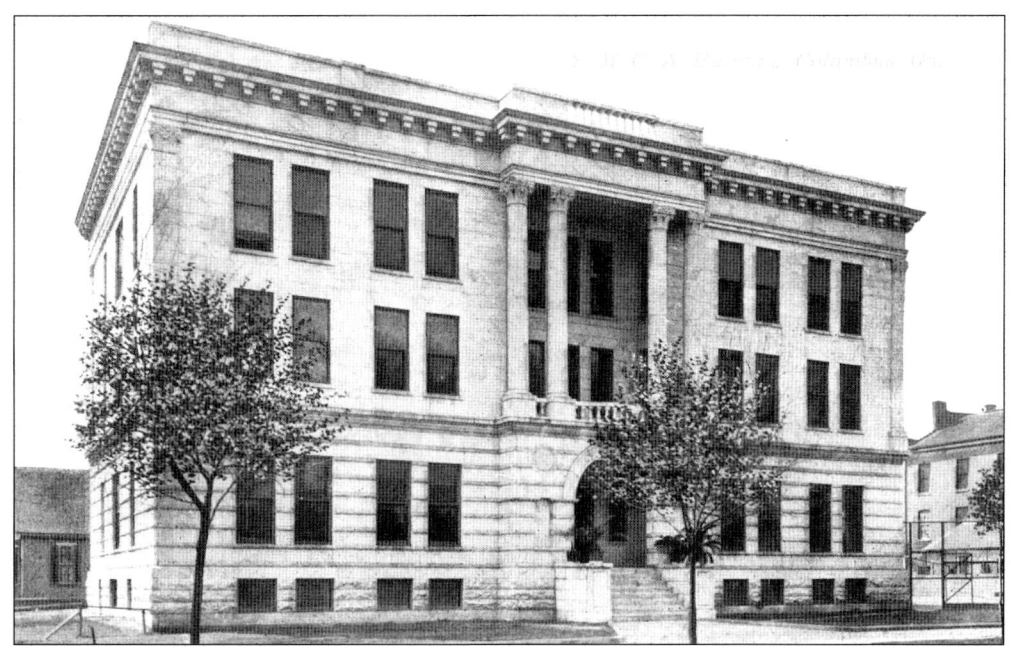

The **YMCA** Building in Columbus.

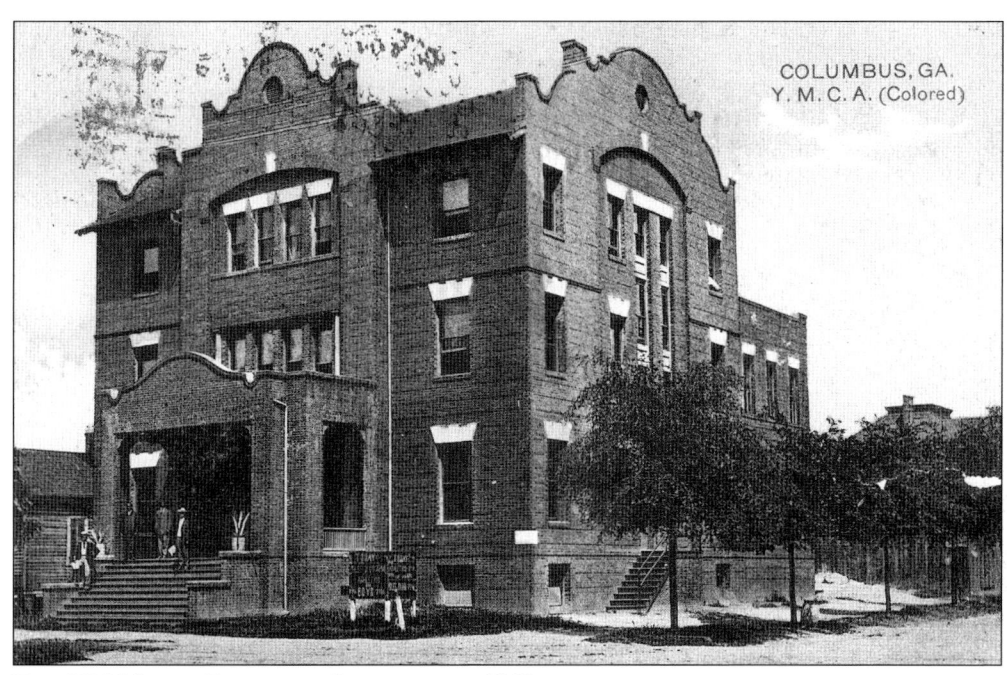

The **YMCA** for Blacks in Columbus, c. 1910.

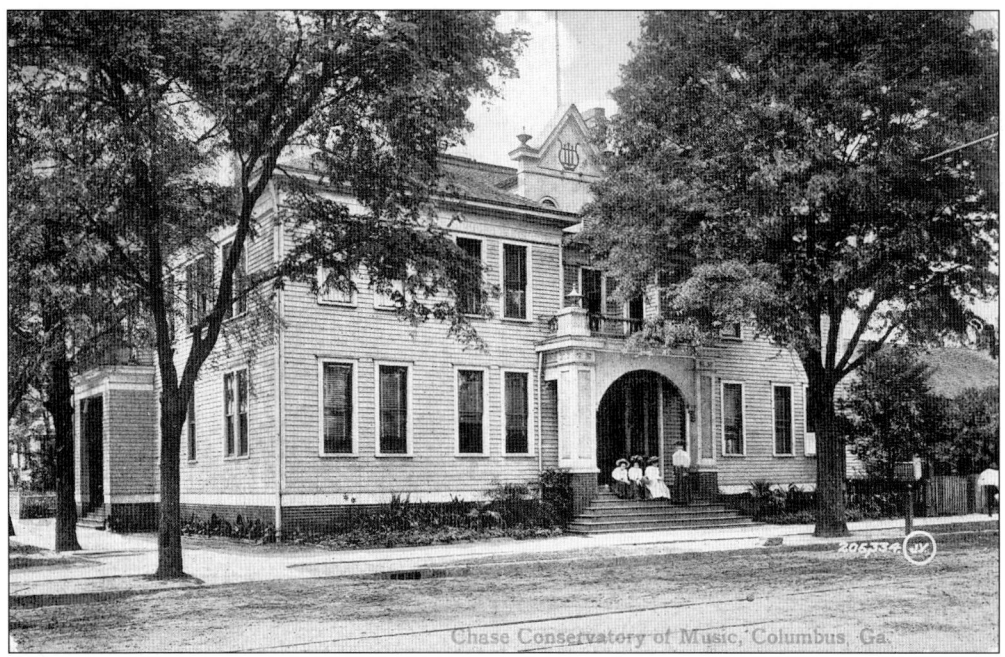

THE CHASE CONSERVATORY OF MUSIC IN COLUMBUS. The card was mailed from Chipley, which is in Harris County north of Columbus, to Box Springs, which is in Talbot County east of Columbus. It carried the following rather serious message: "Dear Hattie: How is Robert? Papa says if you all need him let him know and he will come down and stay several days. Be sure to let us hear from Robert right away please. We are so anxious. Fondly Inez H."

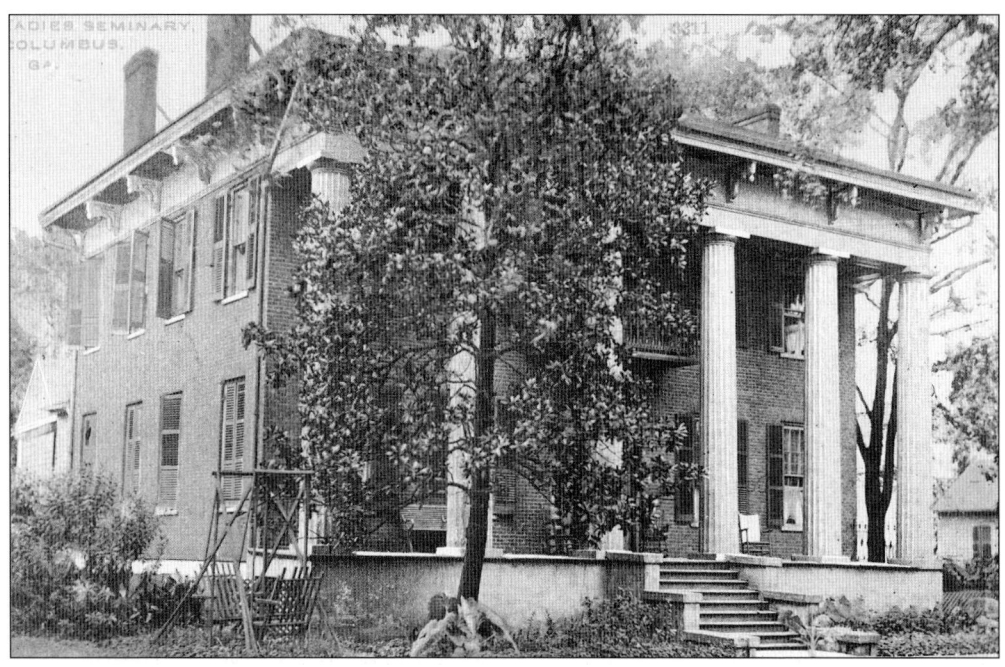

THE LADIES SEMINARY IN COLUMBUS, c. 1912.

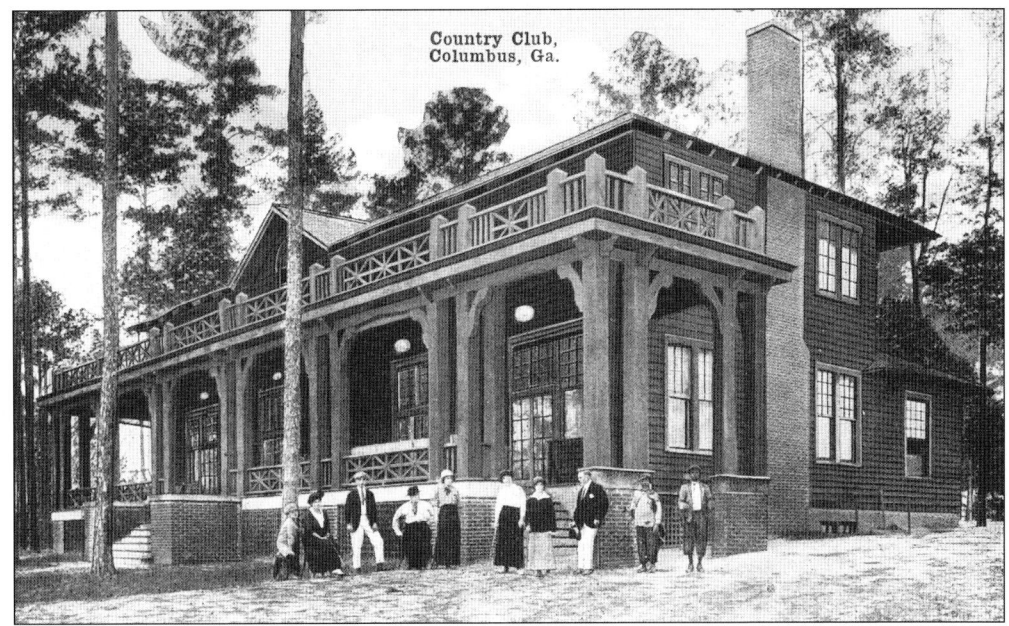

THE COUNTRY CLUB IN COLUMBUS, C. 1920. Three of the ladies in the group are holding golf clubs and the two caddies on the right have golf bags.

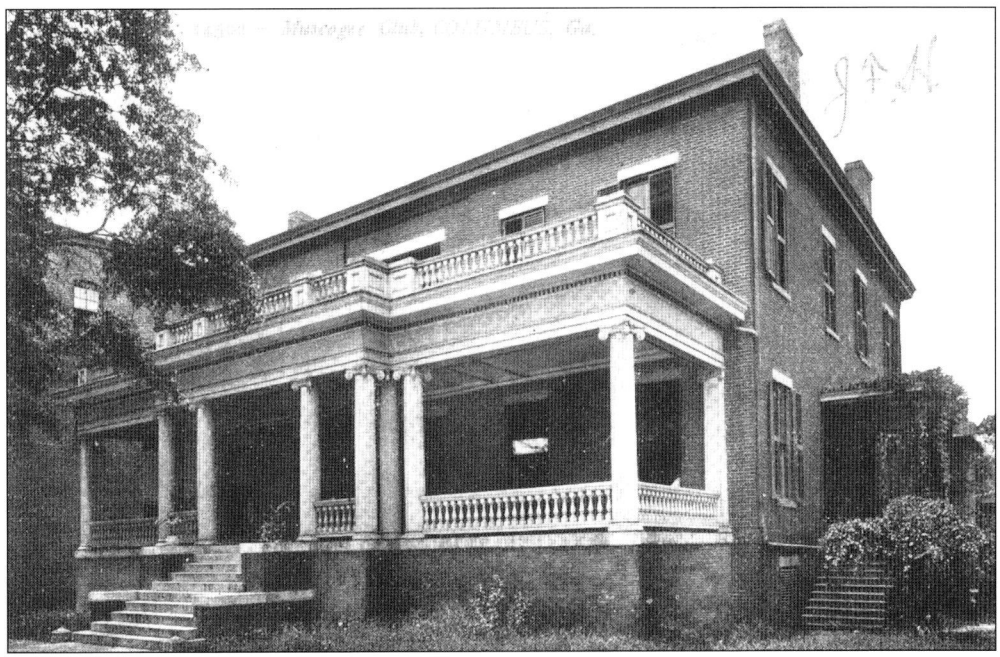

THE MUSCOGEE CLUB IN COLUMBUS, C. 1907.

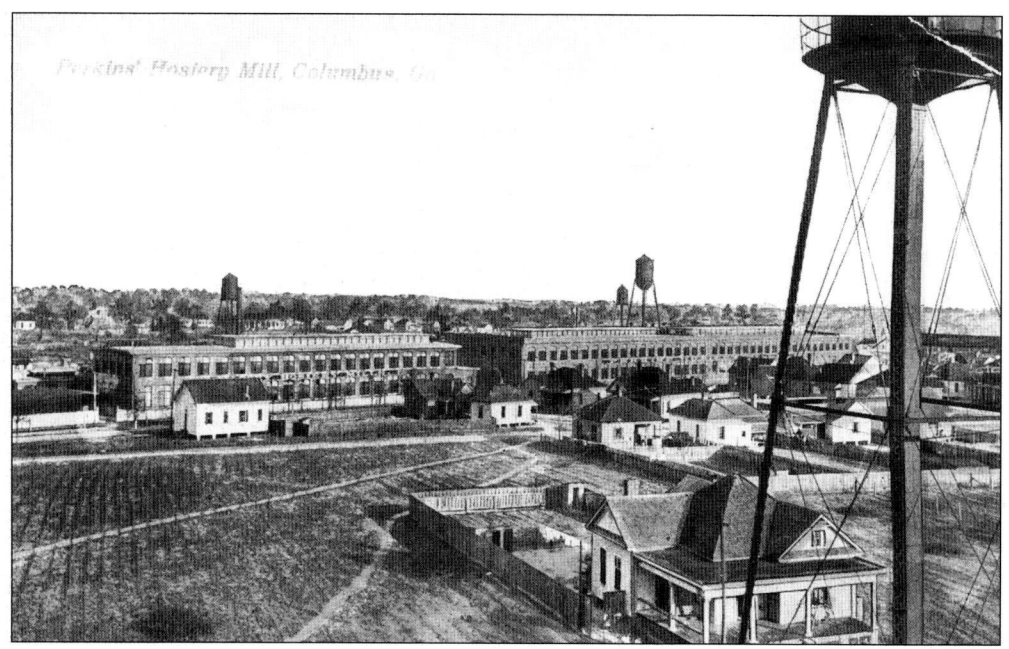

THE PERKINS' HOSIERY MILL IN COLUMBUS WITH SOME OF THE HOMES FOR WORKERS SHOWN NEAR THE BUILDINGS.

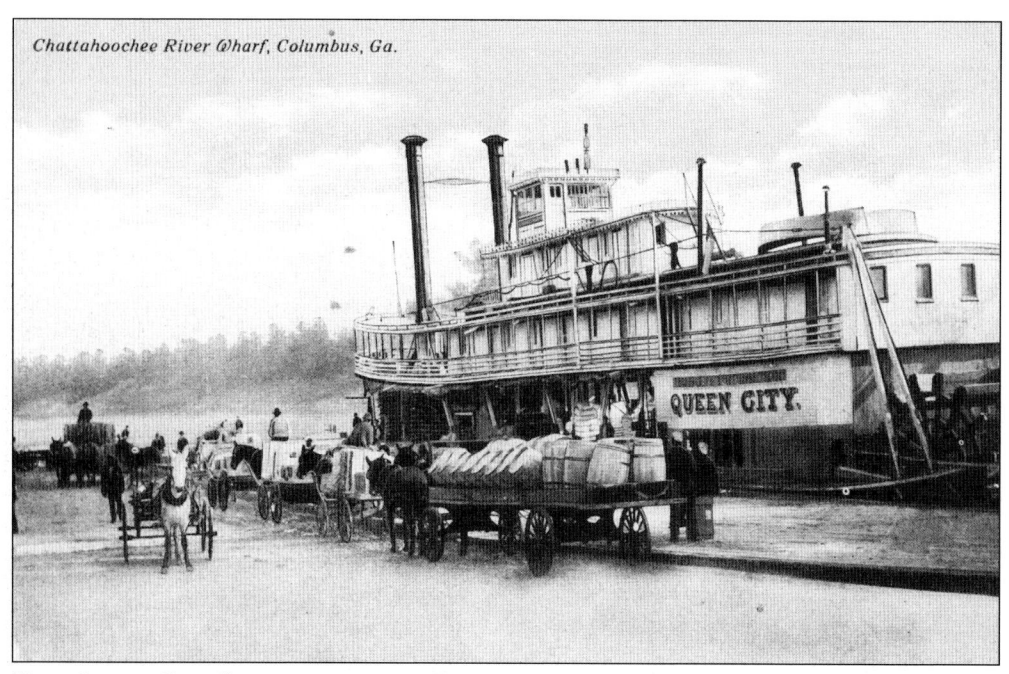

THE *QUEEN CITY* STERNWHEELER AT DOCK AT THE CHATTAHOOCHEE RIVER WHARF IN COLUMBUS, C. 1910.

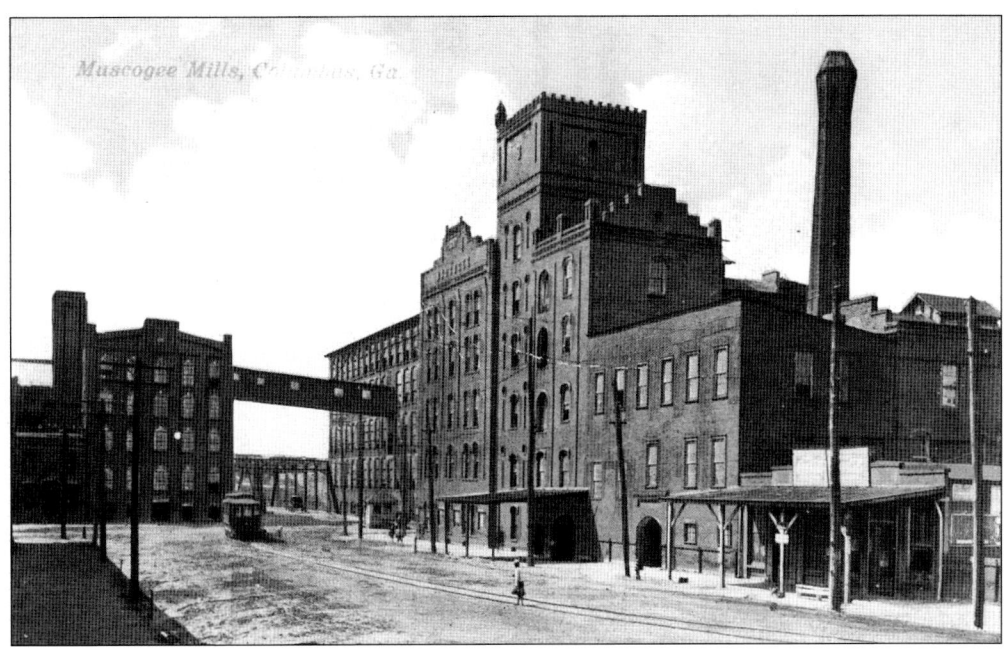
THE MUSCOGEE MILLS AT COLUMBUS, C. 1912.

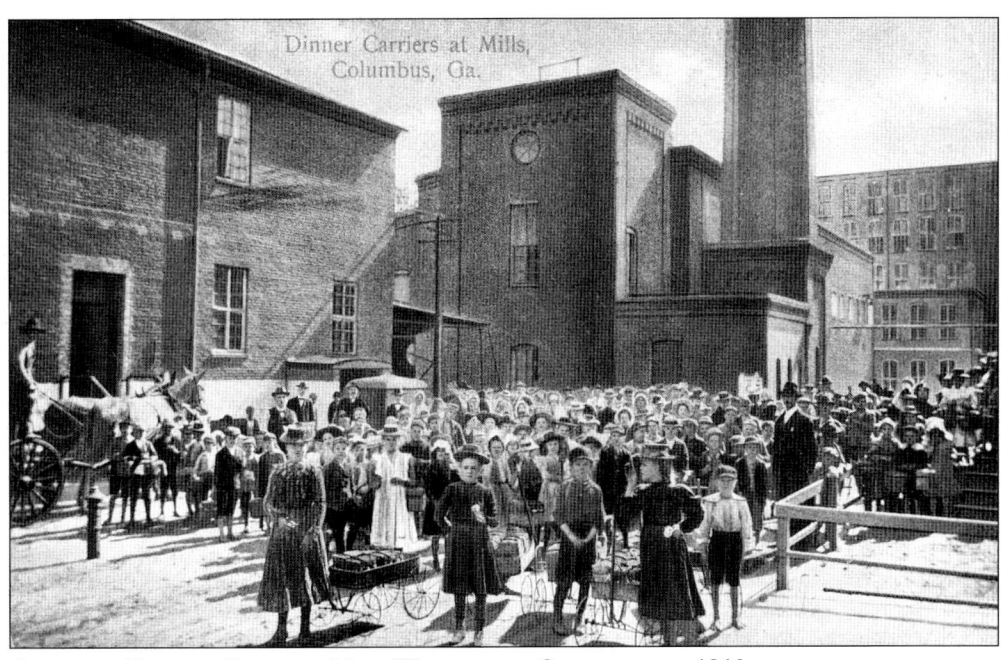
CHILDREN DELIVER FOOD TO MILL WORKERS IN COLUMBUS, C. 1910.

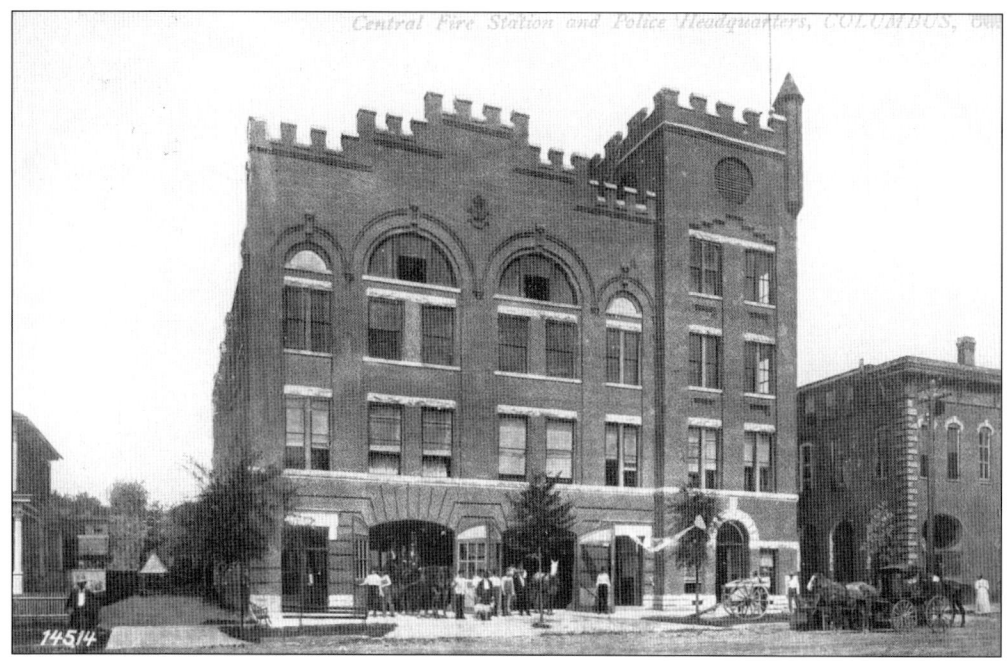

THE CENTRAL FIRE STATION AND POLICE HEADQUARTERS IN COLUMBUS. The message writer probably was an entertainer traveling around the country; the message reads: "April 16, 1909. My Dear Mother: I expect to leave 7:10 Sunday morning and reach Mobile at 4:12 in the afternoon—274 miles. Everything going fine all week. Have been away four months on Sunday. April 19—Crown Theater in Mobile, Alabama. Best love, Tom."

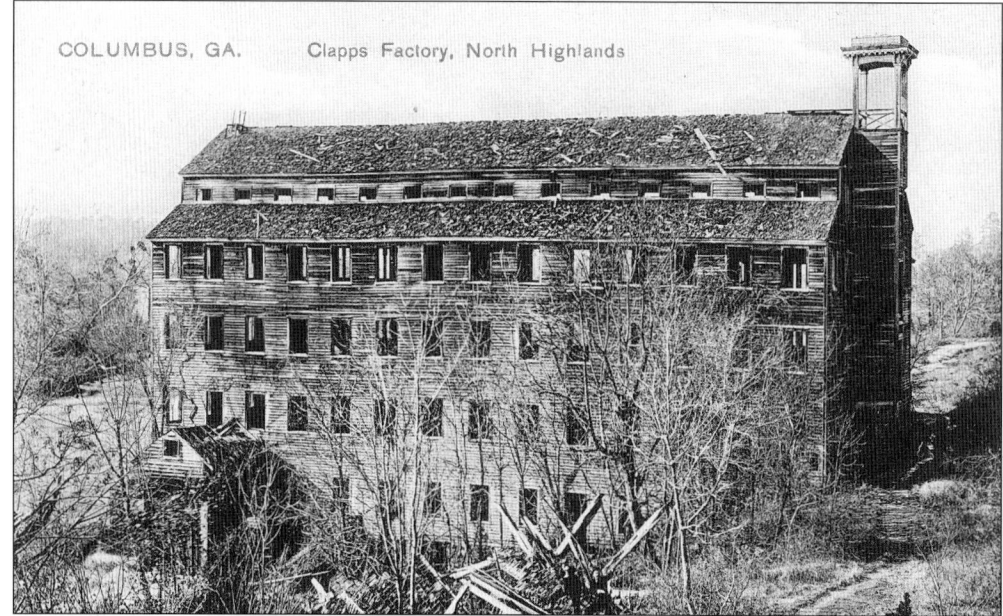

THE SECOND CLAPP'S MILL. The Clapp's mill originally built on this site, on the Chattahoochee near Columbus, was burned by Union soldiers in 1864. This building was put up by J.R. Clapp in 1866 to produce sheeting, shirting, yarn, and thread. The building was burned to the ground March 19, 1910.

Two
MACON AND ENVIRONS

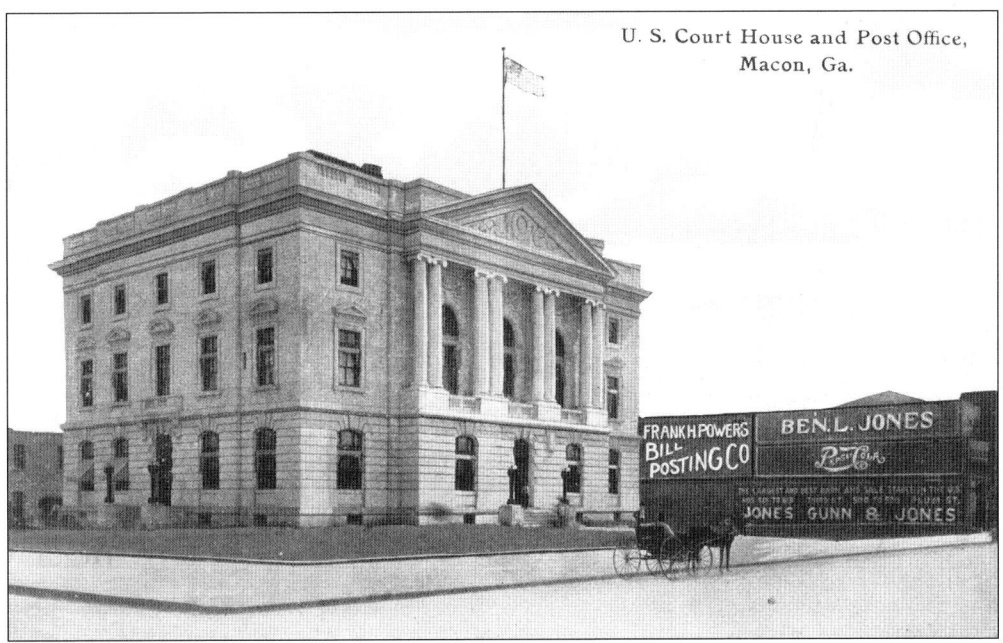

THE U.S. COURTHOUSE AND POST OFFICE IN MACON, C. 1910. Note the early billboards to the right advertising local businesses, including Pepsi Cola.

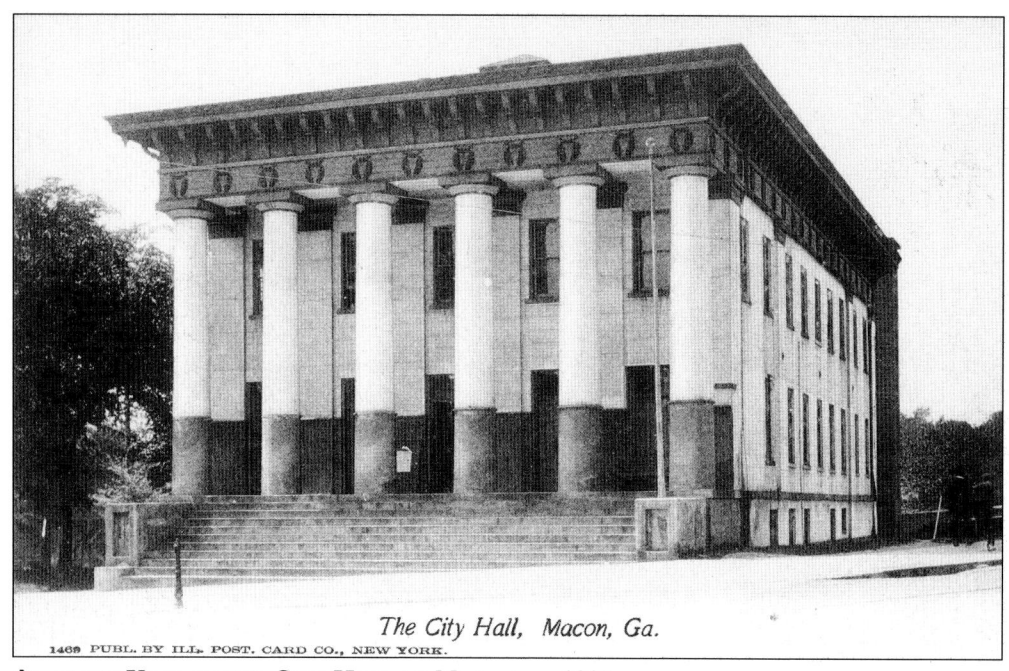

An early View of the City Hall at Macon, c. 1906.

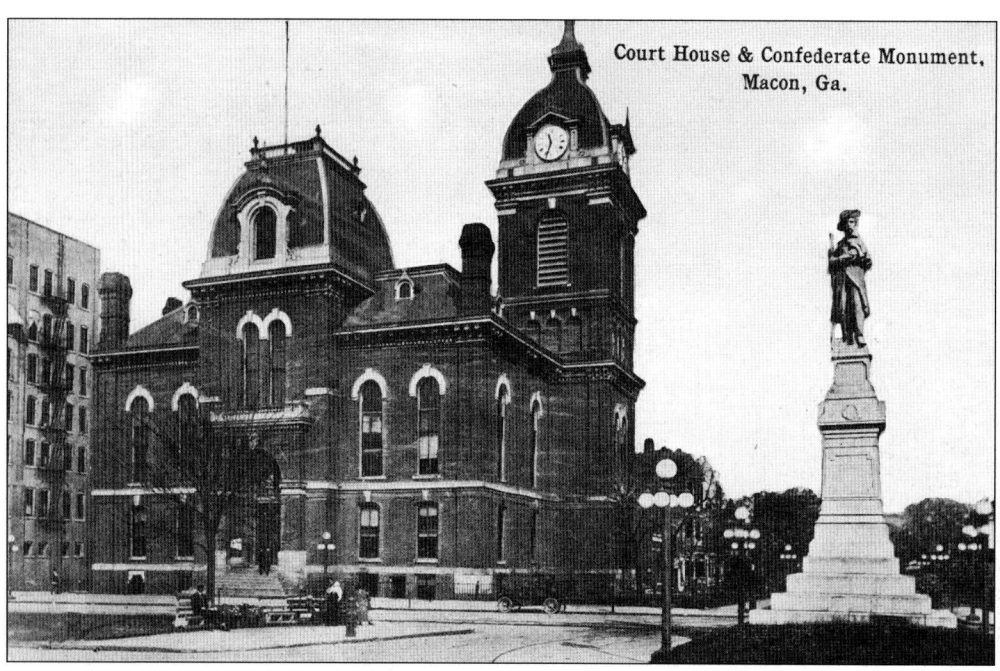

The Bibb County Courthouse at Macon. The courthouse was built at the corner of Mulberry and Second Streets in 1870 at a cost of $100,000. It was used until the new courthouse was completed in 1924. The Confederate Monument was unveiled October 20, 1879, at the intersection of Mulberry and Second Streets. Between 35,000 and 45,000 people were present at the unveiling. The monument was moved to its present location in April 1956.

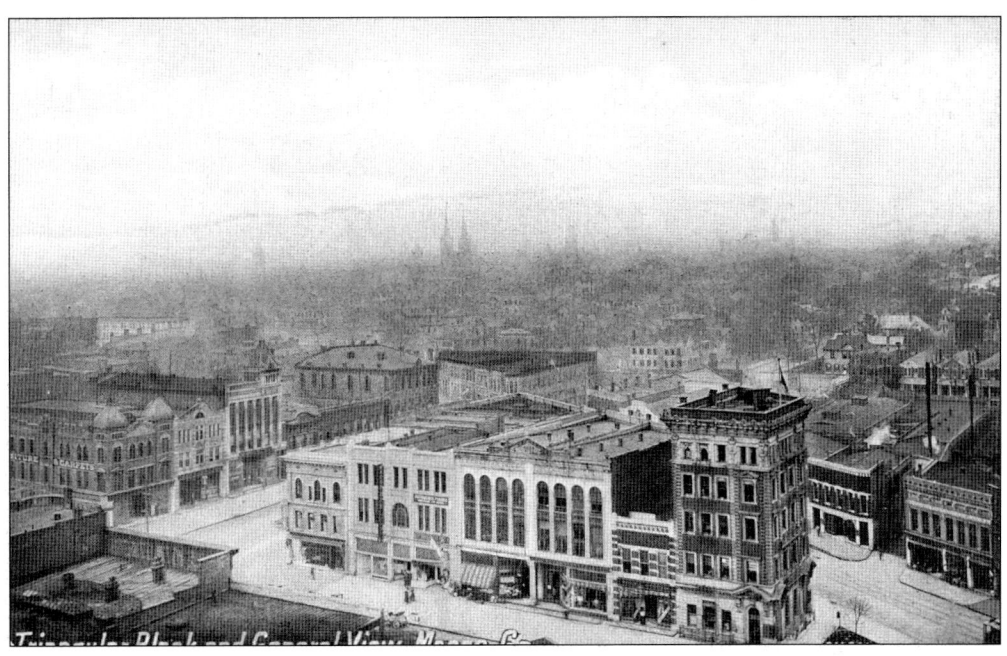

A BIRD'S-EYE VIEW OF MACON, C. 1909, SHOWING THE "TRIANGULAR BLOCK."

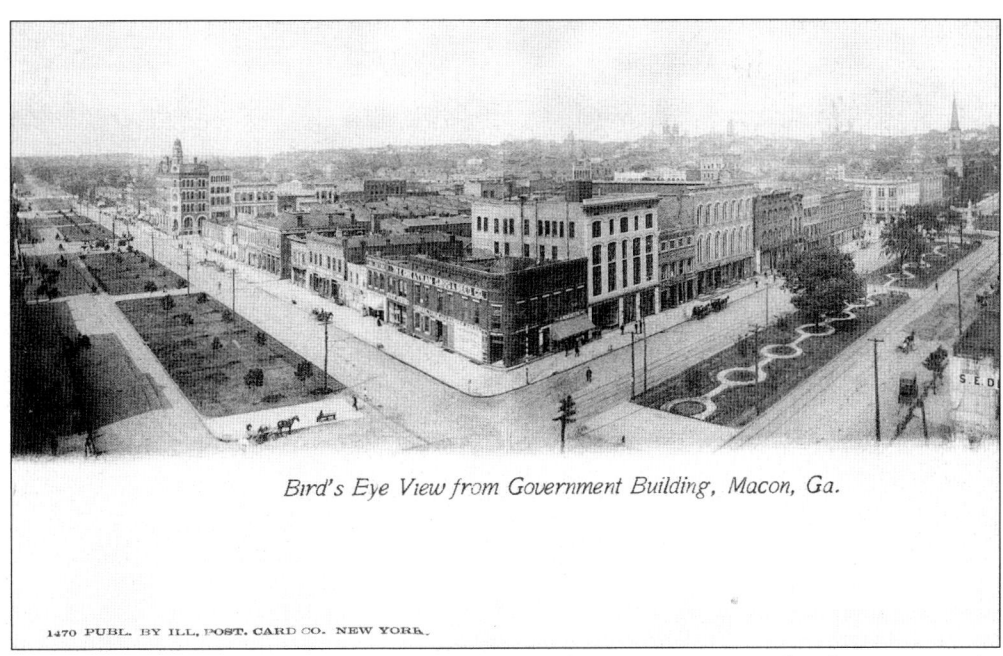

ANOTHER BIRD'S-EYE VIEW OF MACON. This one was made from atop the Government Building.

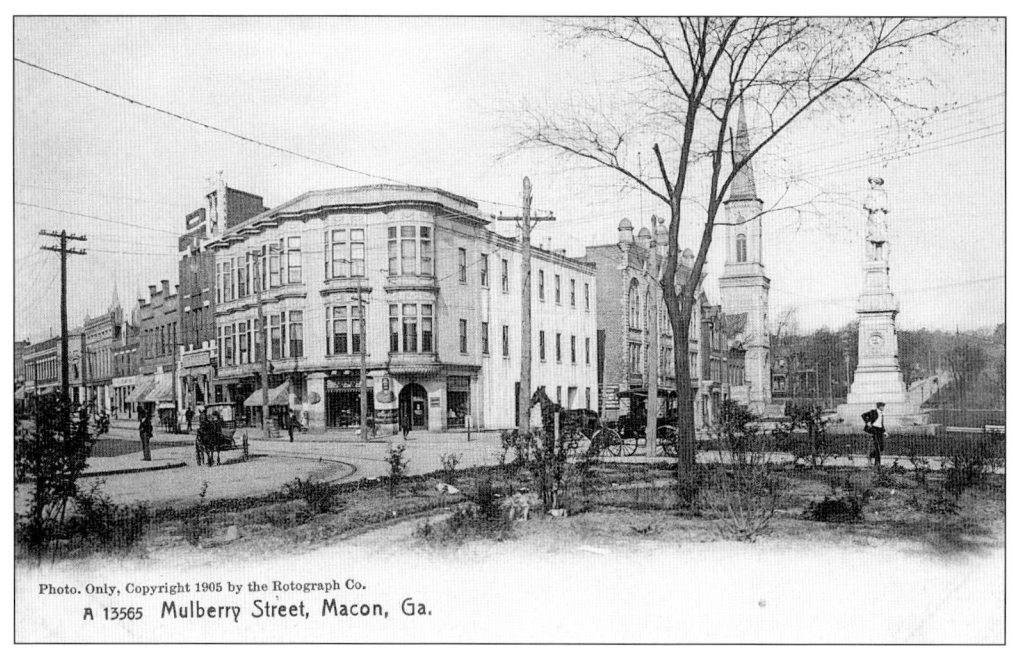

MULBERRY STREET IN MACON IN 1905.

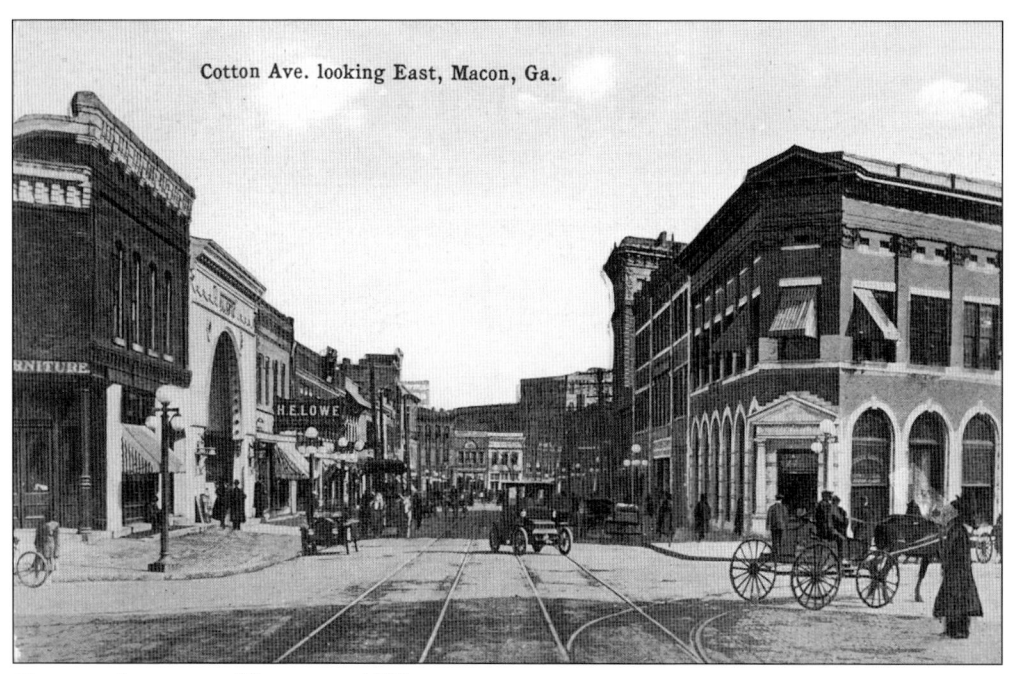

COTTON AVENUE IN MACON, C. 1908.

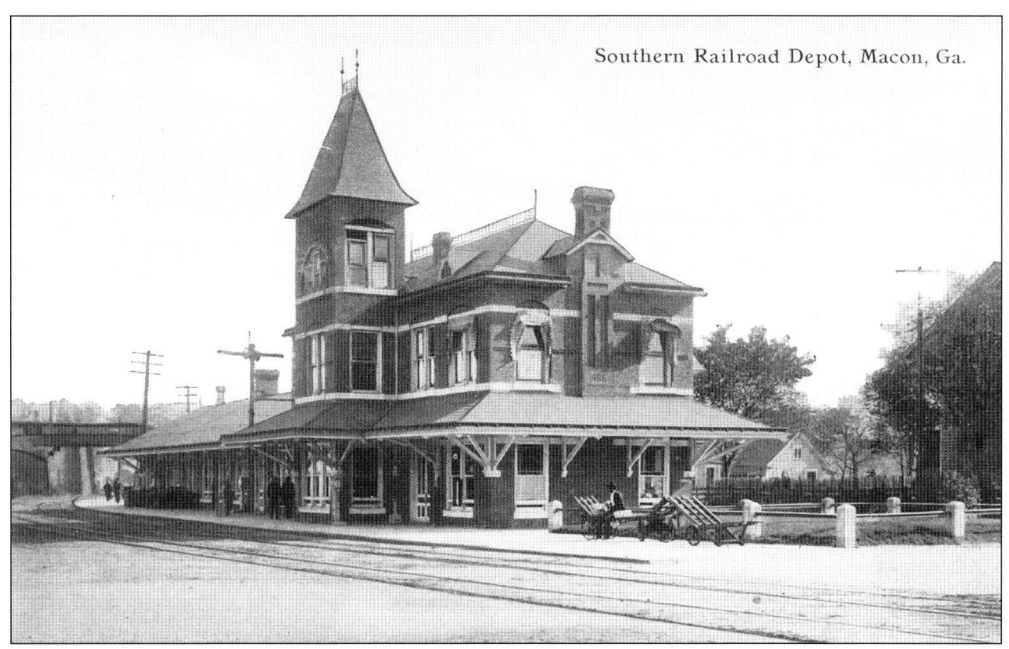

THE SOUTHERN RAILROAD DEPOT IN MACON, C. 1910.

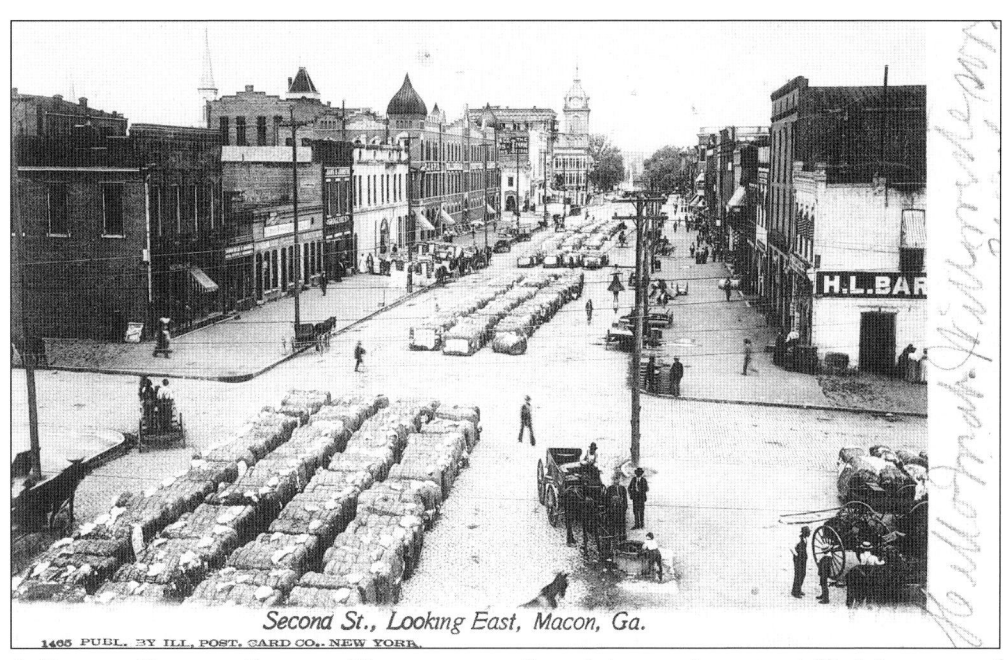

A BUMPER CROP OF COTTON. The cotton overflowed the warehouses and filled the streets of Macon, *c.* 1906.

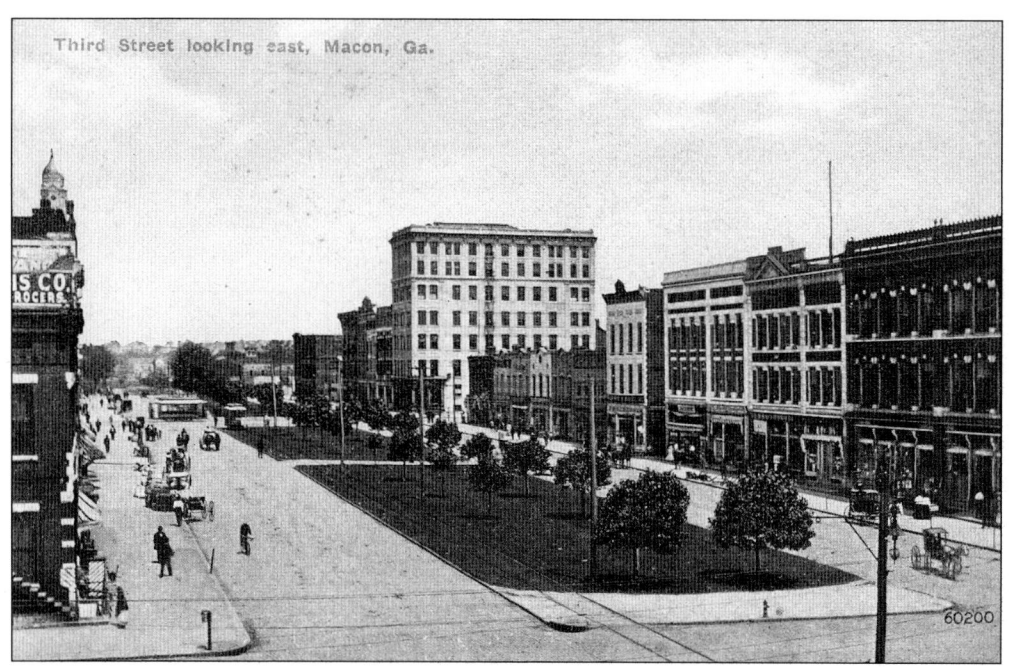

THIRD STREET LOOKING EAST IN MACON, C. 1907.

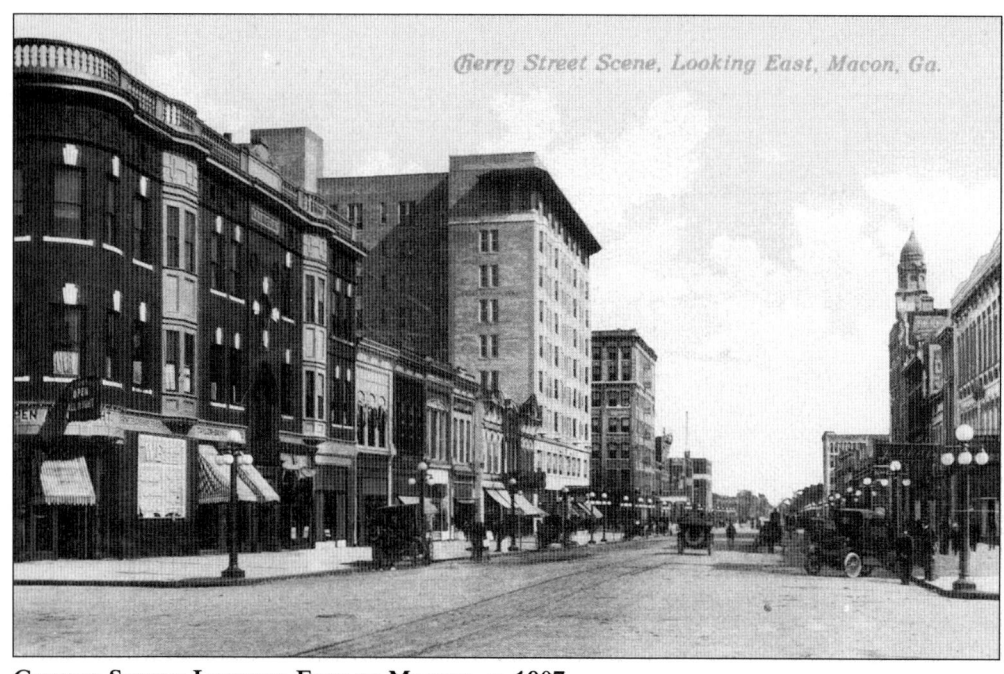

CHERRY STREET LOOKING EAST IN MACON, C. 1907.

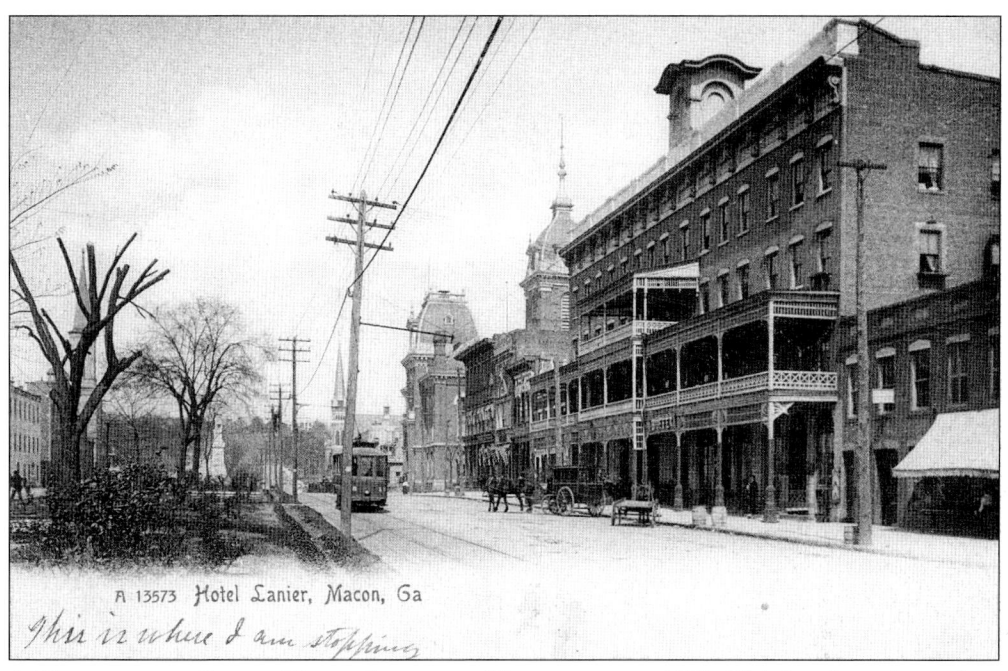

A View of the Grand Hotel Lanier in Macon about 1905. This hotel was located on Mulberry Street between Second and Third Streets.

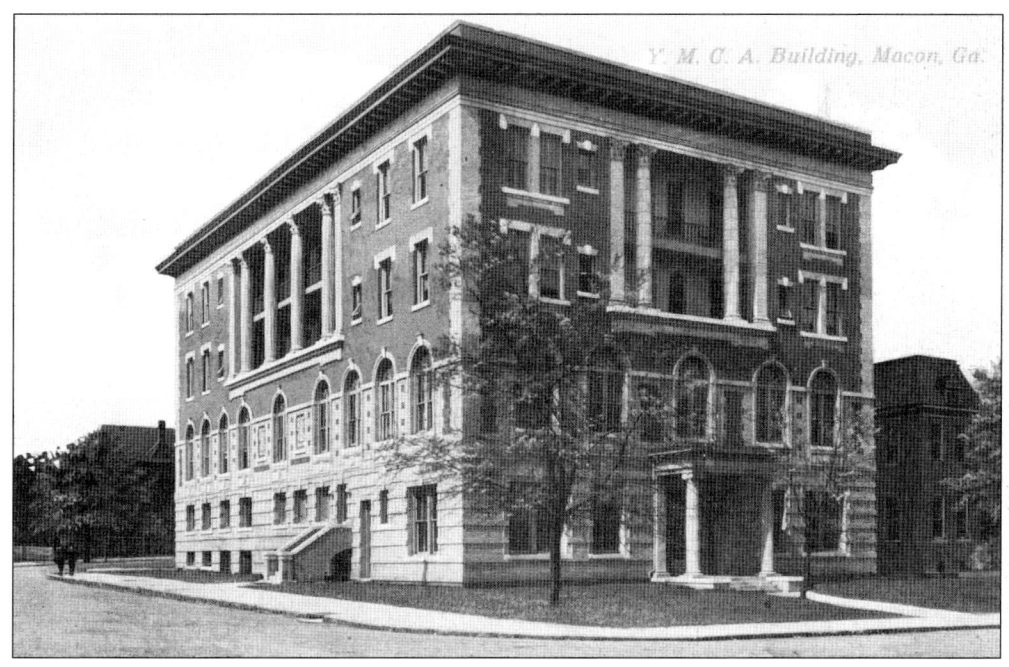

The YMCA in Macon, c. 1912.

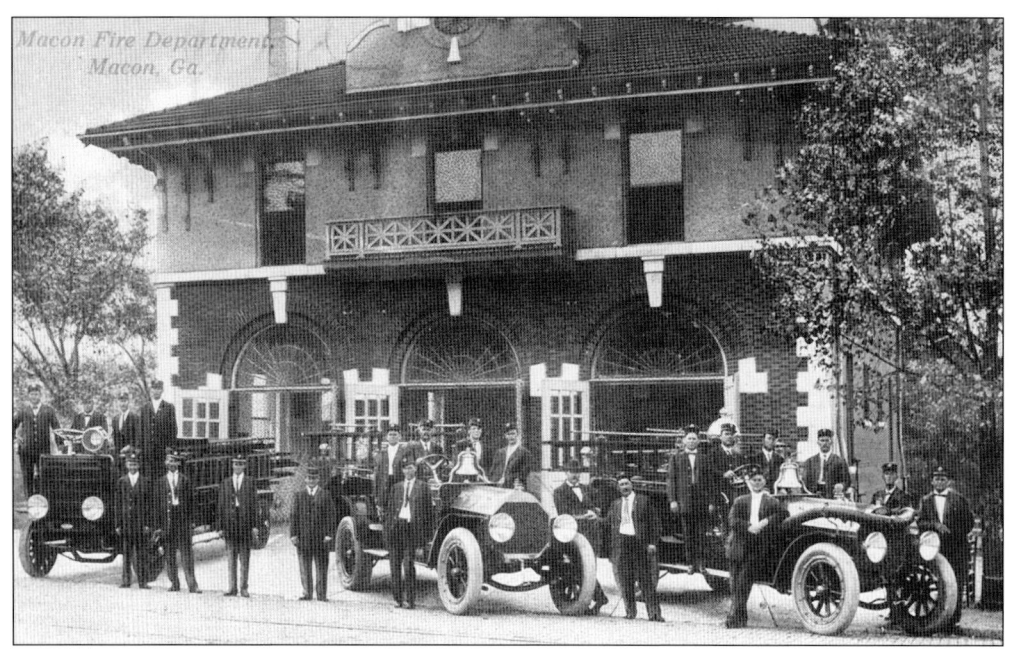

THE MACON FIRE DEPARTMENT IN THE 1910s.

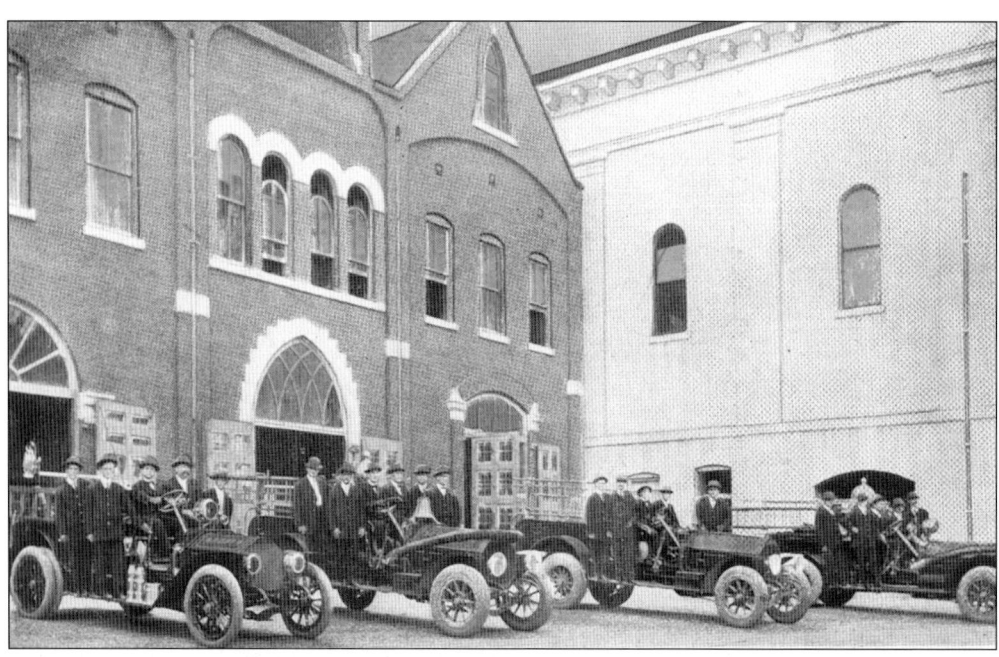

ANOTHER VIEW OF THE MACON FIRE DEPARTMENT IN THE 1910s. This one is identified as the "Headquarters of Auto Fire Department."

THE AMERICAN NATIONAL BANK OF MACON ON THE CORNER OF THIRD AND CHERRY STREETS. Although the card was printed *c.* 1910, it was not used until 1915 and was postmarked Times Square Station, New York, and mailed to Harrinton, Connecticut. The message reads: "Dear Friend. Your card received and was glad to hear from you & to learn that you would take good care of my son. I know you will. For he is dear to me. Would be glad to have a letter from you. Mrs. —."

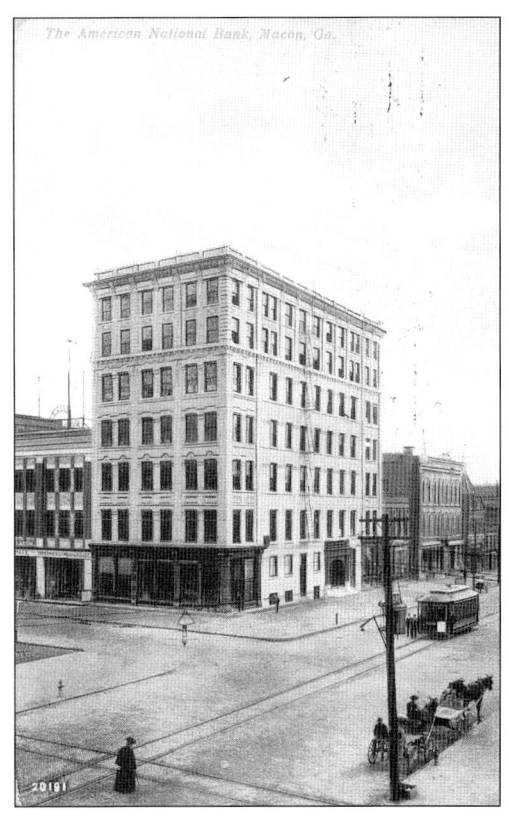

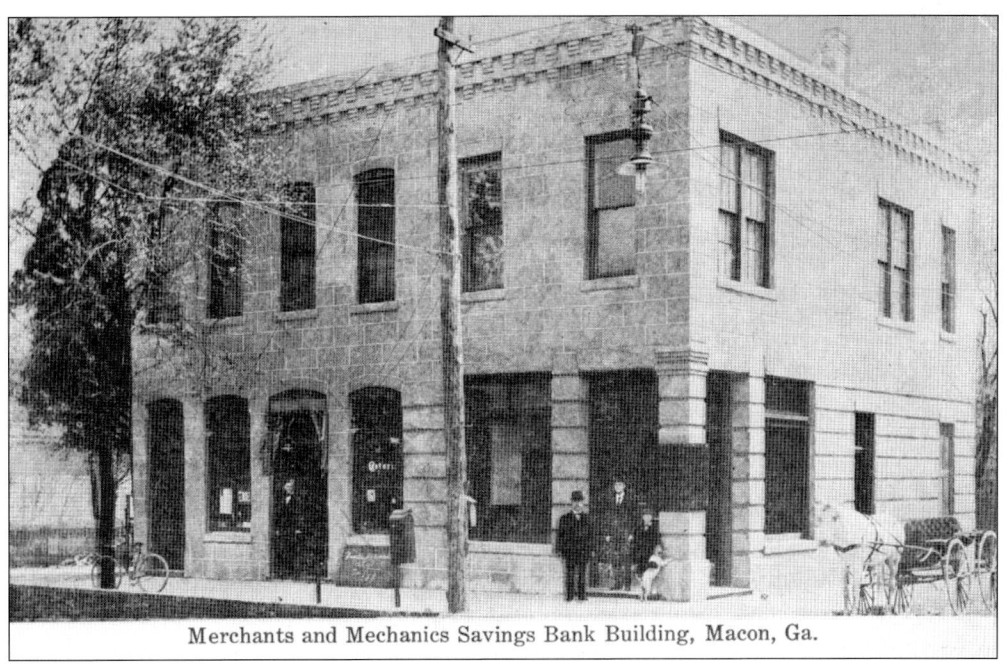

Merchants and Mechanics Savings Bank Building, Macon, Ga.

THE MERCHANTS AND MECHANICS SAVINGS BANK BUILDING IN MACON.

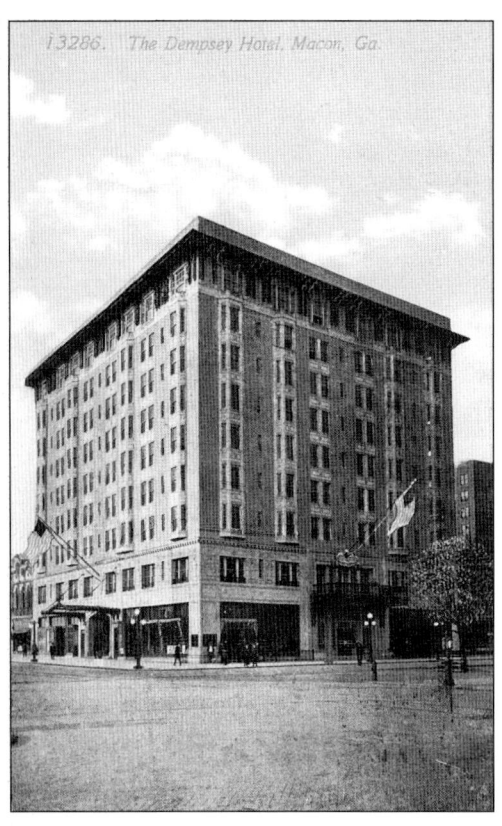

THE FAMOUS DEMPSEY HOTEL IN MACON.

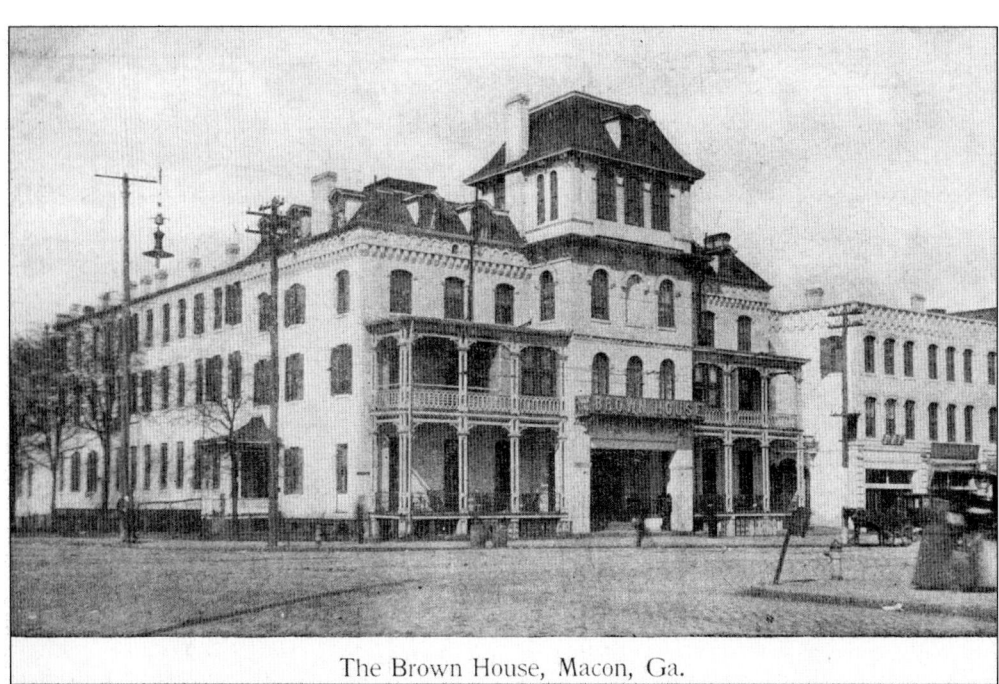

THE BROWN HOUSE, LOCATED ACROSS FROM THE RAILROAD DEPOT IN MACON, C. 1907.

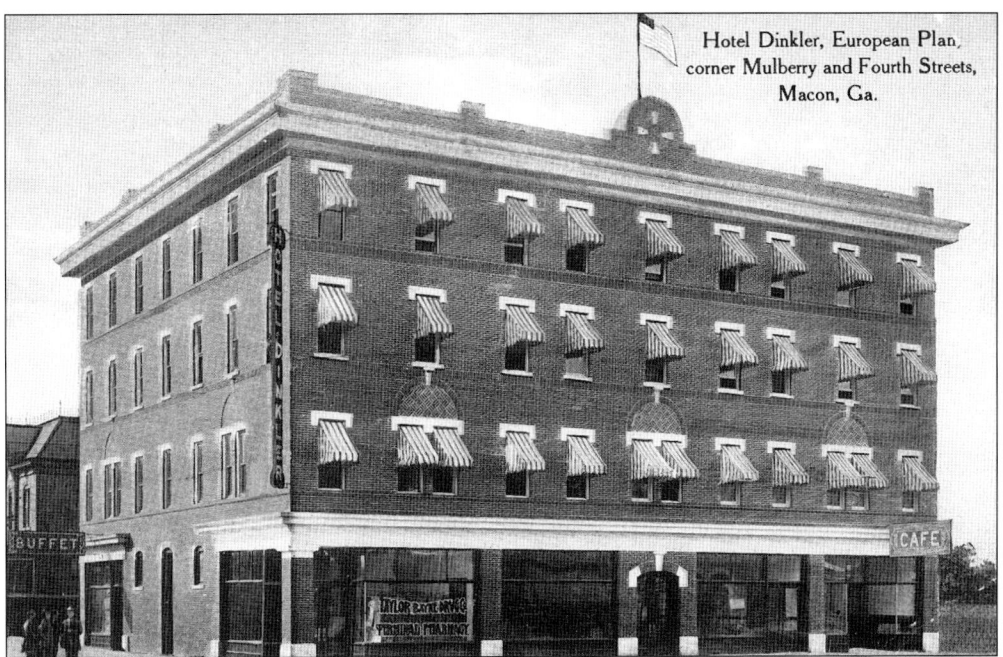

THE HOTEL DINKLER AT THE CORNER OF MULBERRY AND FOURTH STREETS IN MACON.

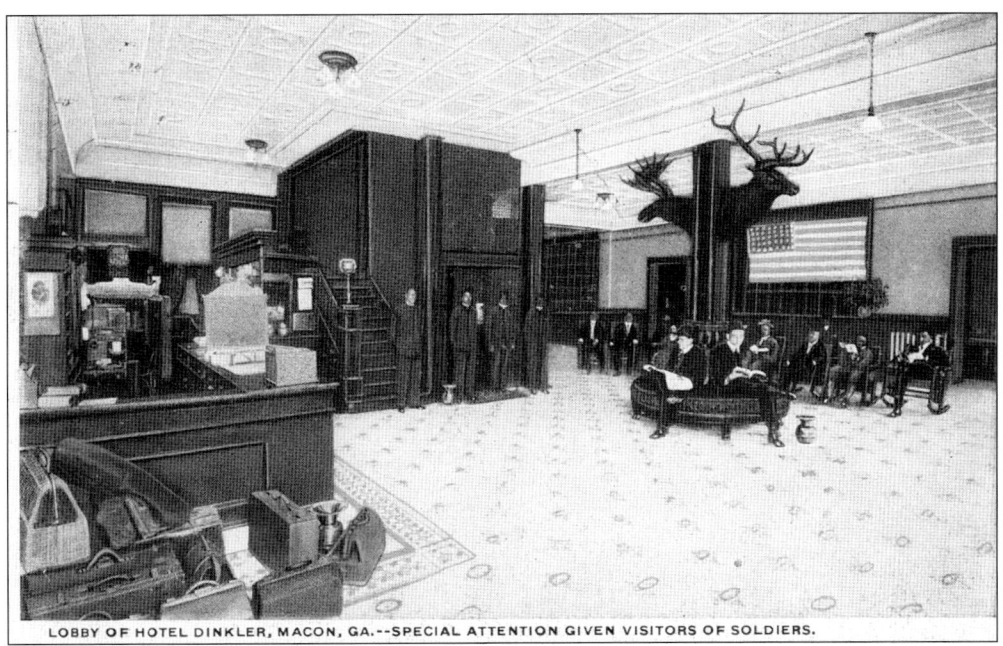

THE LOBBY OF THE HOTEL DINKLER IN MACON, C. 1920, SHOWING MOUNTED ELK AND MOOSE HEADS AND PLENTY OF CUSPIDORS. The writer has penned an interesting message to friends in Bangor, Maine, as follows: "Macon Ga. Dec. 3 [1920] Left our first town in Georgia this morning with frost on the ground and gorgeous roses growing in the back-yard! This is the first warm spot we've come to & the first time we have been obliged to stop longer that to eat or sleep, due to repairs on truck. Everything has gone wonderfully well, except for frightful roads all thru the Carolinas. Dorothy H."

St. Paul's Church in Macon.

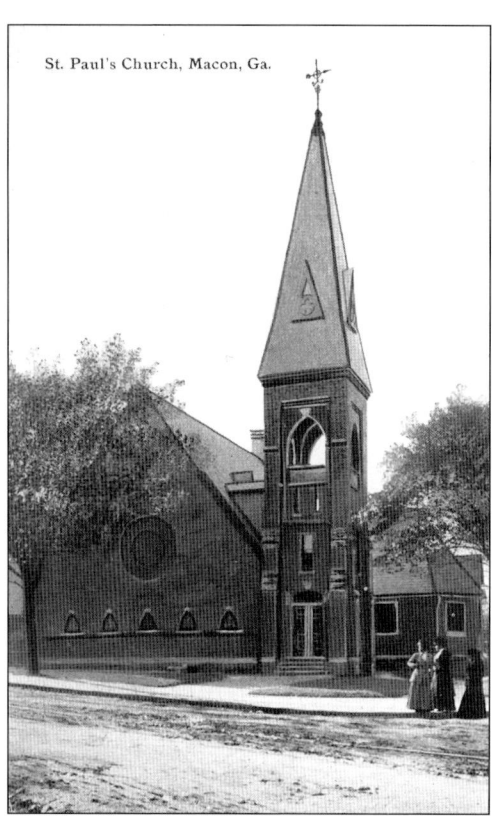

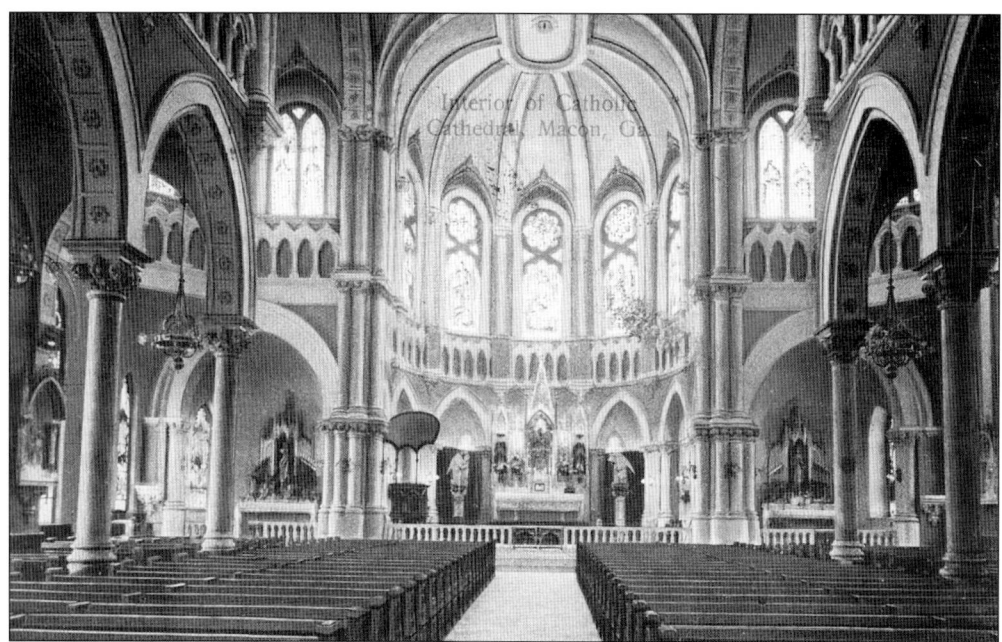

An Interior View of the Catholic Cathedral in Macon.

One of the Buildings of Mercer University in Macon, c. 1906.

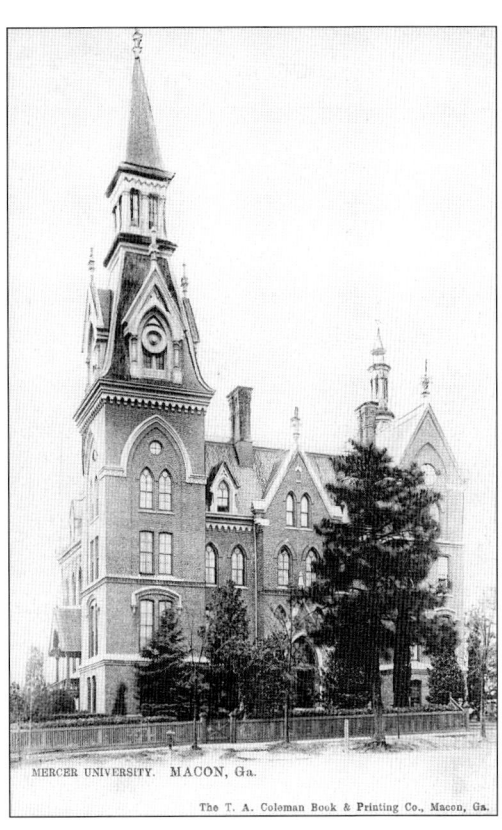

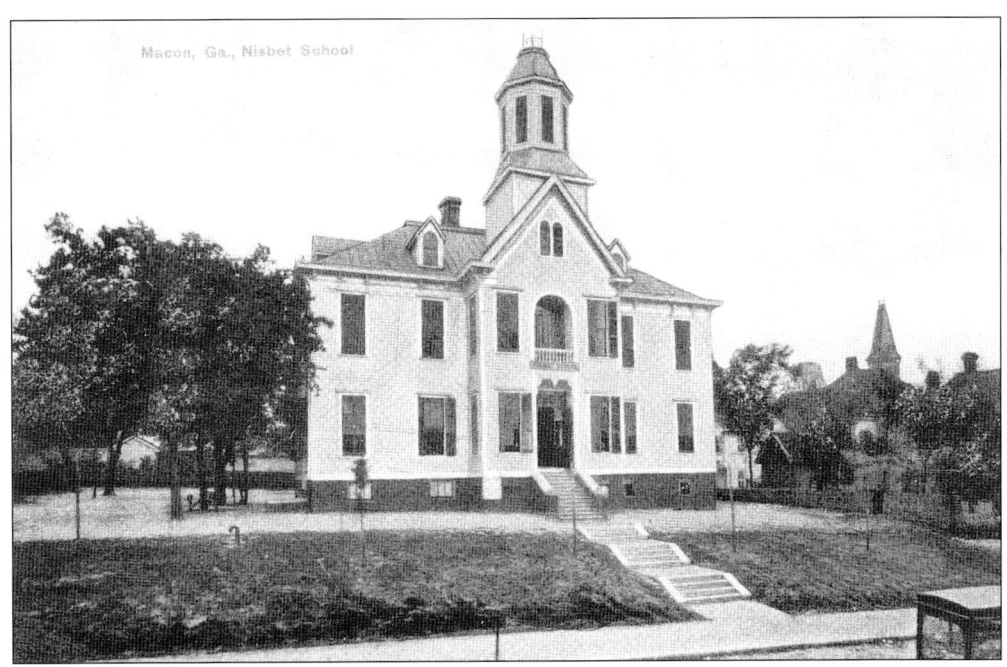

Nisbet School in Macon, c. 1912.

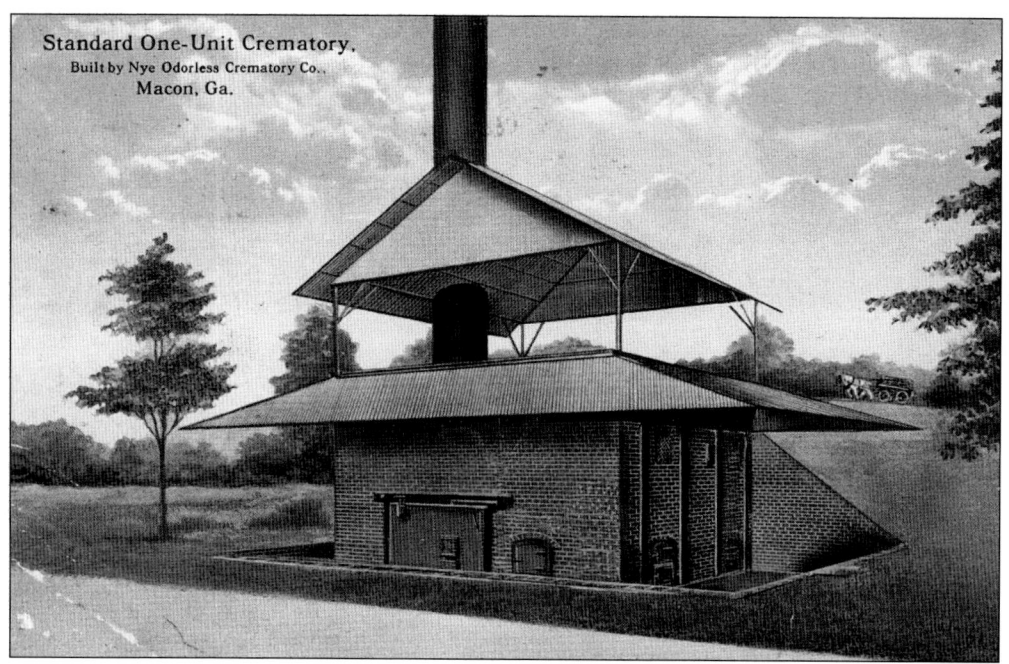

A STANDARD ONE-UNIT CREMATORY, BUILT BY NYE ODORLESS CREMATORY, MACON, GA.
This was not for human cremations, but was built to burn garbage. A printed ad on the message side states that the unit came in three sizes and that they were so reasonably priced that "This company has put garbage crematories within the reach of every town and city."

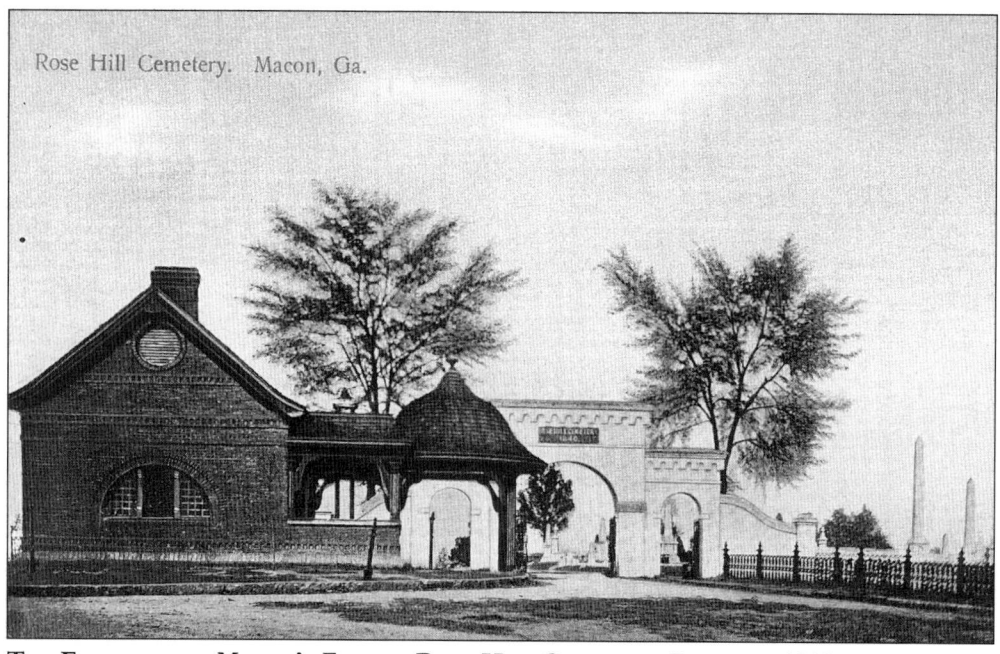

THE ENTRANCE TO MACON'S FAMOUS ROSE HILL CEMETERY, BEGUN IN 1840.

Three
BUTTS COUNTY

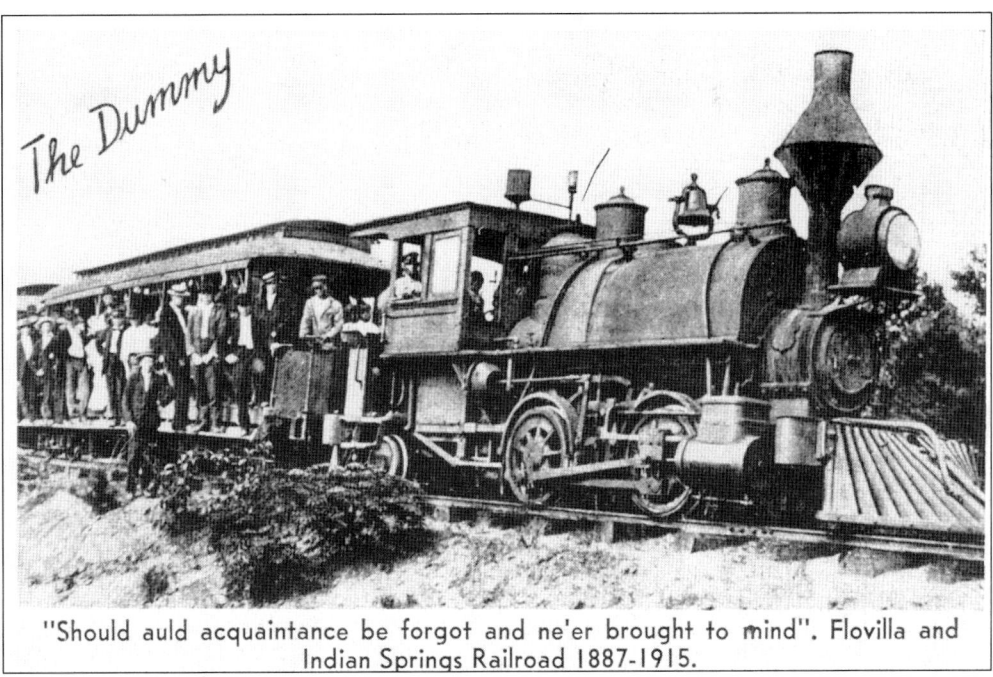

"Should auld acquaintance be forgot and ne'er brought to mind". Flovilla and Indian Springs Railroad 1887-1915.

THE INDIAN SPRINGS AND FLOVILLA RAILROAD. The railroad ran only 3 miles, from the railroad depot in Flovilla to the popular resort hotels at Indian Springs.

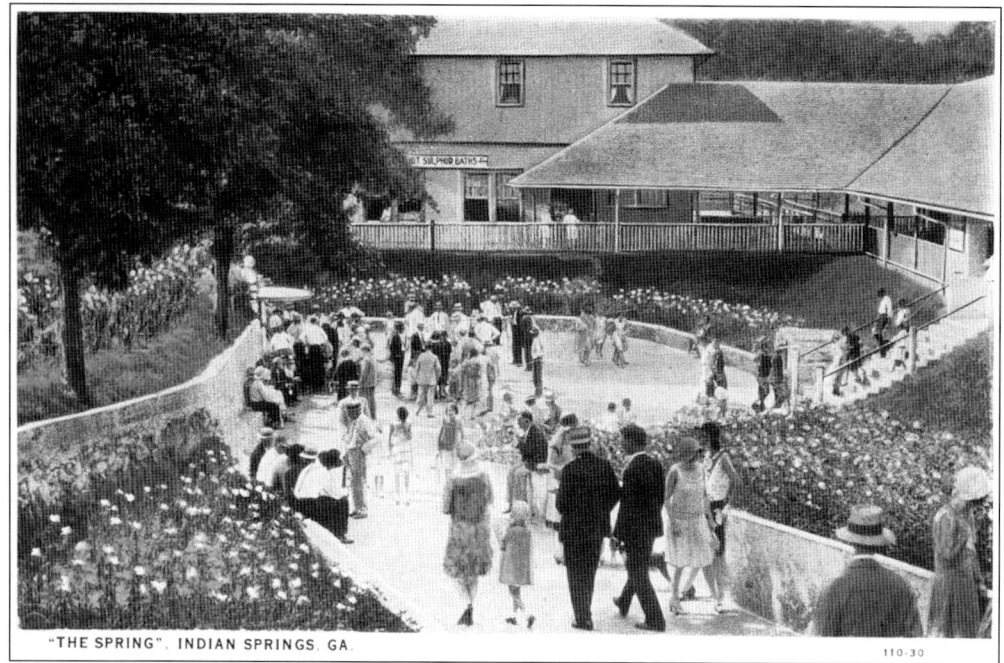

THE ENTRANCE TO THE SPRINGS AND BATH HOUSE AT INDIAN SPRINGS, C. 1918. A printed message reads: "Indian Springs famed 125 years for its curative properties of water. On Southern Railway and State Route 42, scenic and shortest route between Atlanta and Macon."

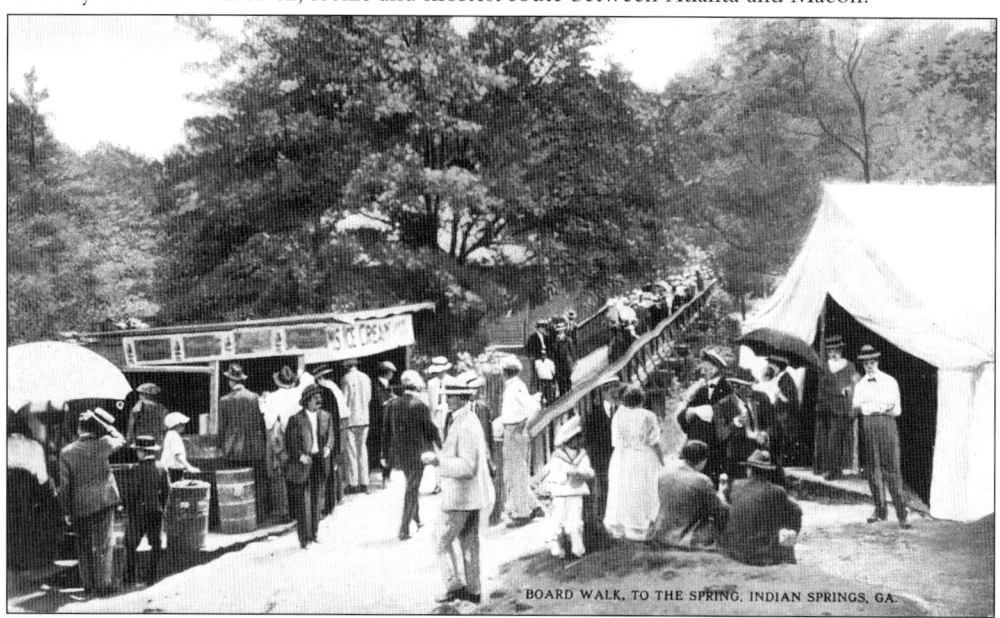

INDIAN SPRINGS. This was a popular place, as this crowd shows. A printed message reads in part: "Indian Springs Water is the greatest health giver on earth, and has been for a hundred years. It is famous for it unlimited cures of Acute Brights Disease, Catarrhal Diseases of the Stomach, Intestines and Bladder, Skin Diseases, Acute and Chronic Rheumatism, Insomnia, Indigestion, Malaria, Liver and Nerve Trouble, Diabetes, and many others." The U.S. Food and Drug Administration probably would take issue with these claims today!

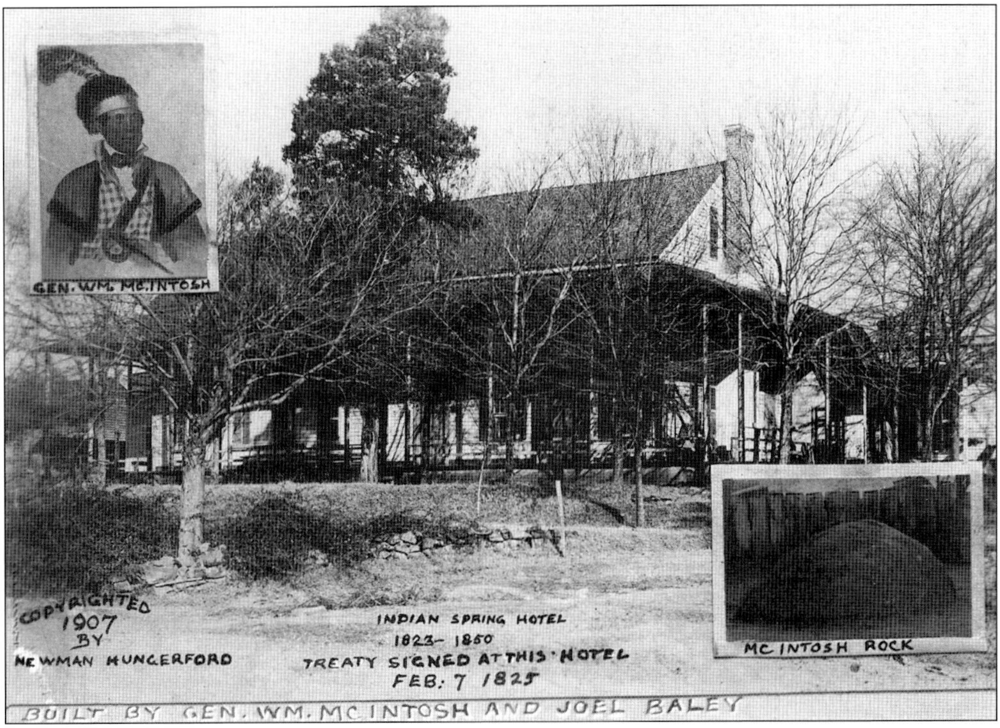

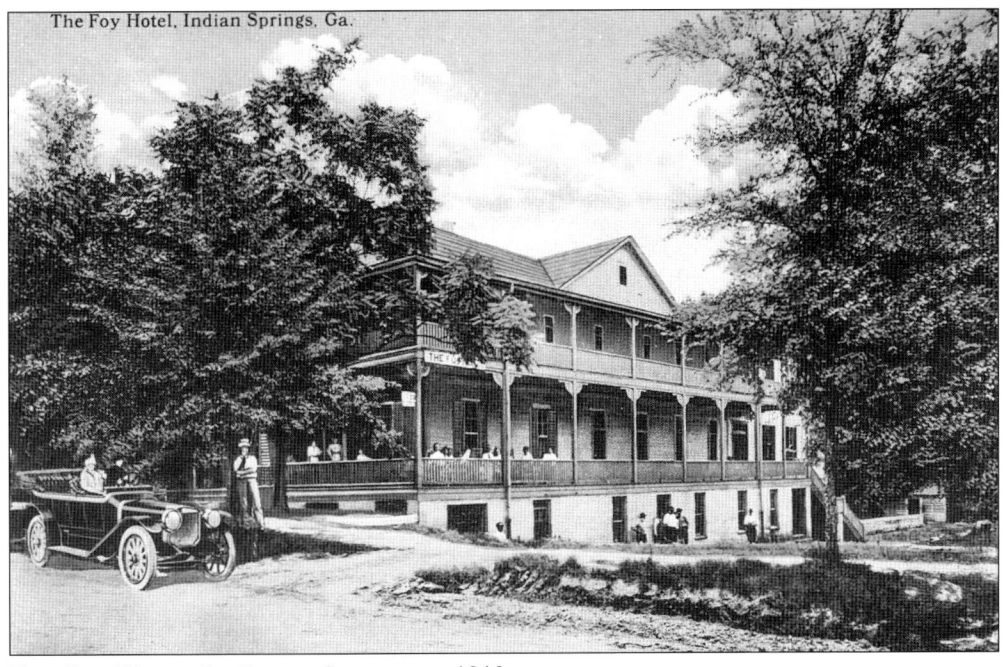

THE HOME OF CREEK INDIAN CHIEF WILLIAM MCINTOSH. This home was built in 1823 and stands today as a museum.

THE FOY HOTEL AT INDIAN SPRINGS, C. 1910.

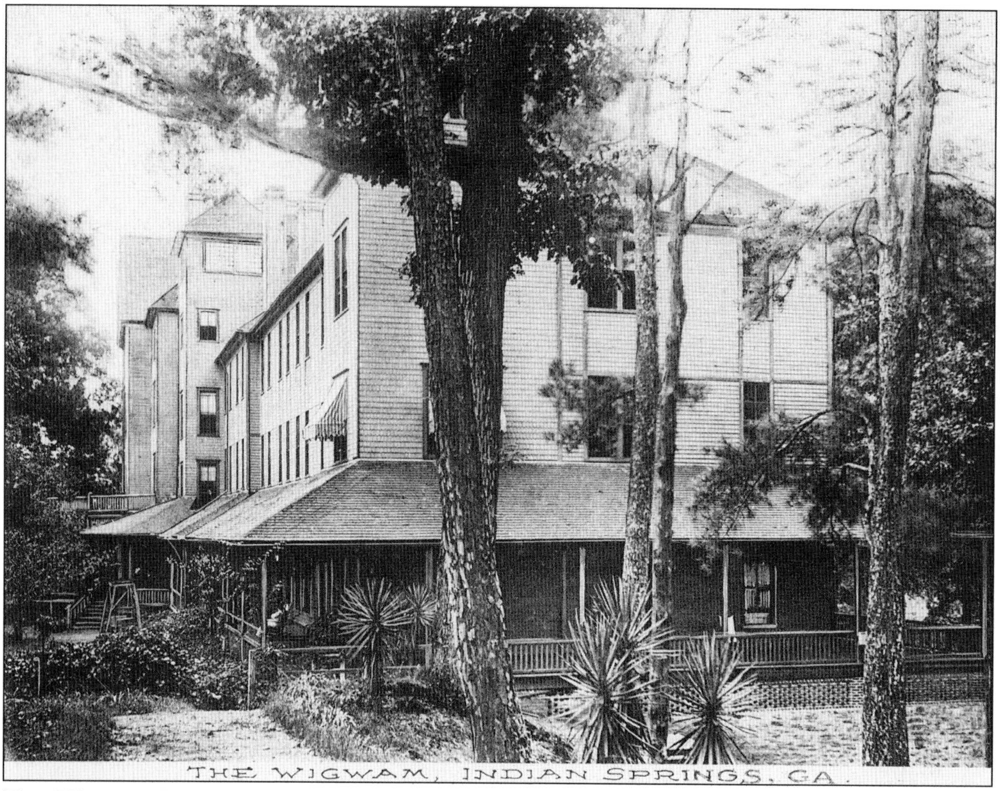

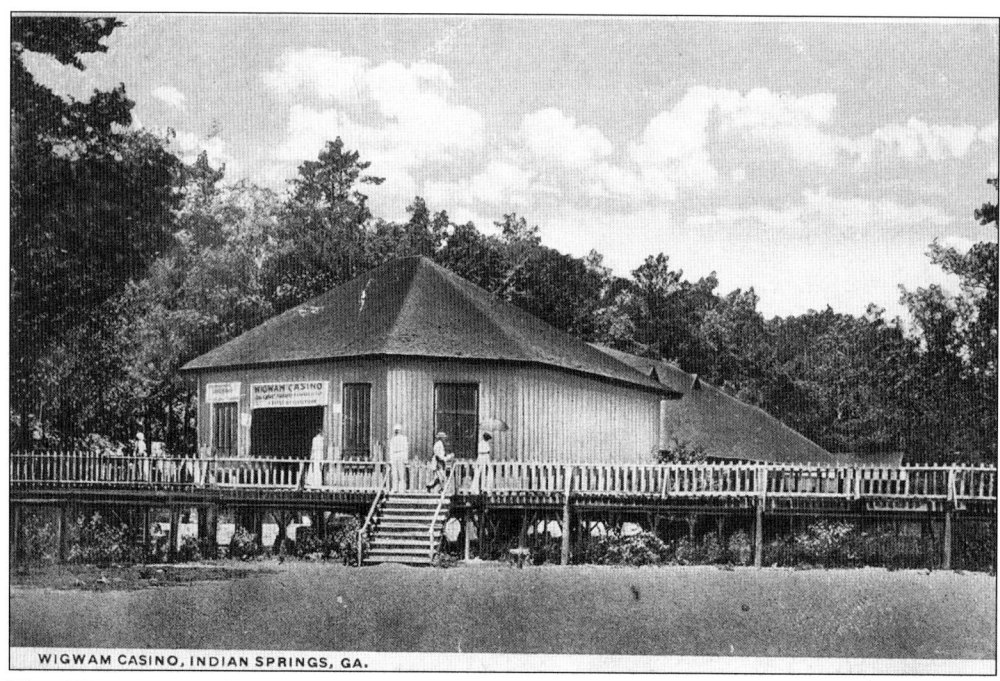

THE WIGWAM HOTEL AT INDIAN SPRINGS, C. 1907.

THE WIGWAM CASINO AT INDIAN SPRINGS.

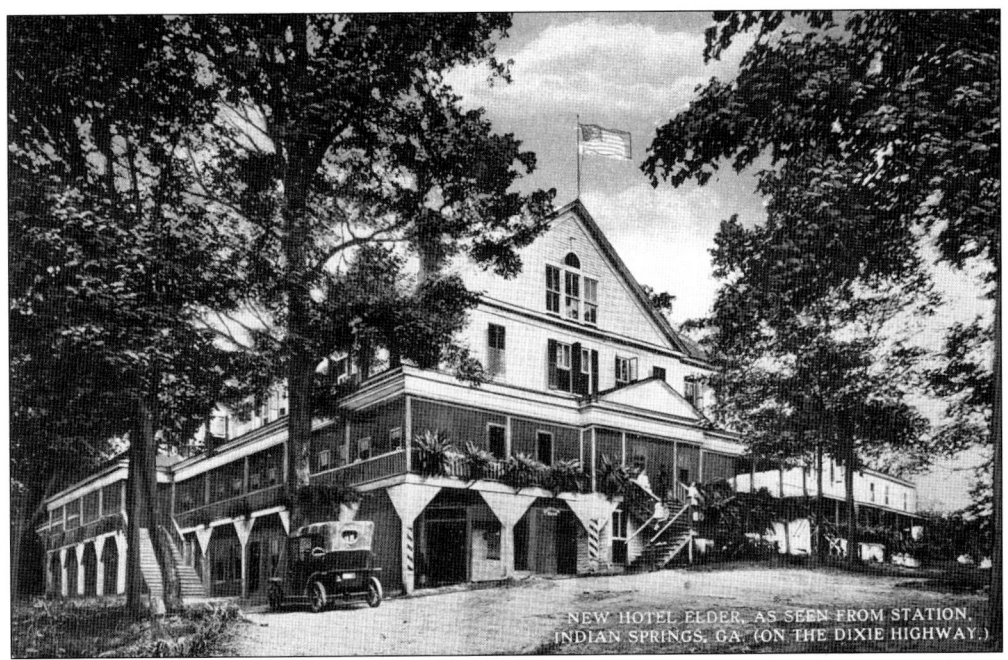

THE NEW HOTEL ELDER AT INDIAN SPRINGS. All of these beautiful old wooden hotel buildings in Indian Springs fell victim to fires over the years and none remain today.

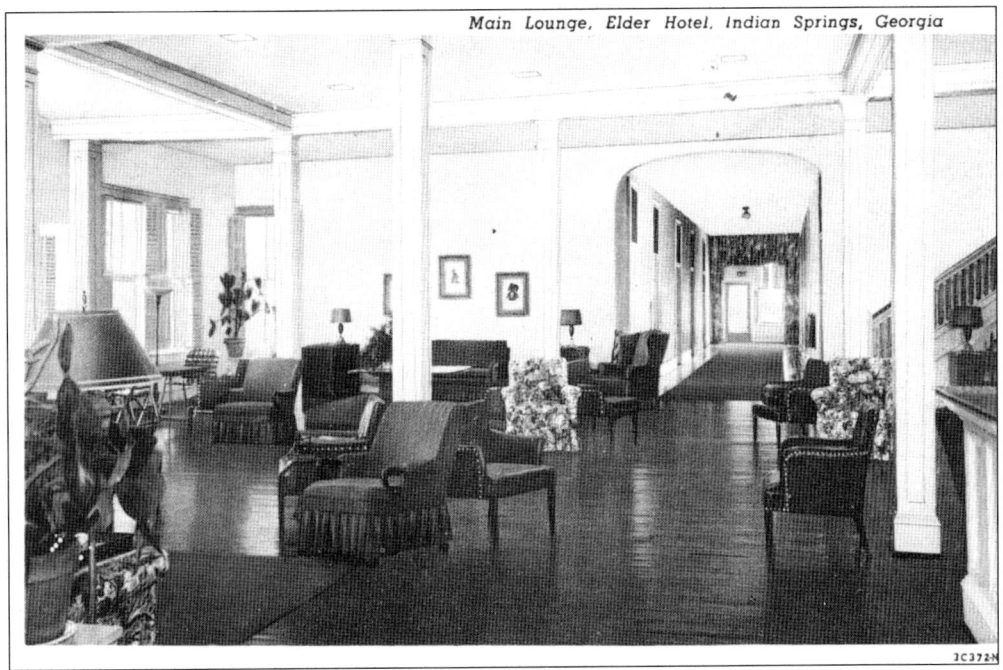

THE MAIN LOUNGE OF THE ELDER HOTEL IN INDIAN SPRINGS.

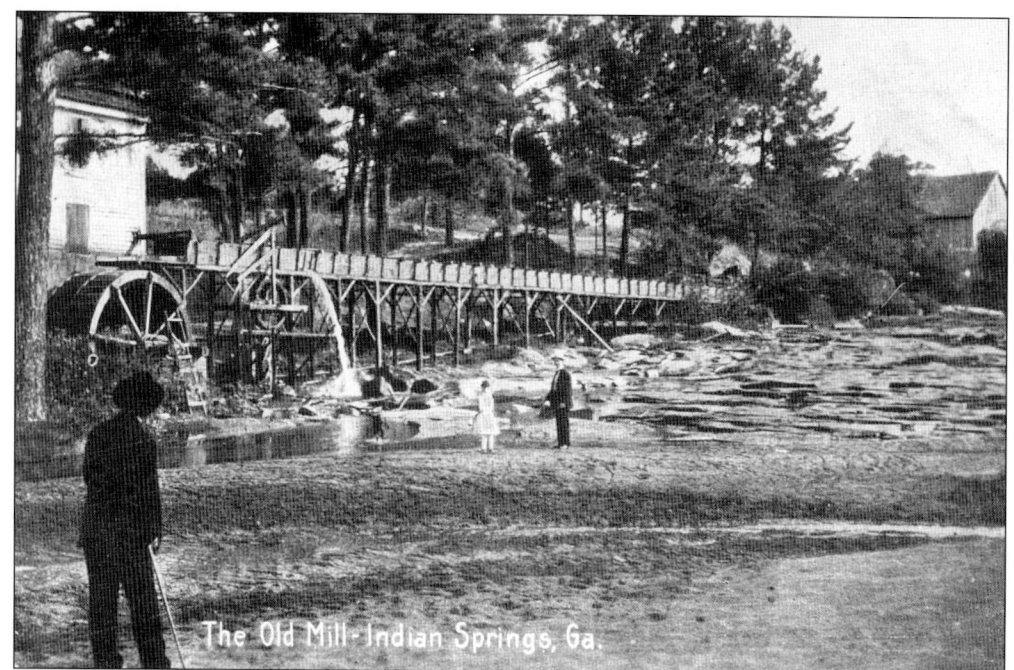

A Long Water Flume. The flume provided water to the overshot wheel at the old mill at Indian Springs *c.* 1908. The writer wrote to Athens: "How I wish all of my Athens friends were here with me. Everything is lovely—having good time, of course. M.C.B."

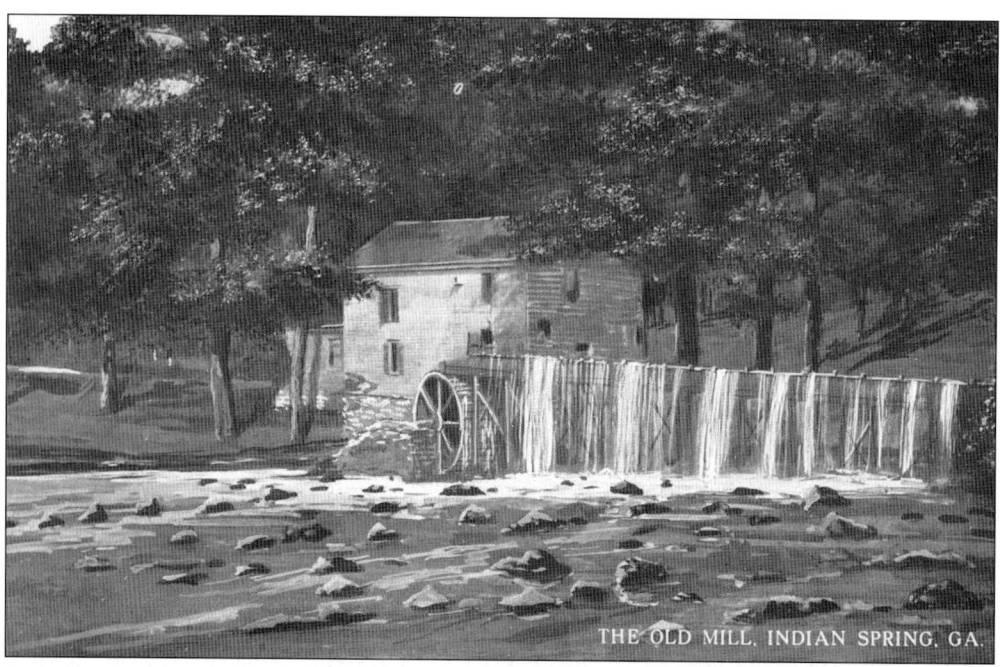

Another View of the Old Mill from a Different Angle. The writer's message reads in part: "This is a fine place to be. Know you would like it. Sincerely B.J."

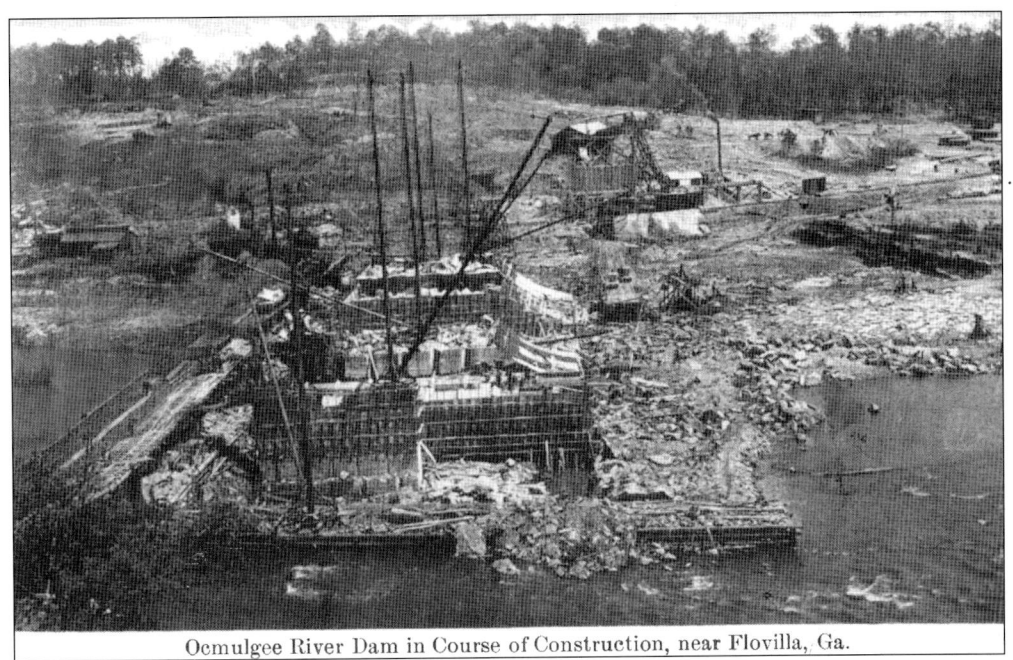

Ocmulgee River Dam in Course of Construction, near Flovilla, Ga.

AN INTERESTING AND UNUSUAL VIEW OF THE DAM UNDER CONSTRUCTION ON THE OCMULGEE RIVER, WHICH FORMED LAKE JACKSON.

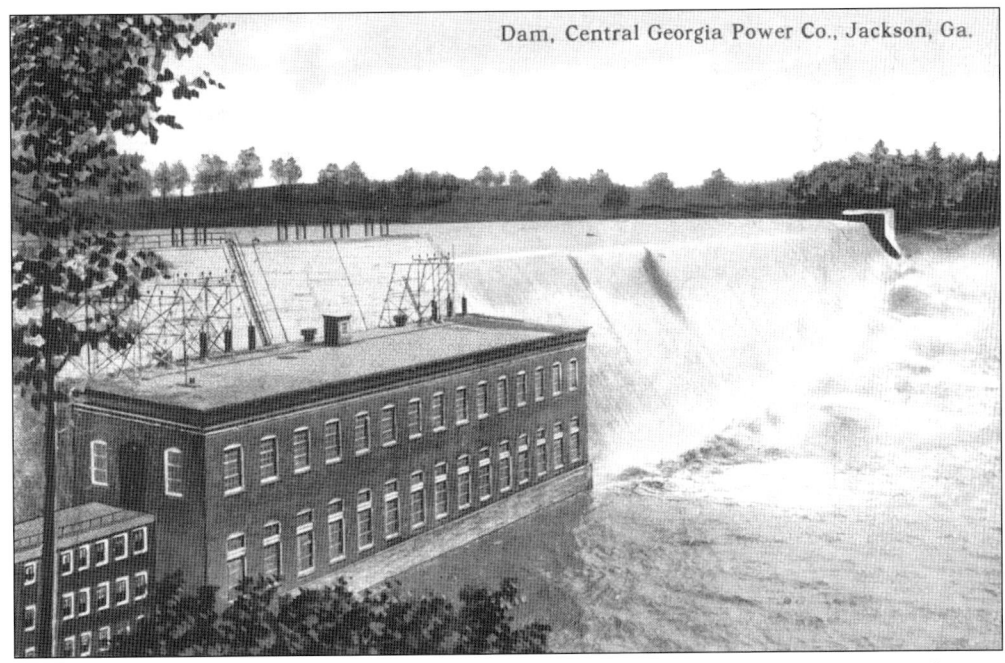

Dam, Central Georgia Power Co., Jackson, Ga.

THE LAKE JACKSON DAM AND POWER PLANT AFTER COMPLETION BY THE GEORGIA POWER COMPANY.

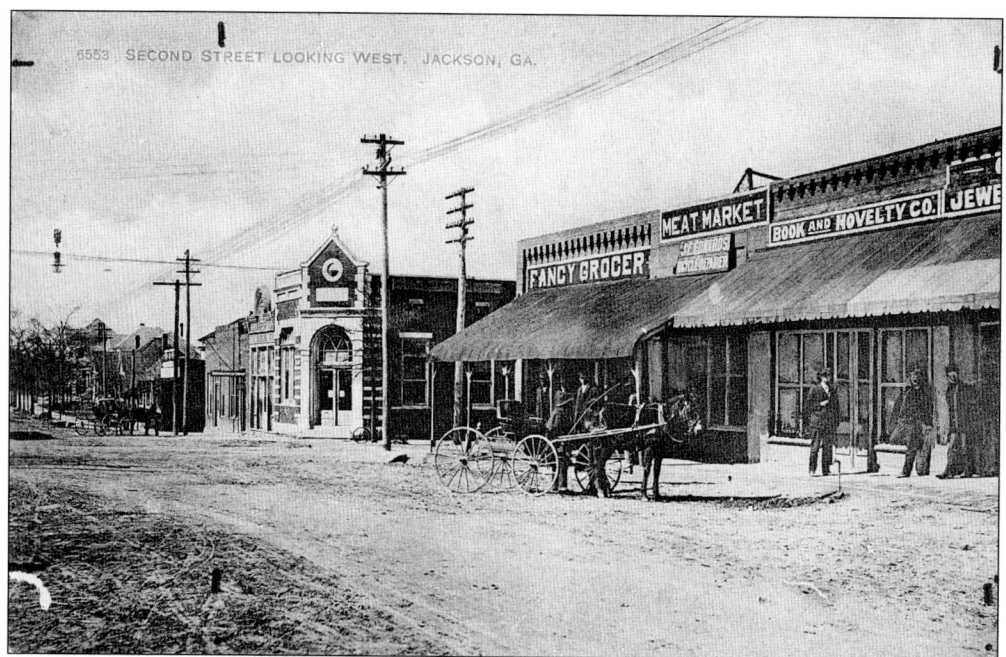

A VIEW OF SECOND STREET LOOKING WEST IN JACKSON, C. 1907. Several Jackson businesses can be seen, including the bank with the catercornered doorway.

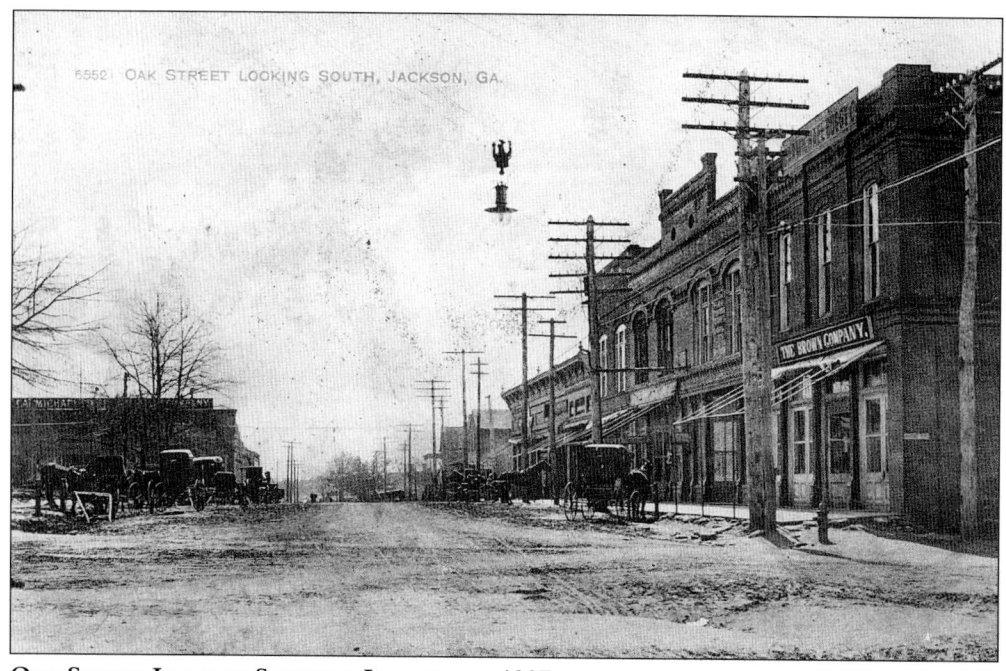

OAK STREET LOOKING SOUTH IN JACKSON, C. 1907.

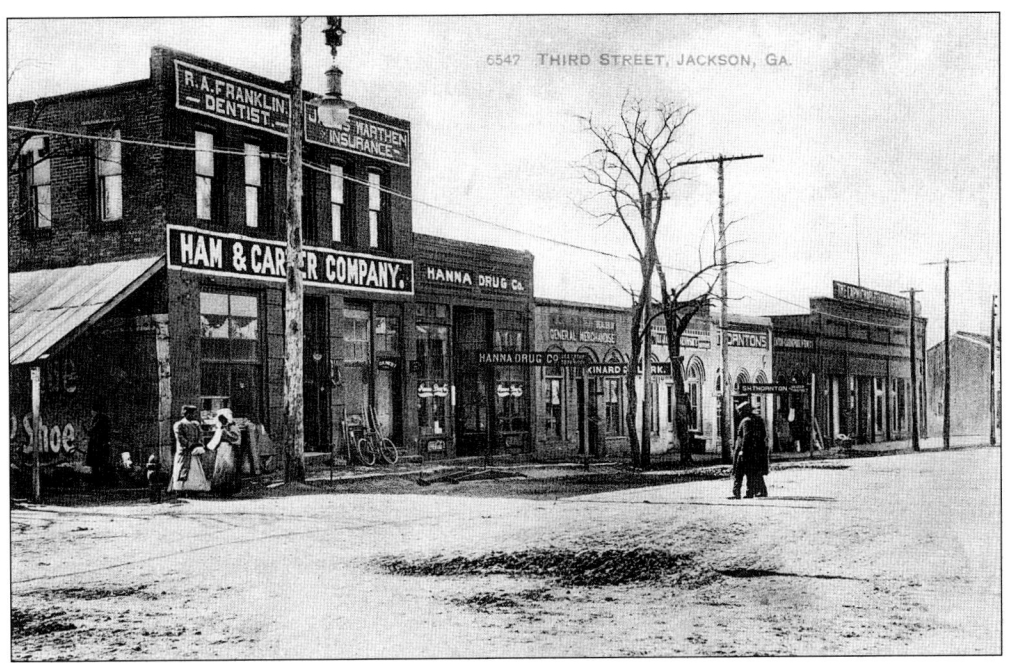

A c. 1907 View of Third Street. Several Jackson businesses can be identified in this card.

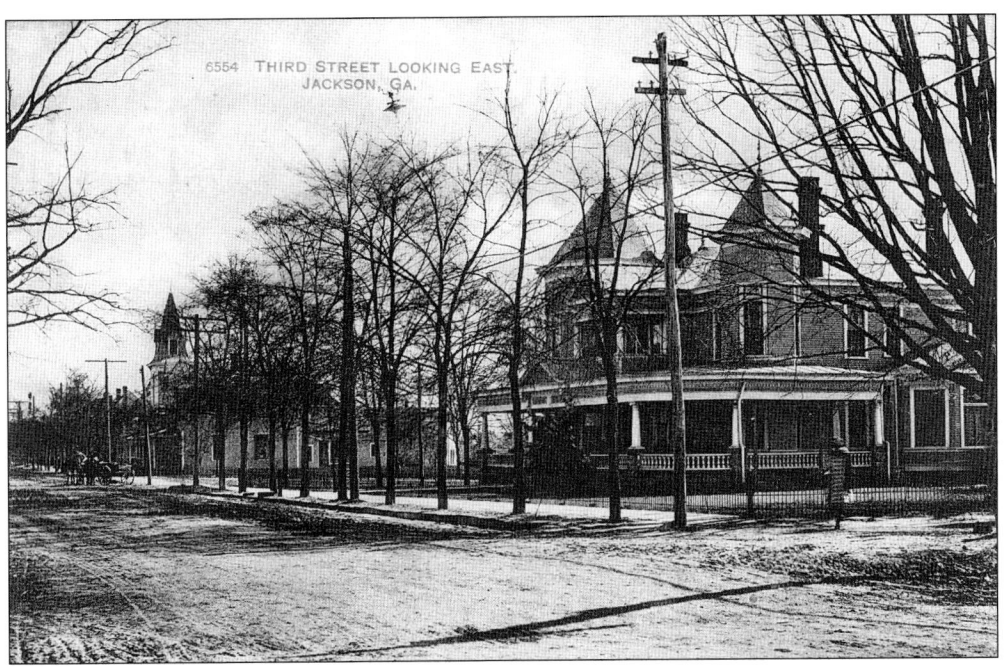

Third Street Looking East in Jackson. This was a residential area.

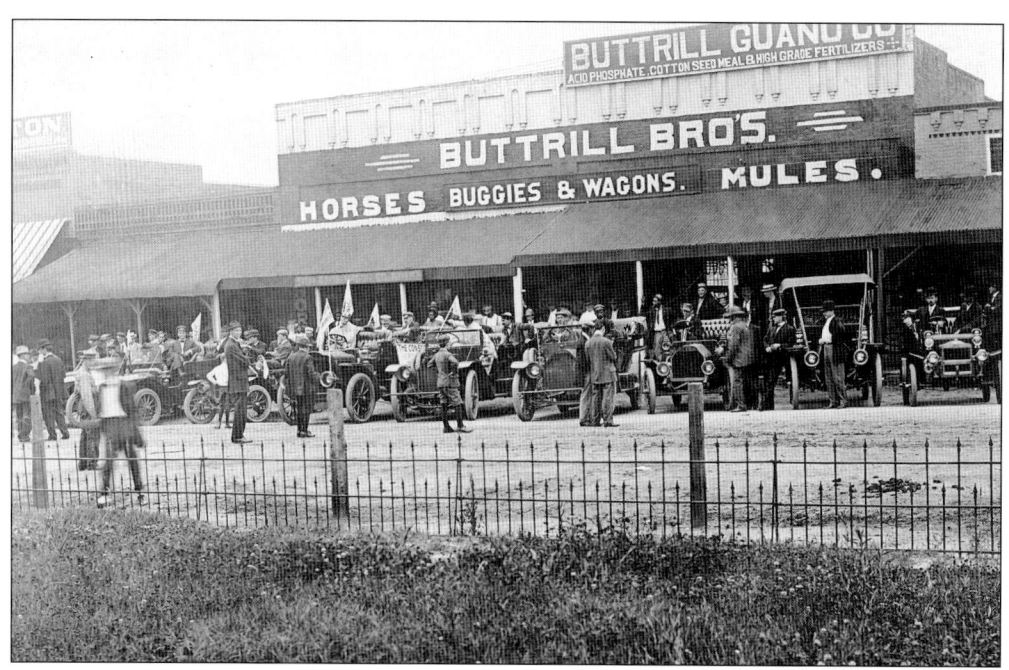

A Wonderful Real-Photo View of the Buttrill Brothers' Store on Jackson Street in Jackson, c. 1908.

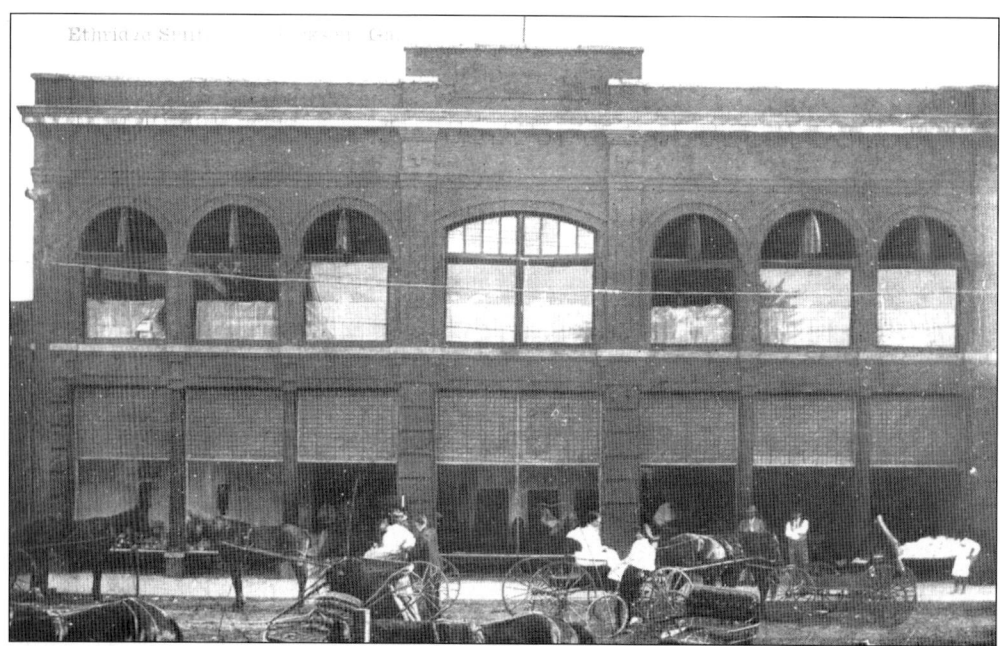

A Busy Day at the Ethridge-Smith Company on the Corner of Oak and Third Streets in Jackson, c. 1910. Ethridge and Smith were cotton brokers.

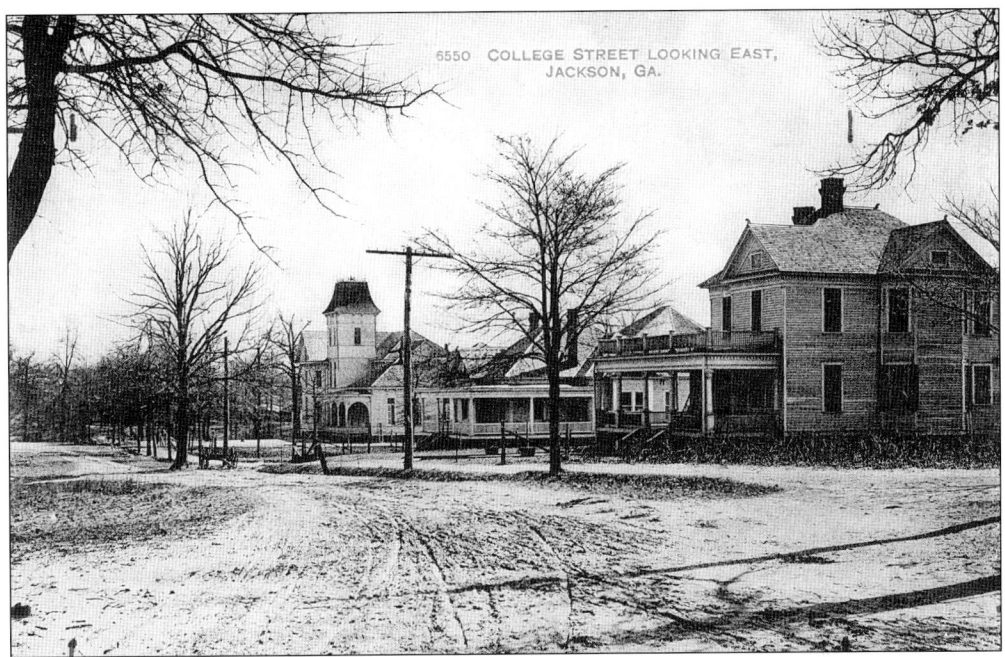

A VIEW DOWN COLLEGE STREET, LOOKING EAST IN JACKSON. This view shows some of the town's beautiful homes.

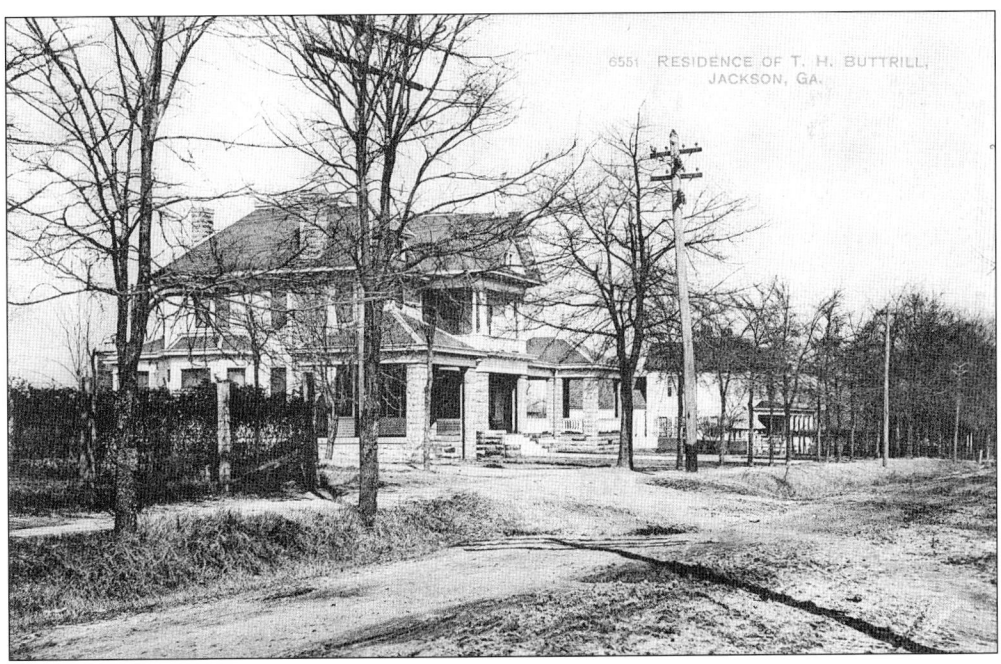

THE RESIDENCE OF MR. T.H. BUTTRILL, COTTON BUYER, IN JACKSON.

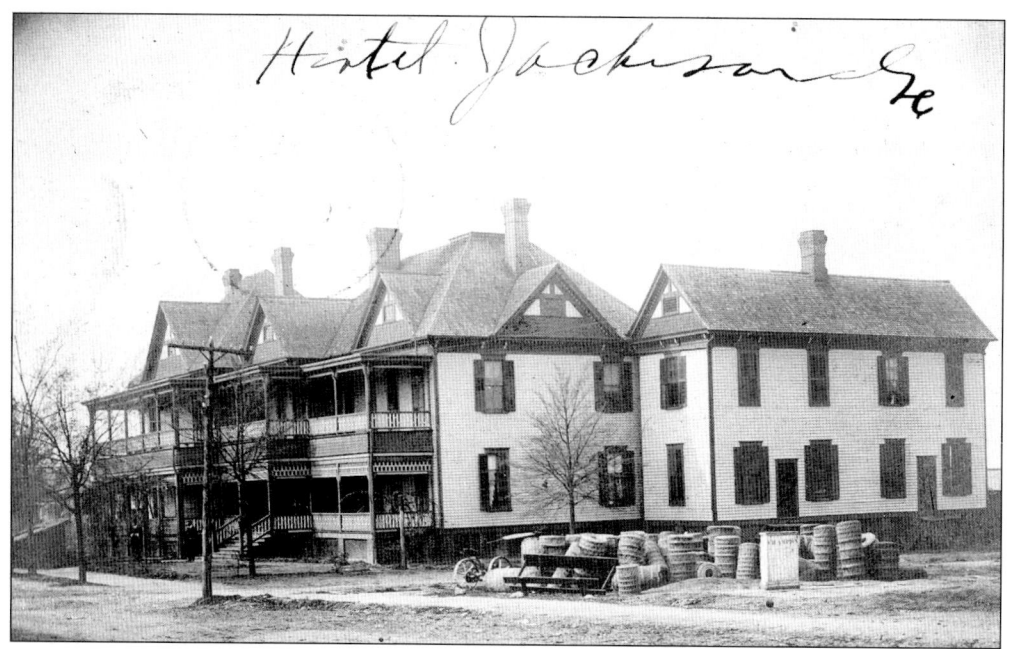

A GRAND REAL-PHOTO VIEW OF THE HOTEL JACKSON IN 1906.

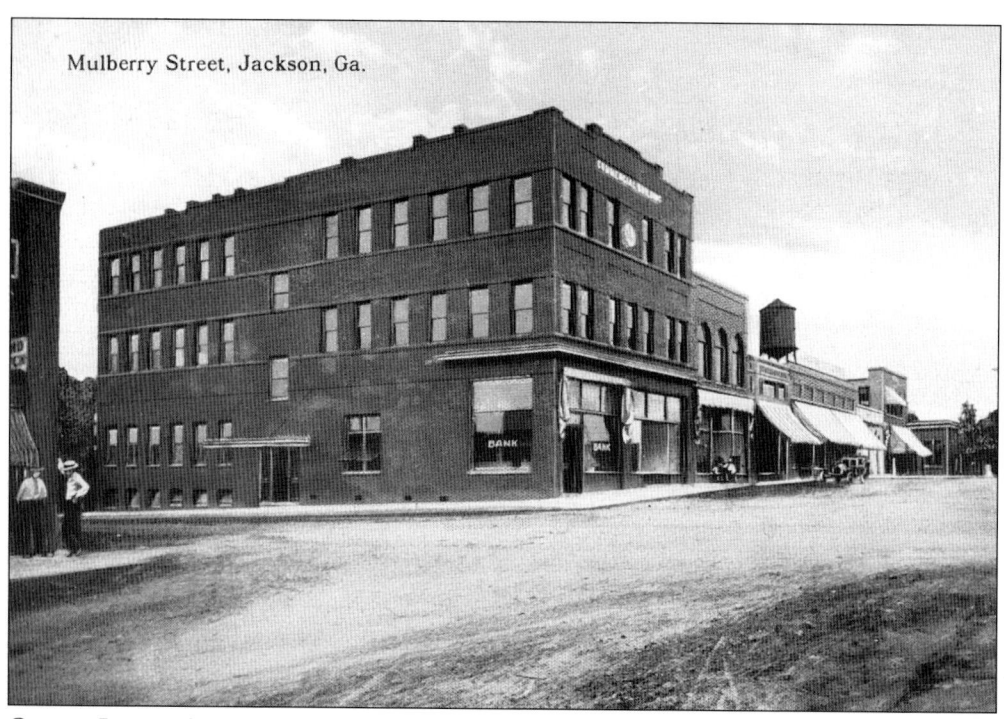

ONE OF JACKSON'S THREE BANKS IN 1910. This one was located in the Commercial Building.

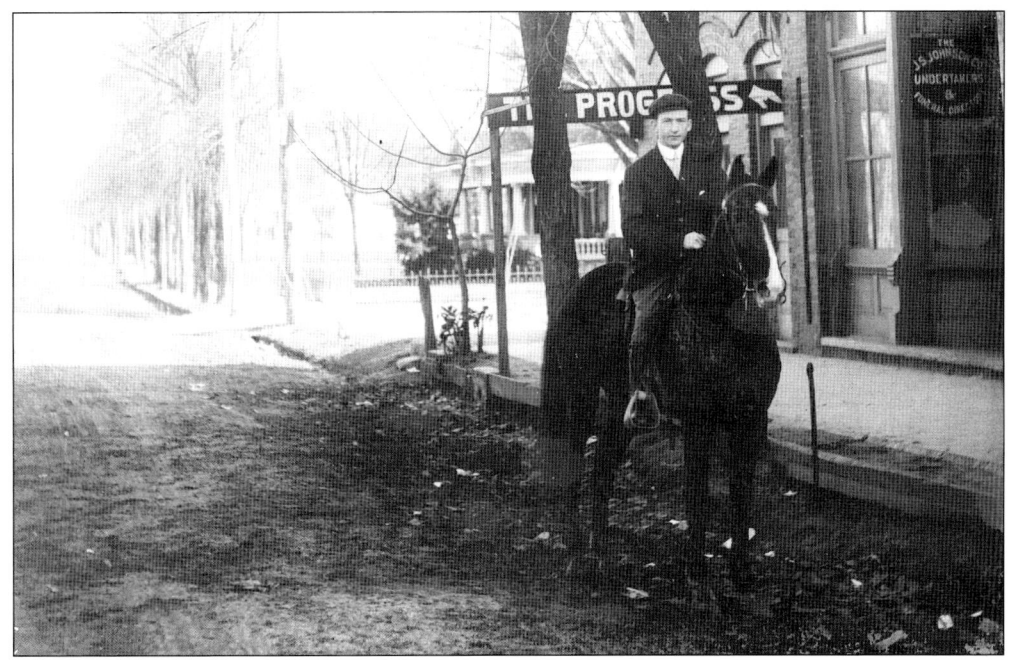

A Gentleman on Horseback in Front of J.S. Johnson's Funeral Parlor on Third Street in Jackson, c. 1910. The office of the *Butts County Progress*, a local newspaper, is next door.

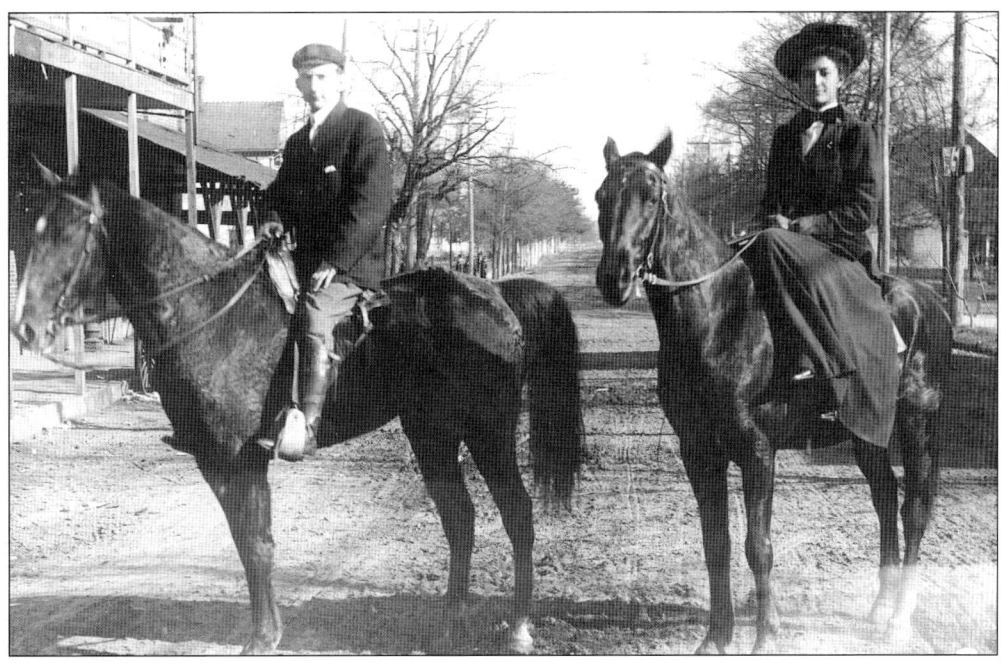

A Gentleman Rider. He is joined by a lady rider on the streets of Jackson *c.* 1910. Note that the lady is mounted sidesaddle.

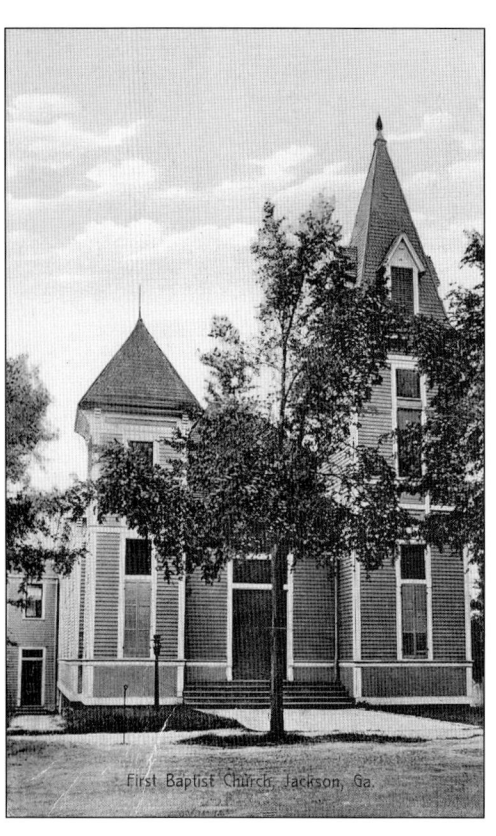

THE FIRST BAPTIST CHURCH BUILDING IN JACKSON. This charming little building is seen in a *c.* 1908 view.

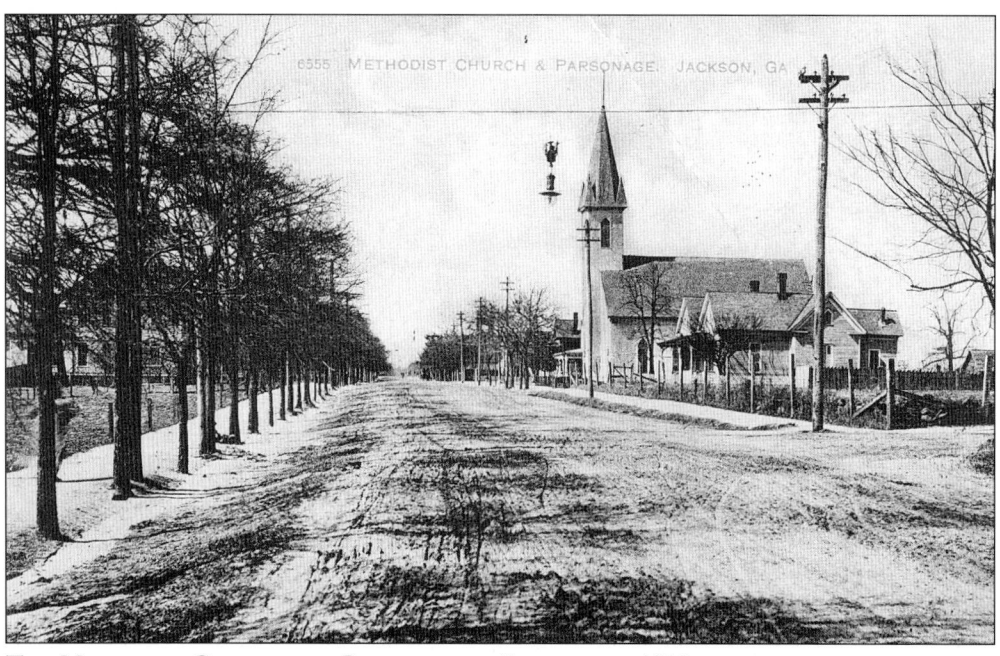

THE METHODIST CHURCH AND PARSONAGE IN JACKSON, *c.* **1908.**

Four

CLAYTON, COWETA, HEARD, AND HENRY COUNTIES

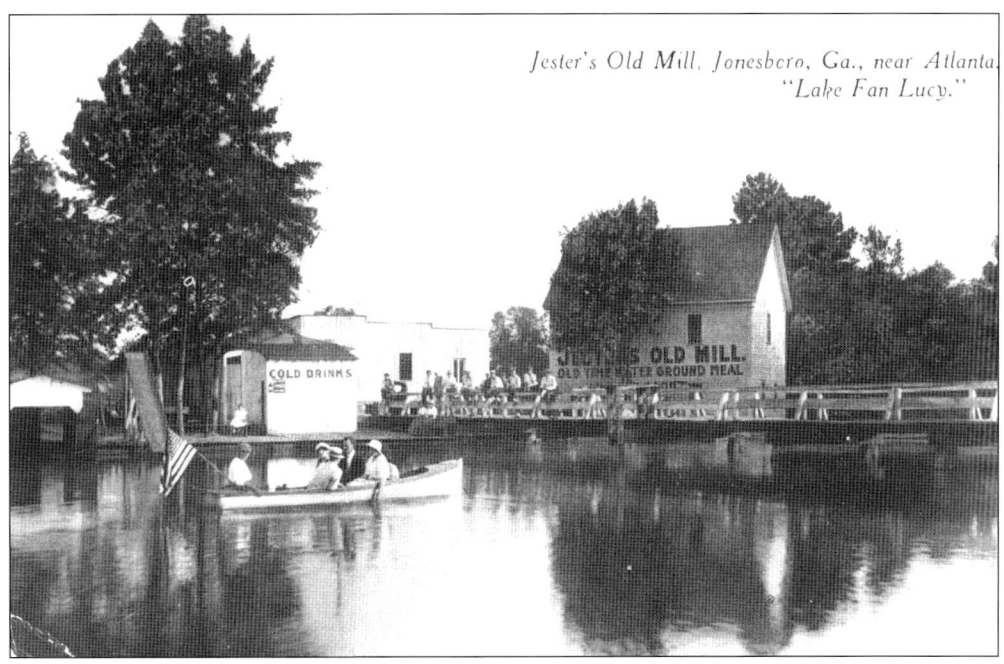

JESTER'S MILL ON LAKE FAN LUCY AT JONESBORO. This was already referred to as "Old" in this *c.* 1908 view.

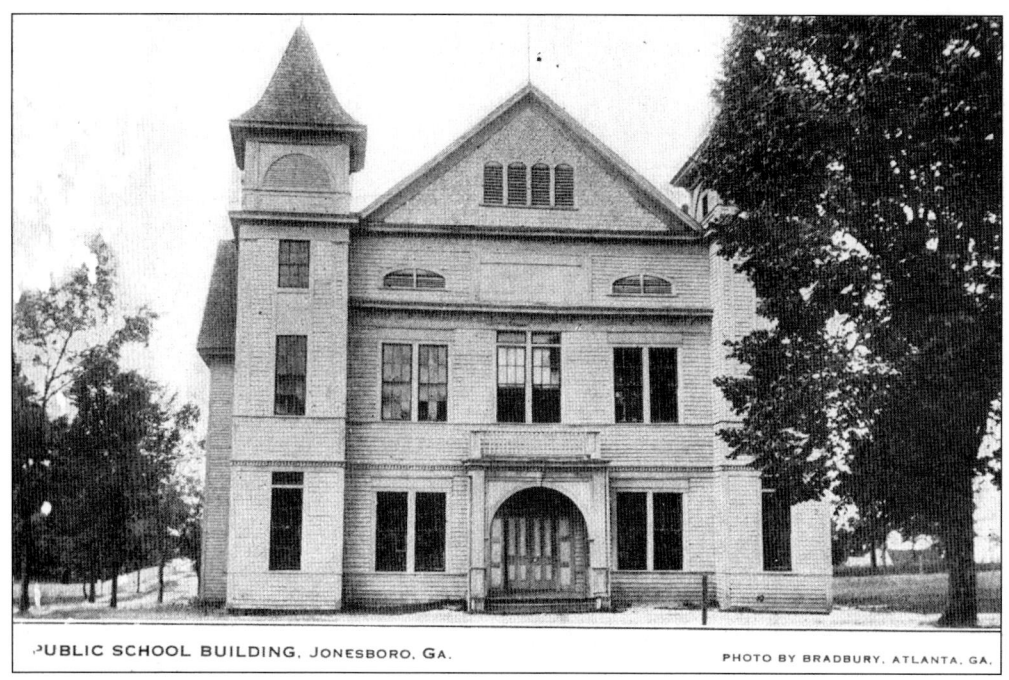

AN EARLY VIEW CARD SHOWING THE PUBLIC SCHOOL BUILDING AT JONESBORO. This card was mailed to Atlanta. The message reads: "Say! Would like to see you at your home Sun. P.M. (Aug. 9). What say you. Will be glad to have you come to Jonesboro most any time. Always A.S.M."

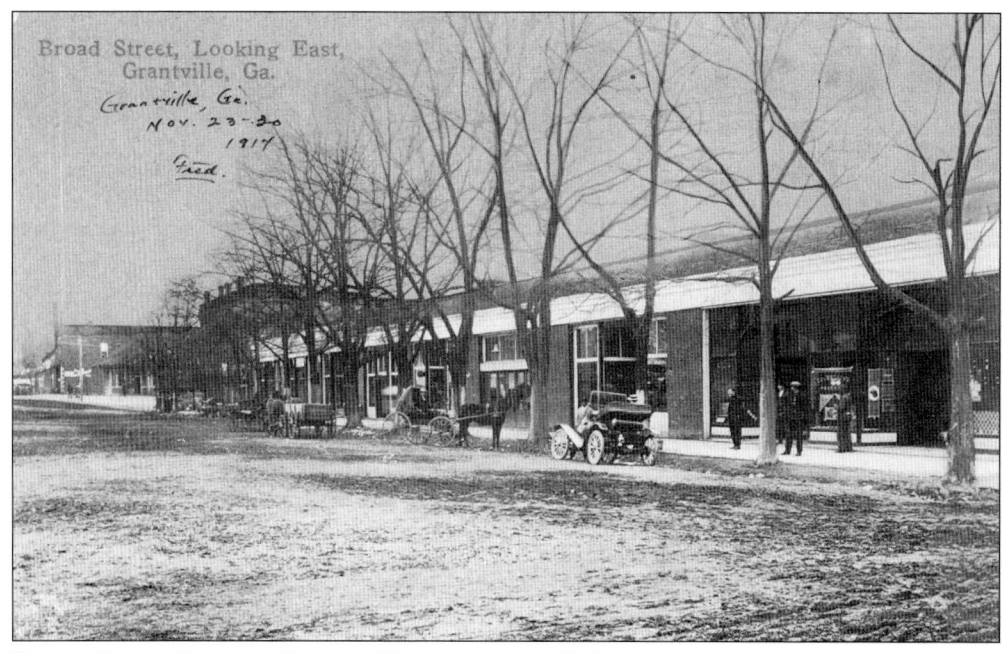

BROAD STREET LOOKING EAST IN GRANTVILLE, C. 1914.

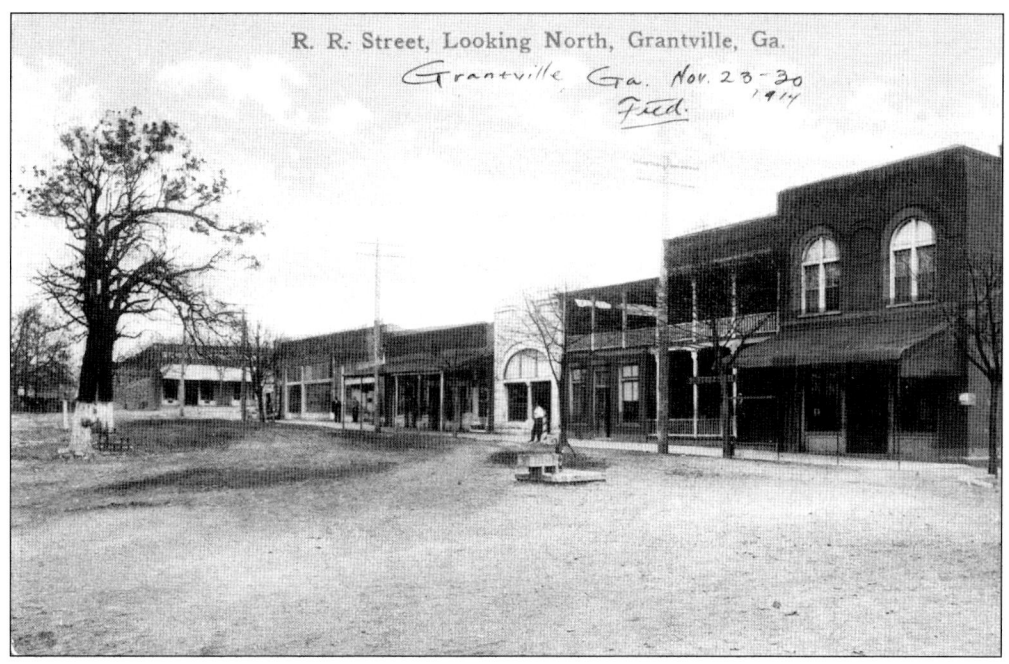

ANOTHER STREET SCENE IN GRANTVILLE, C. 1914. This view shows the stores along Railroad Street, looking north.

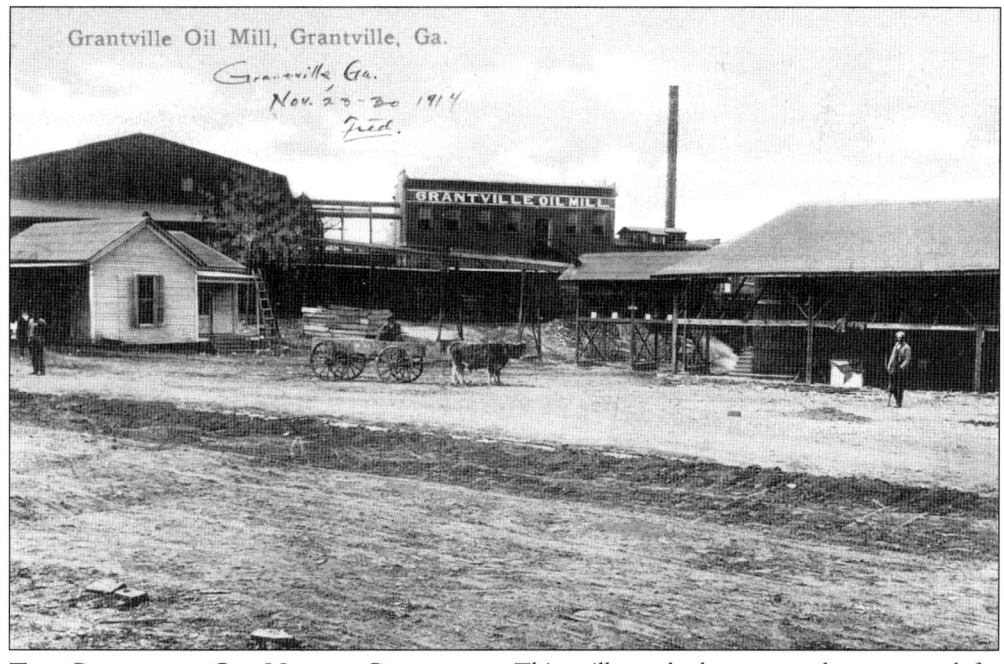

THE GRANTVILLE OIL MILL IN GRANTVILLE. This mill no doubt processed cotton seed for its oil.

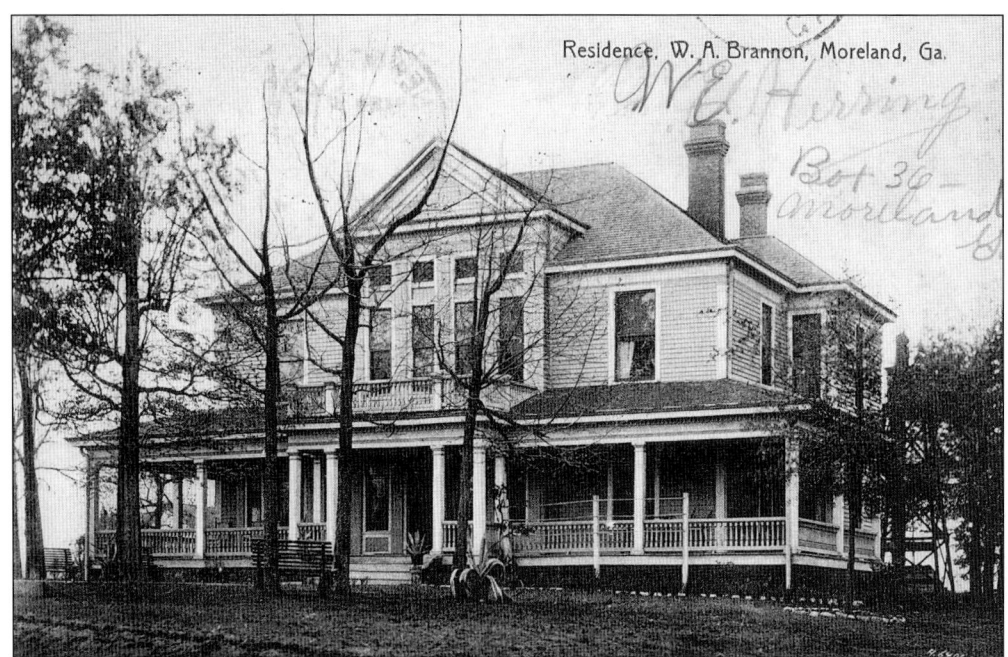

THE RESIDENCE OF W.A. BRANNON, WHO OPERATED A GENERAL MERCHANDISE AND JEWELRY STORE IN MORELAND. This card was mailed to Carrollton and the message written in pencil reads in part: "Helo Miss Allice I would Be glad to meet you for I have heard of You and your Kindness. I will Be over there the fourth Satturday in this month and would Be glad to Meet you. W.E.H."

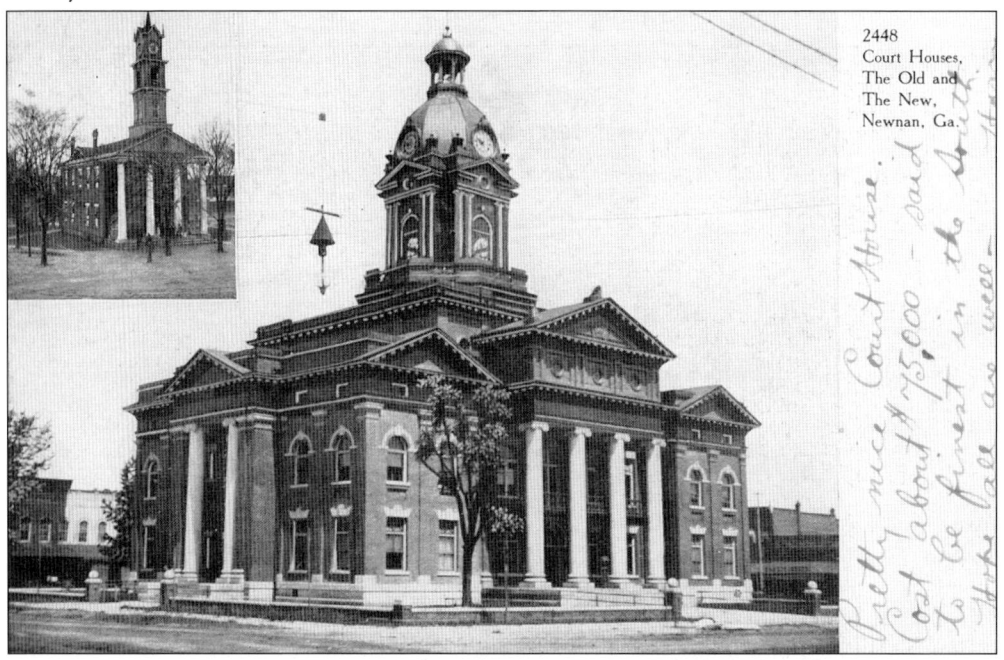

A COMPOSITE VIEW SHOWING THE "NEW" COWETA COUNTY COURTHOUSE, BUILT IN NEWNAN IN 1904. The inset in the upper left shows the old courthouse, built in 1829 and demolished in 1904.

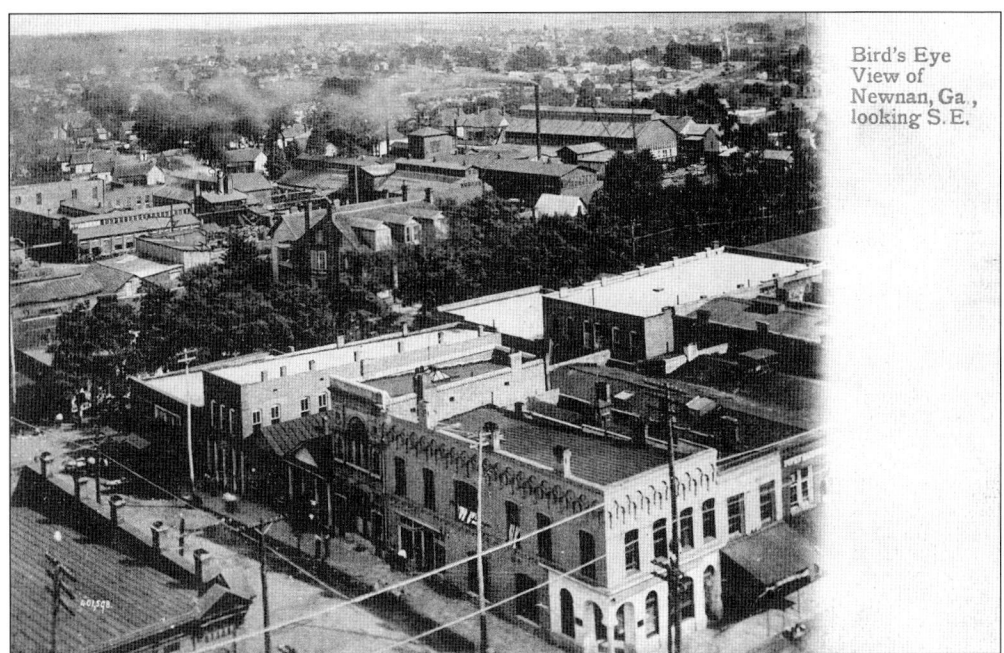

A Bird's-eye View of Newnan Looking toward the Southeast, c. 1907.

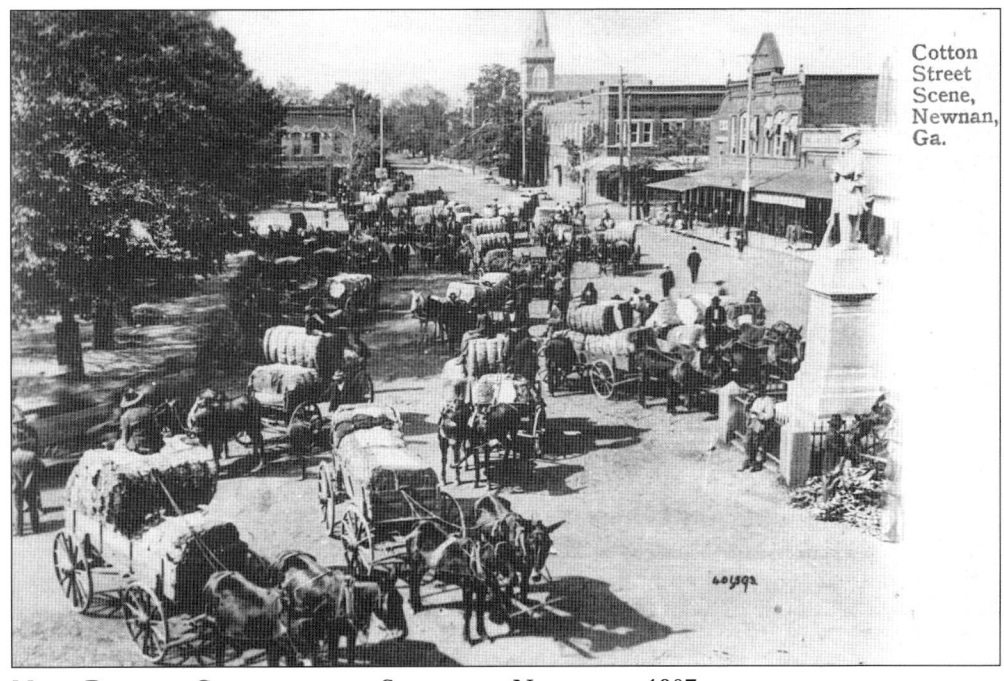

Many Bales of Cotton on the Streets of Newnan in 1907.

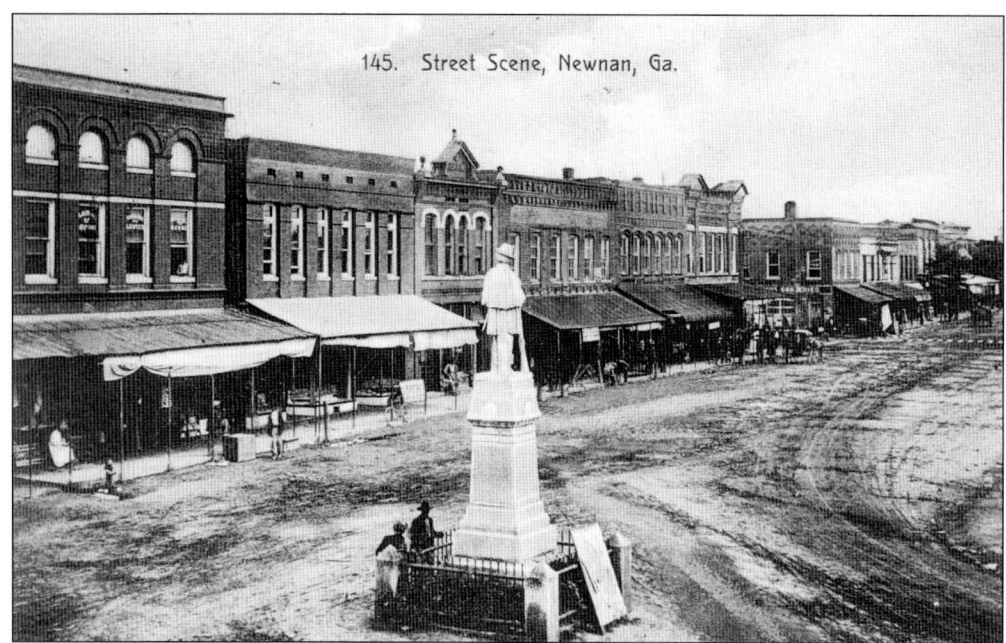

The Confederate Monument in Newnan, Dedicated on December 29, 1885. About 1914, the monument was moved from the middle of the street to its present location east of the courthouse.

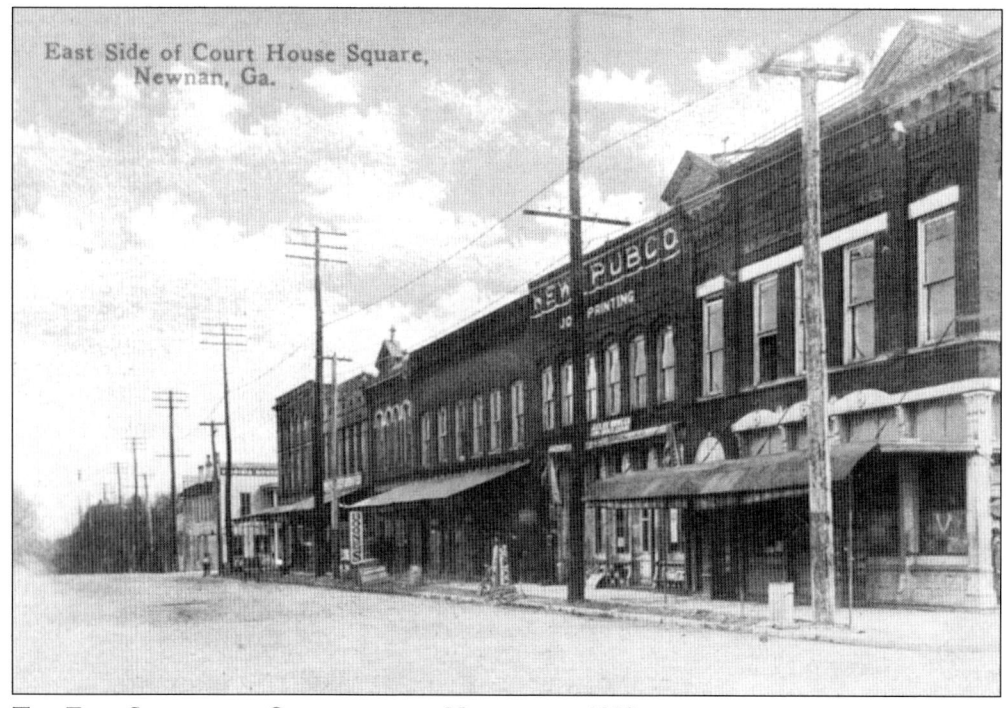

The East Side of the Courthouse in Newnan, c. 1909.

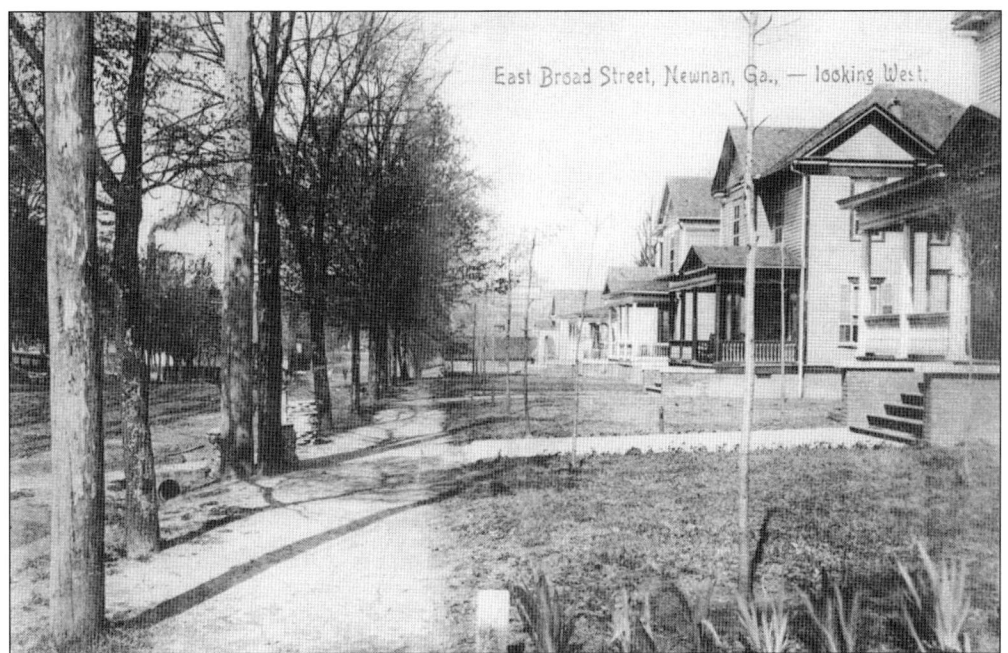

EAST BROAD STREET LOOKING WEST IN NEWNAN IN 1907, SHOWING SOME OF NEWNAN'S FINE HOMES.

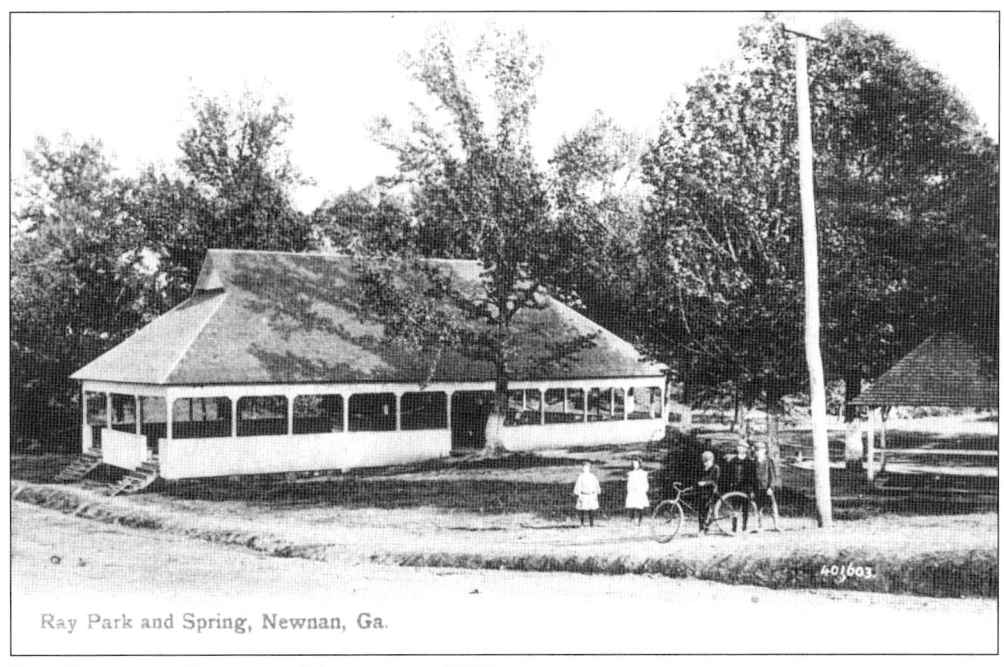

RAY PARK AND SPRING AT NEWNAN, C. 1909.

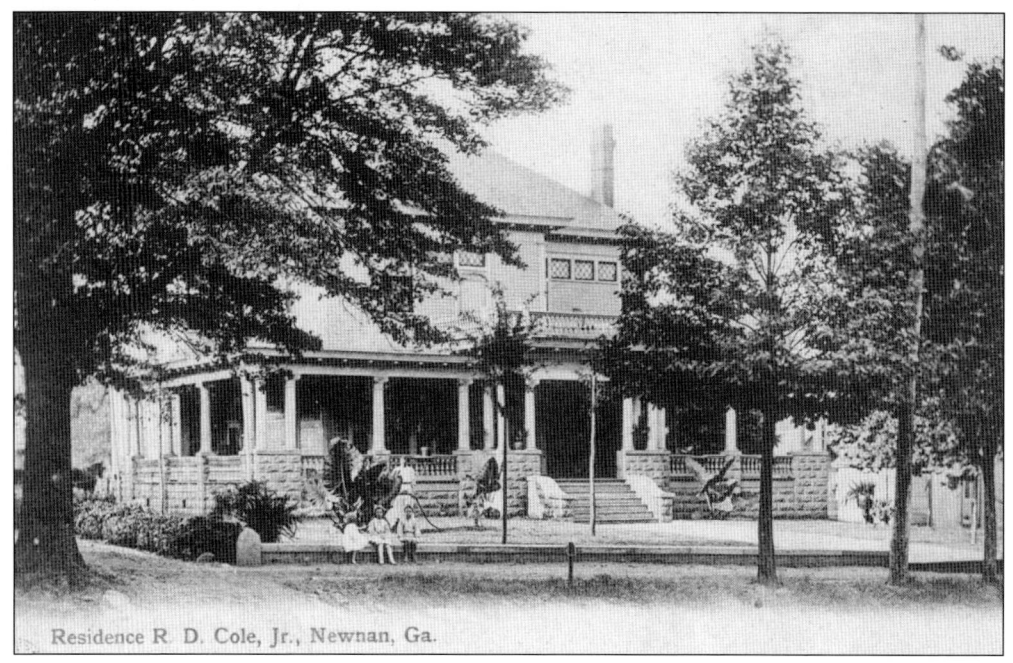

THE RESIDENCE OF MR. R.D. COLE JR. IN NEWNAN IN 1906.

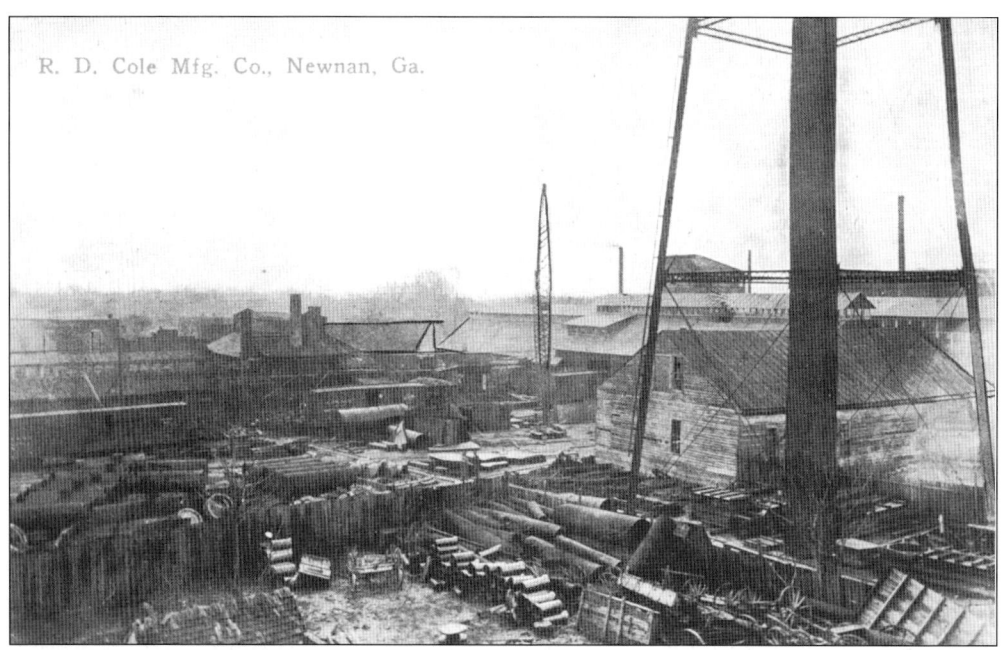

THE R.D. COLE MANUFACTURING COMPANY, AT 57 E. BROAD STREET IN NEWNAN. The company manufactured engines and boilers.

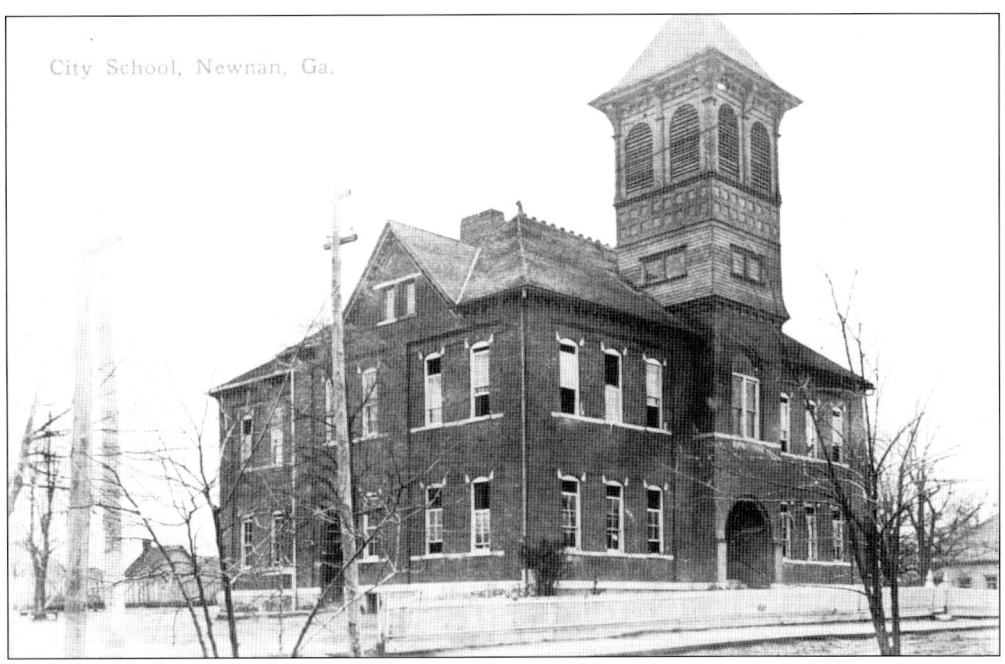

THE CITY SCHOOL IN NEWNAN. The school had a grandiose bell tower.

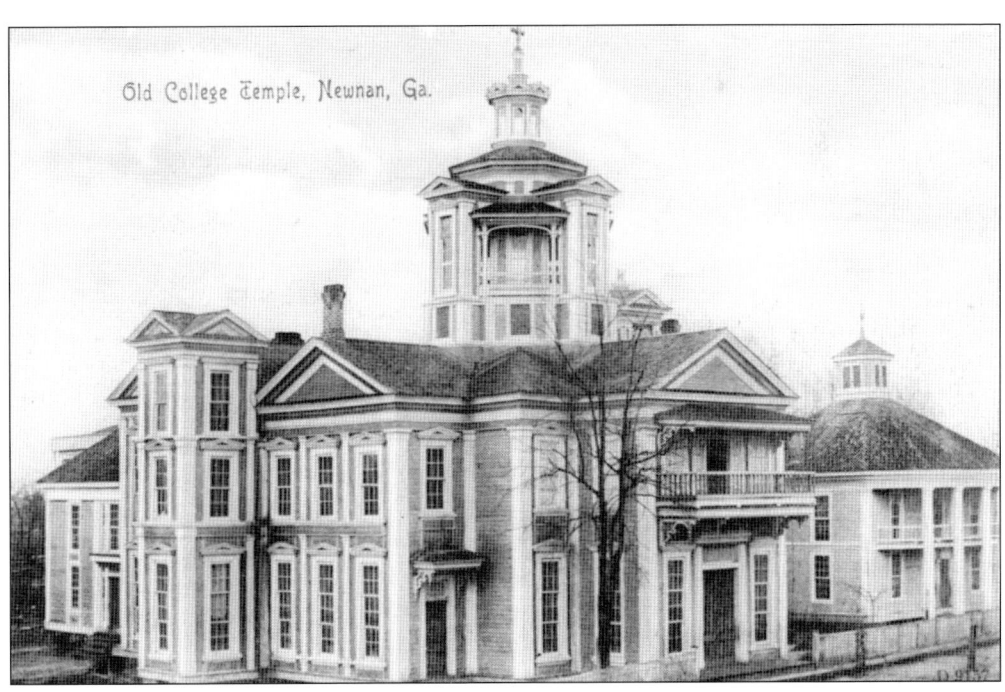

THE OLD COLLEGE TEMPLE IN NEWNAN, C. 1909.

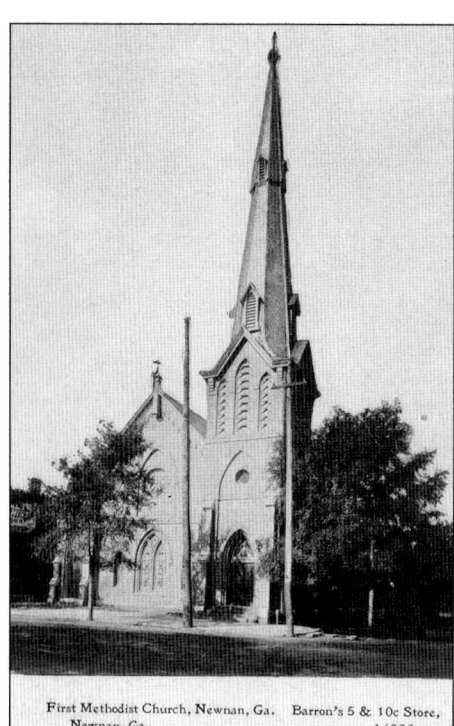

THE FIRST METHODIST CHURCH IN NEWNAN, C. 1907.

THE CENTRAL BAPTIST CHURCH IN NEWNAN, C. 1907.

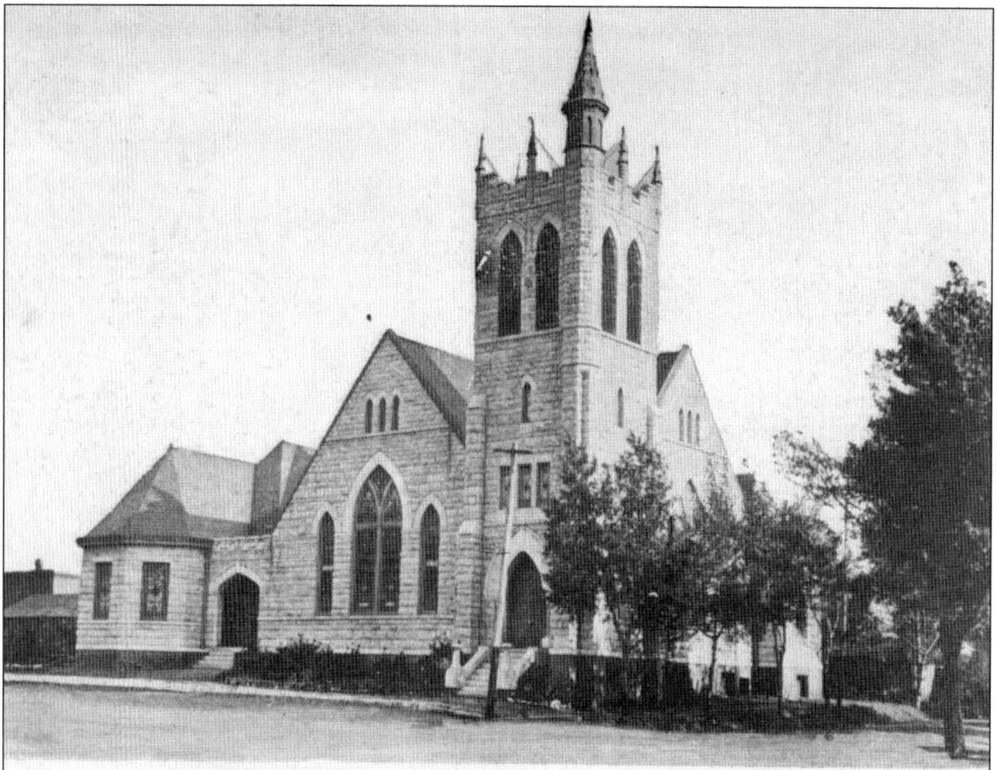

THE FIRST BAPTIST CHURCH IN NEWNAN, C. 1907.

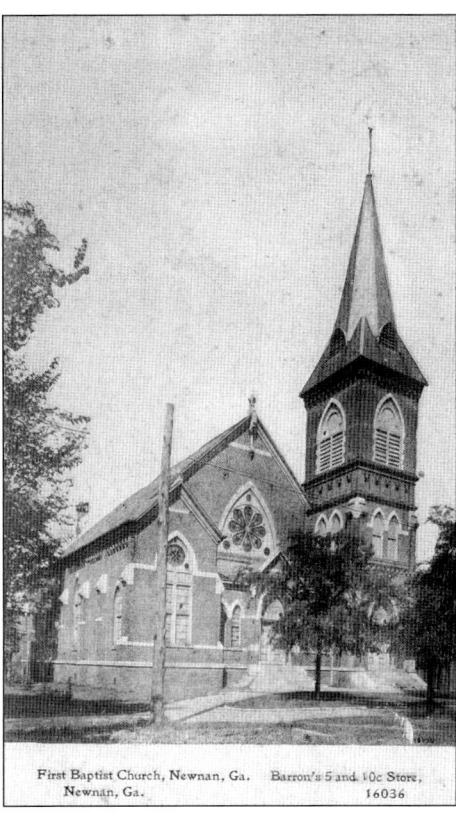

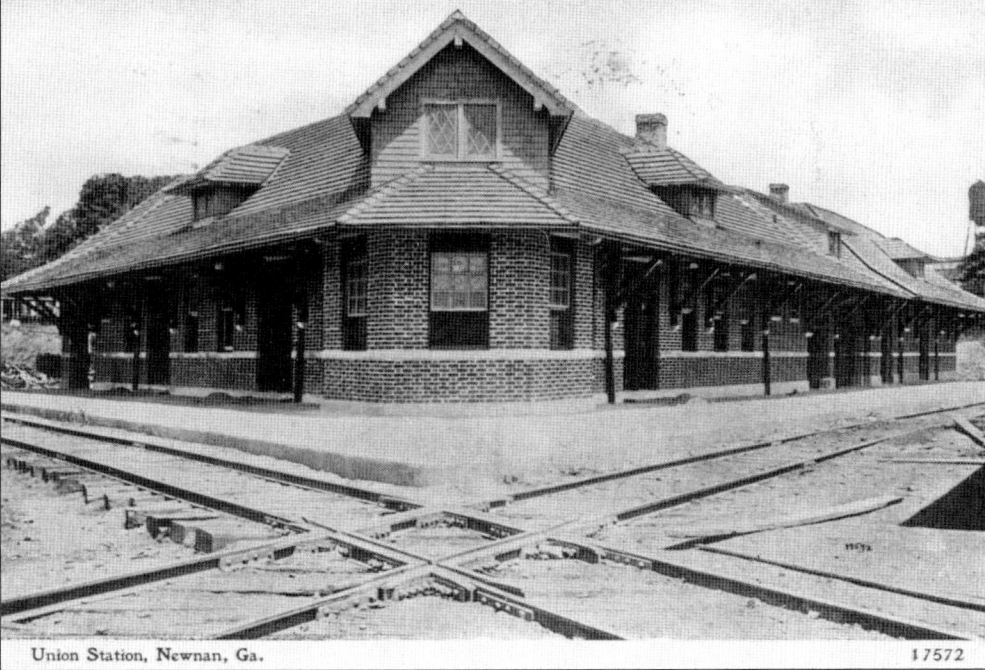

THE UNION STATION RAILROAD DEPOT IN NEWNAN, C. 1912. Newnan was served by the Atlanta and West Point Railroad and the Central of Georgia Railroad.

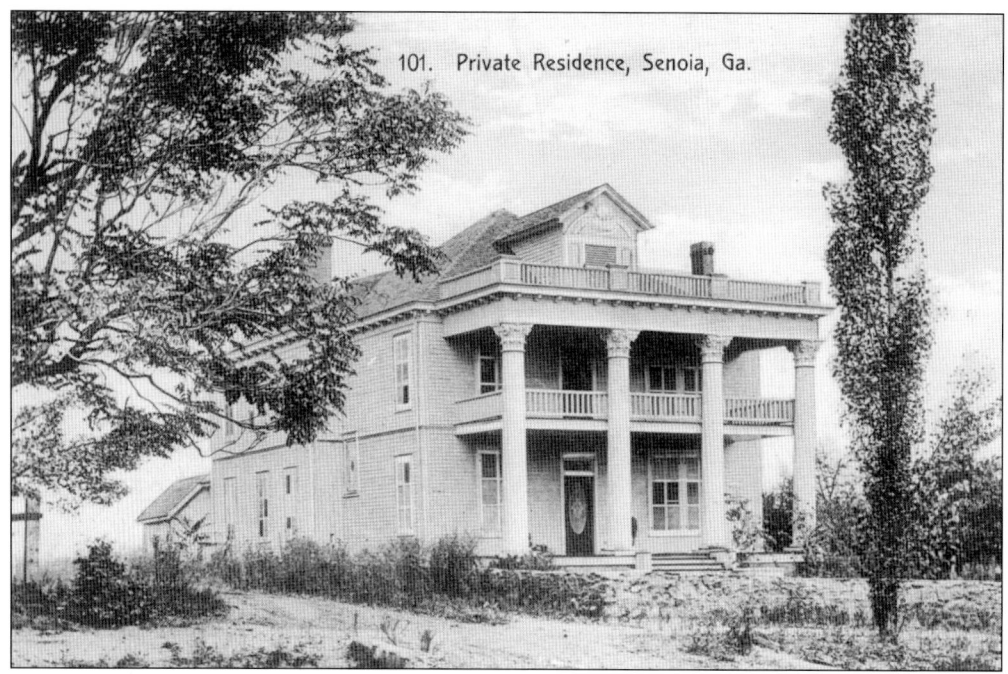

A Private Residence in Senoia, c. 1912.

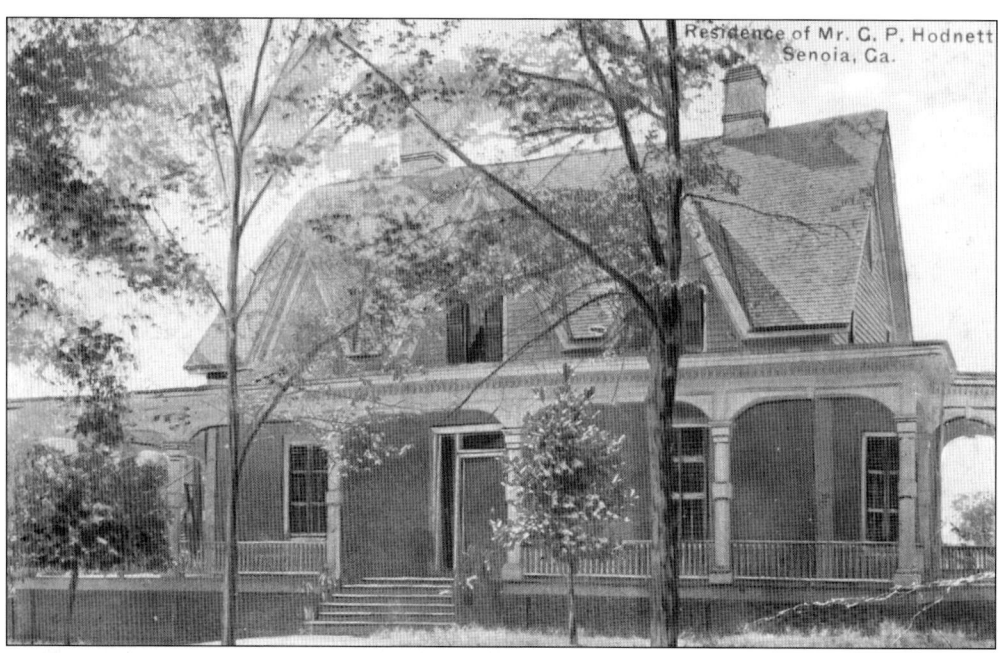

The Residence of Mr. G.P. Hodnett in Senoia.

THE METHODIST CHURCH AT SENOIA ABOUT 1914.

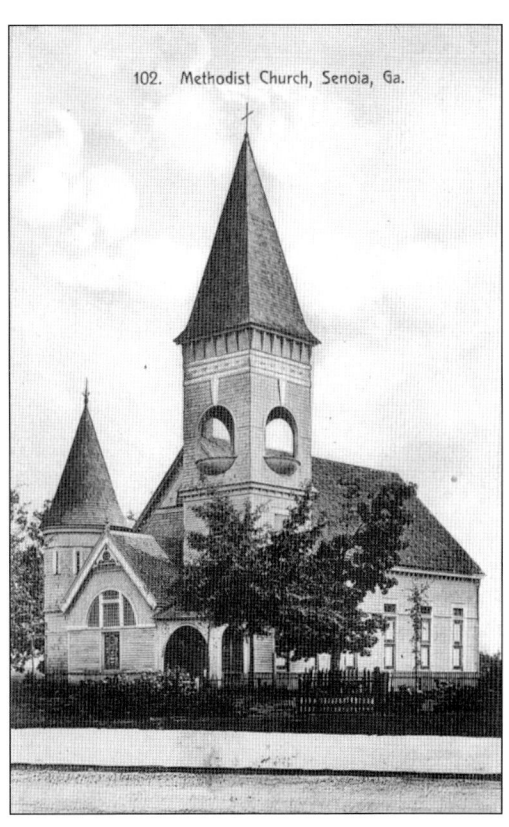

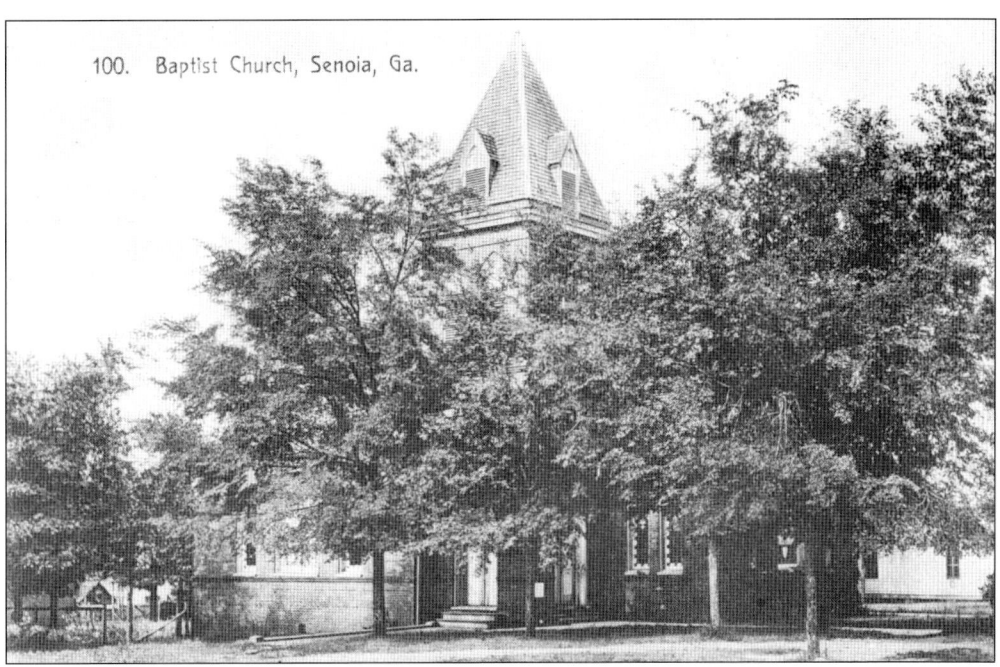

THE BAPTIST CHURCH AT SENOIA ABOUT 1914.

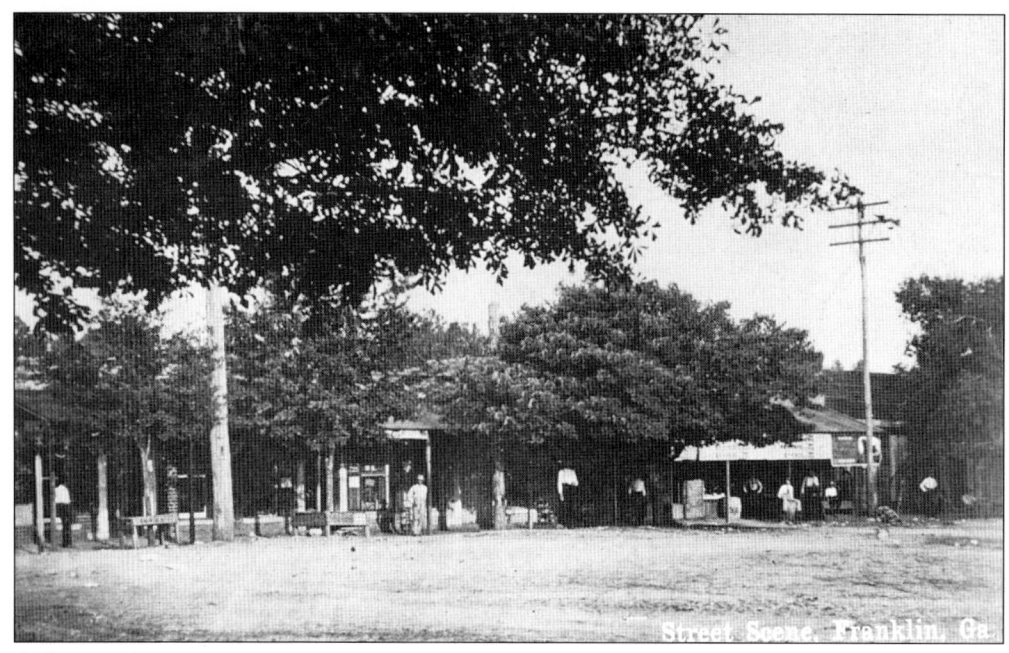
A STREET SCENE IN FRANKLIN ABOUT 1910.

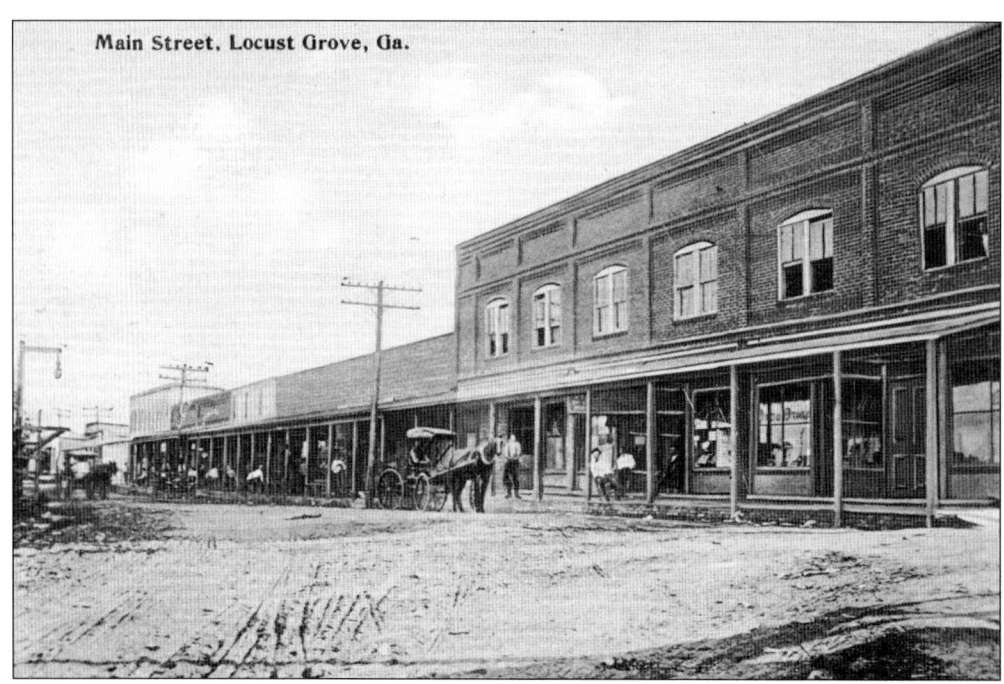
THE MAIN STREET IN LOCUST GROVE, C. 1912.

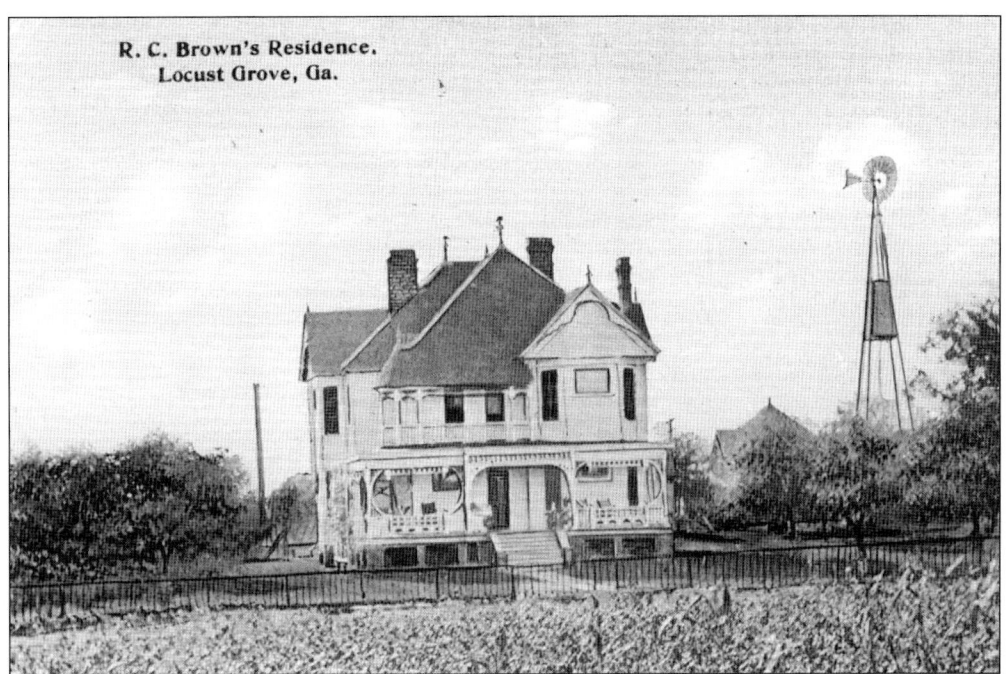

R.C. BROWN'S RESIDENCE IN LOCUST GROVE, c. 1912. Mr. Brown operated a lumber and grain business in Locust Grove.

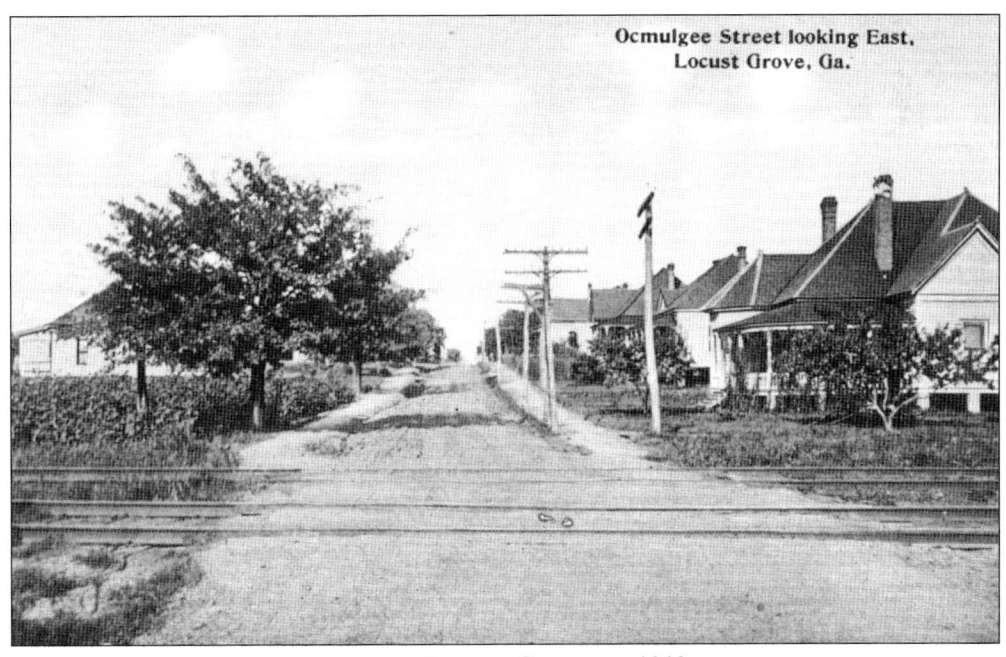

OCMULGEE STREET LOOKING EAST IN LOCUST GROVE, c. 1912.

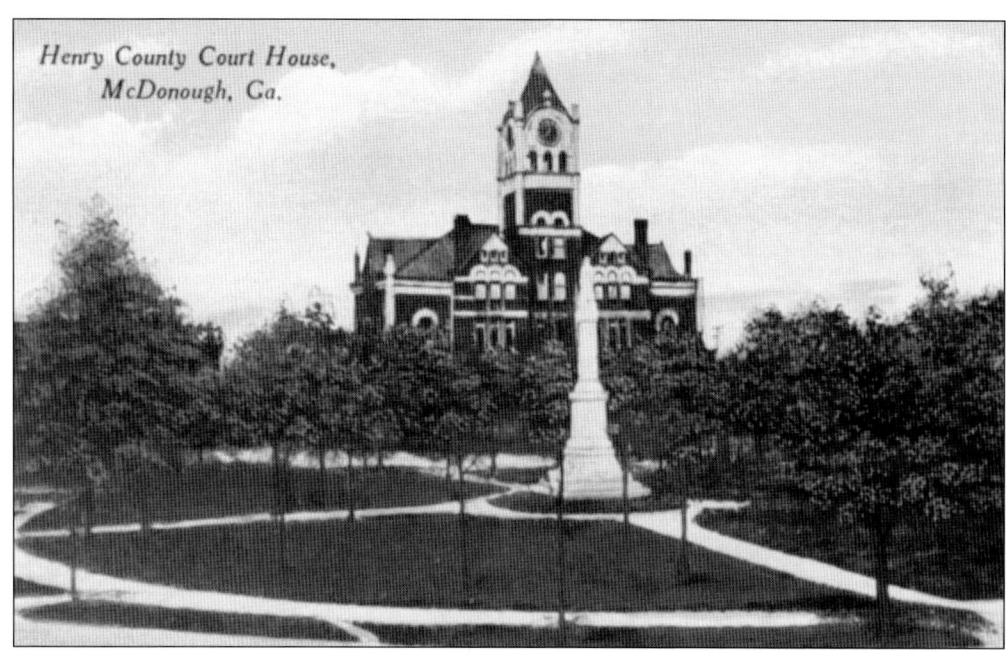

THE HENRY COUNTY COURTHOUSE IN MCDONOUGH. The courthouse was built in 1897 at a cost of $13,794.48, and remains in use. The Confederate Monument was dedicated on Confederate Memorial Day, April 26, 1910.

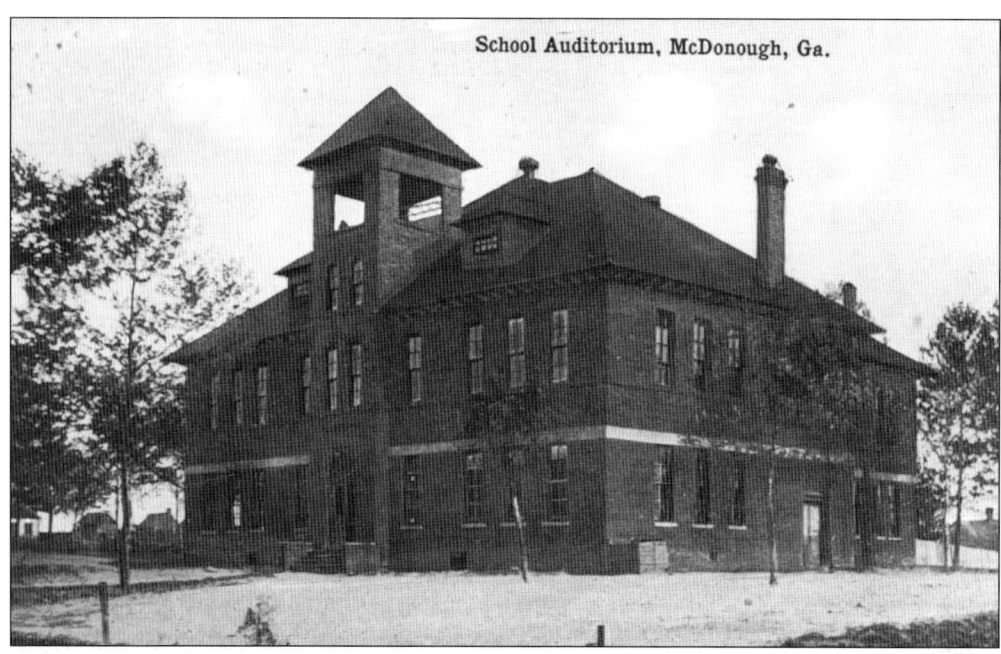

THE SCHOOL AUDITORIUM IN MCDONOUGH ABOUT 1912. The writer of the message which was sent to New Jersey begins: "Way down in Dixie!"

Five
Crawford, Houston, Macon, Peach, Schley, Talbot, and Taylor Counties

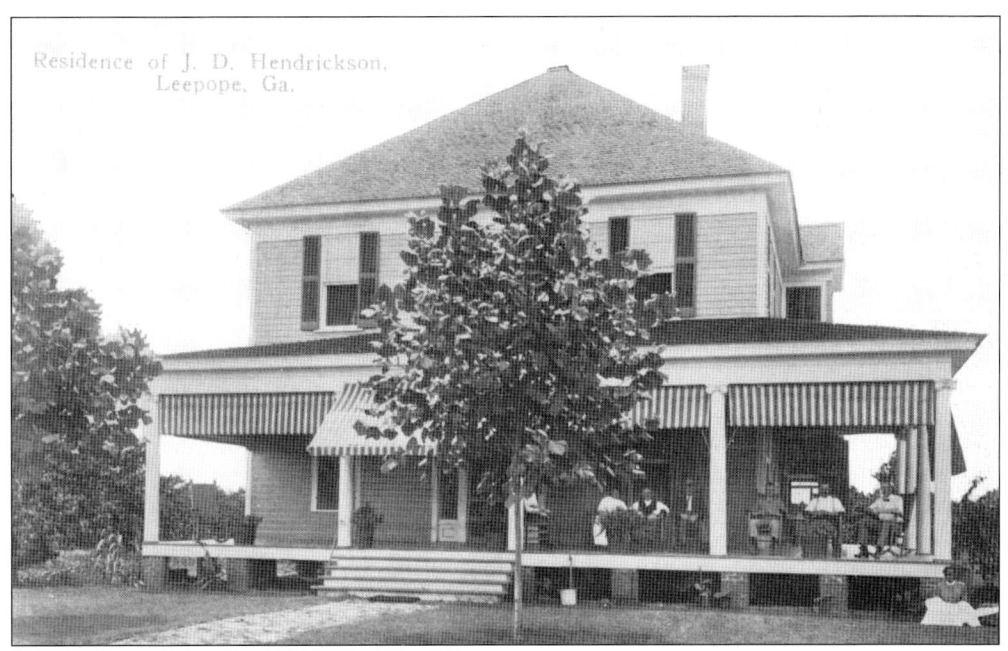

The Residence of J.D. Hendrickson at Leepope.

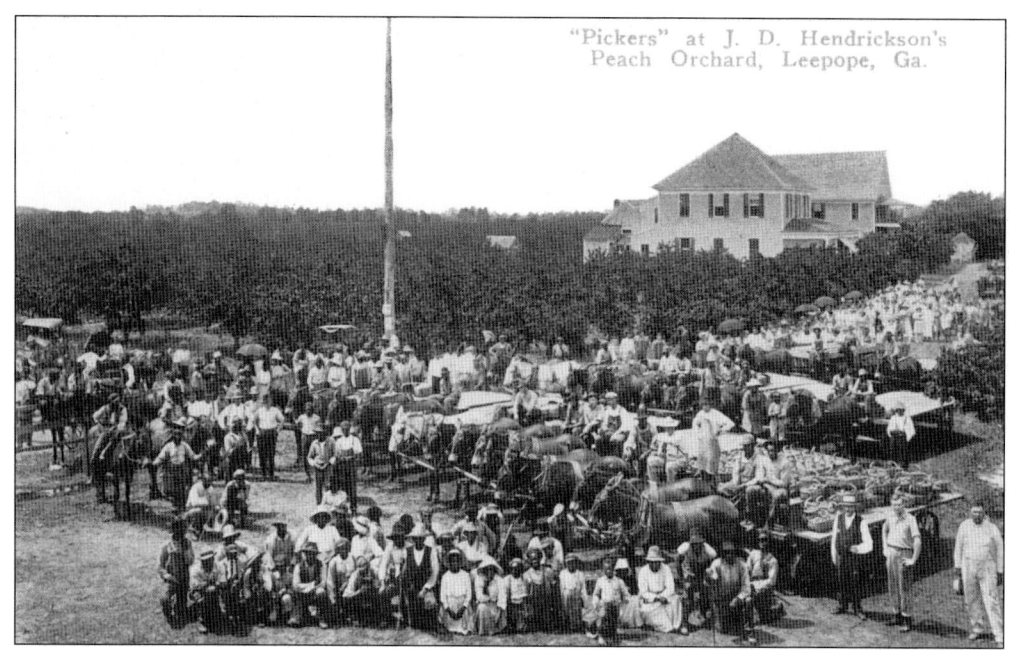

PEACH PICKERS CONGREGATED AT J.D. HENDRICKSON'S PEACH ORCHARD AT LEEPOPE.

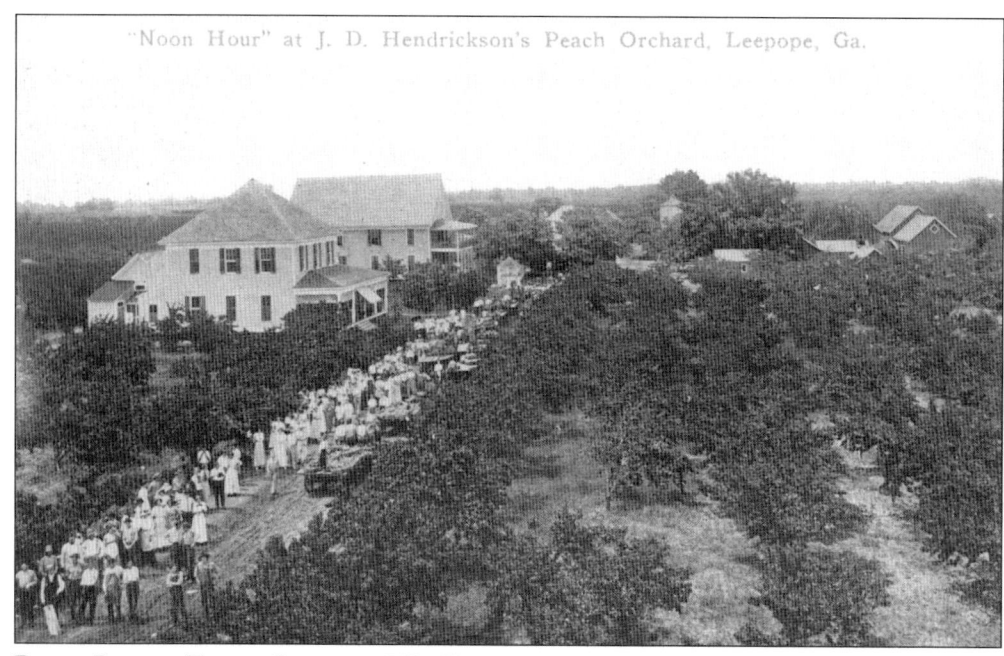

PEACH PICKERS TAKE A BREAK AT J.D. HENDRICKSON'S PEACH ORCHARD AT LEEPOPE.

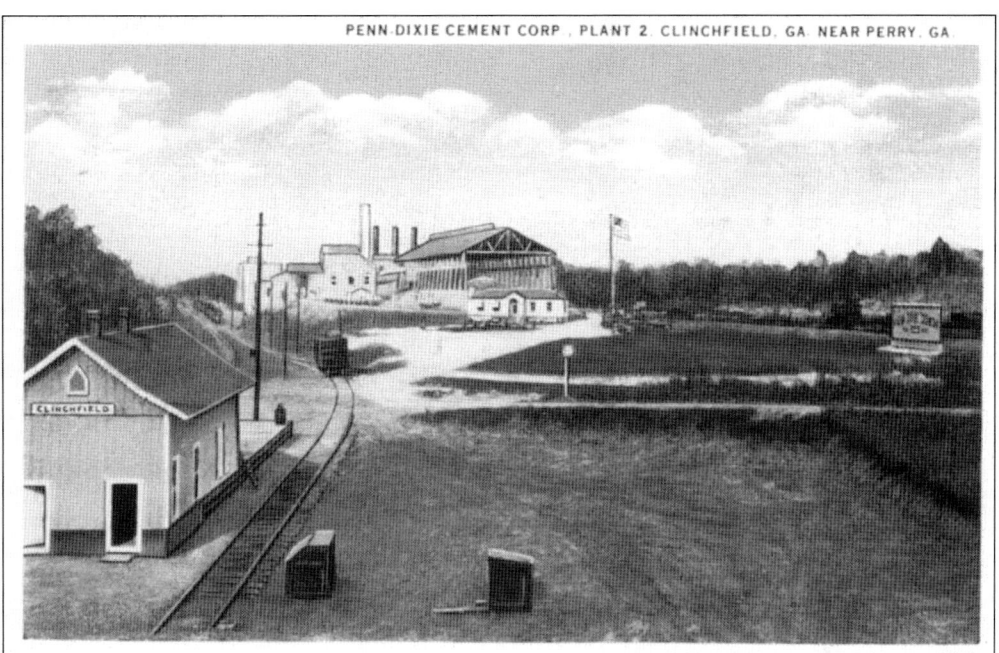

PLANT 2 OF THE PENN-DIXIE CEMENT CORPORATION, SEEN BEYOND THE CLINCHFIELD RAILROAD DEPOT NEAR PERRY. This card probably was printed in the 1920s but was not used until 1938, when it was mailed to Flint, Michigan. The message reads in part: "Well we toddled down this far and have surely put in three hard days work. Kentucky roads are just up and down and around all the time. Fellow rammed into us Fri, not much damage tho. come thru Atlanta today, some big berg. We must be around 125 miles from the Fla line, so it wont take another week to get there. Quite some party here tonight. Ind, Ohio, and Mich in the tourist home. From Dad."

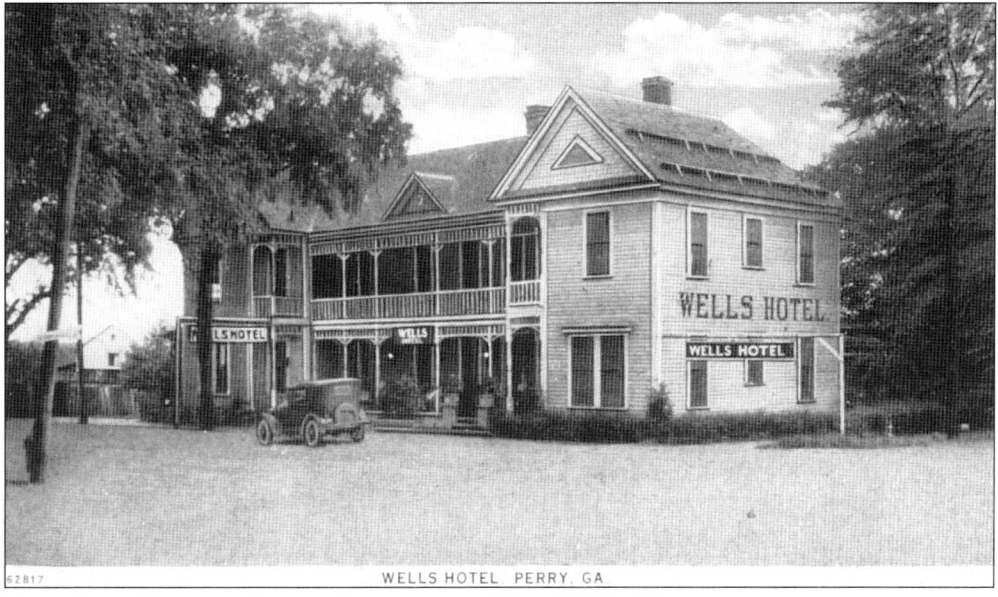

THE WELLS HOTEL IN PERRY, OPERATED BY MRS. W.M. WELLS.

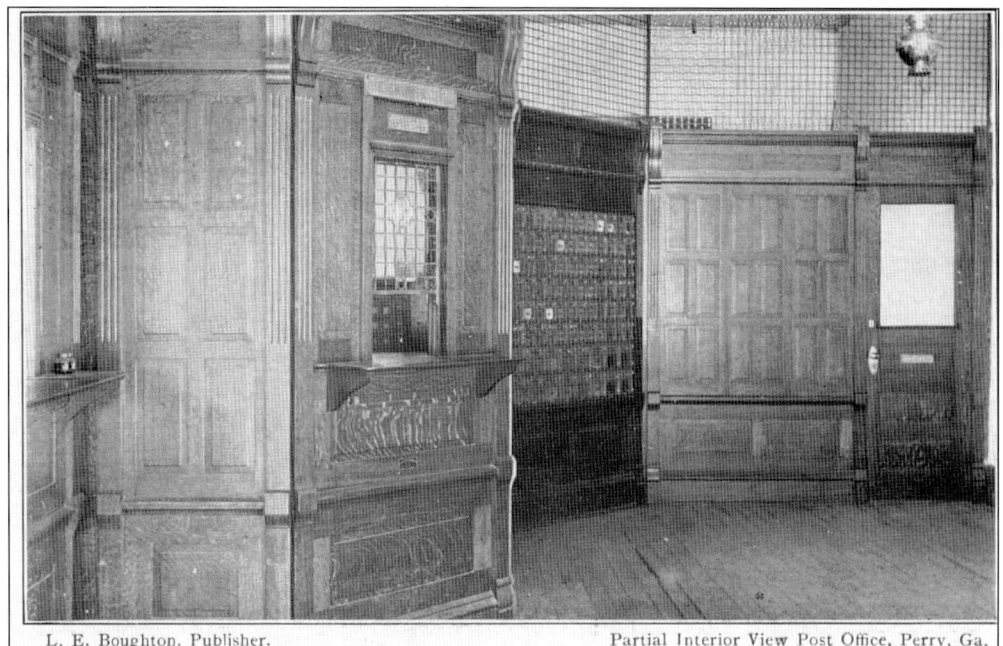

An Interior View of the Post Office at Perry, c. 1913.

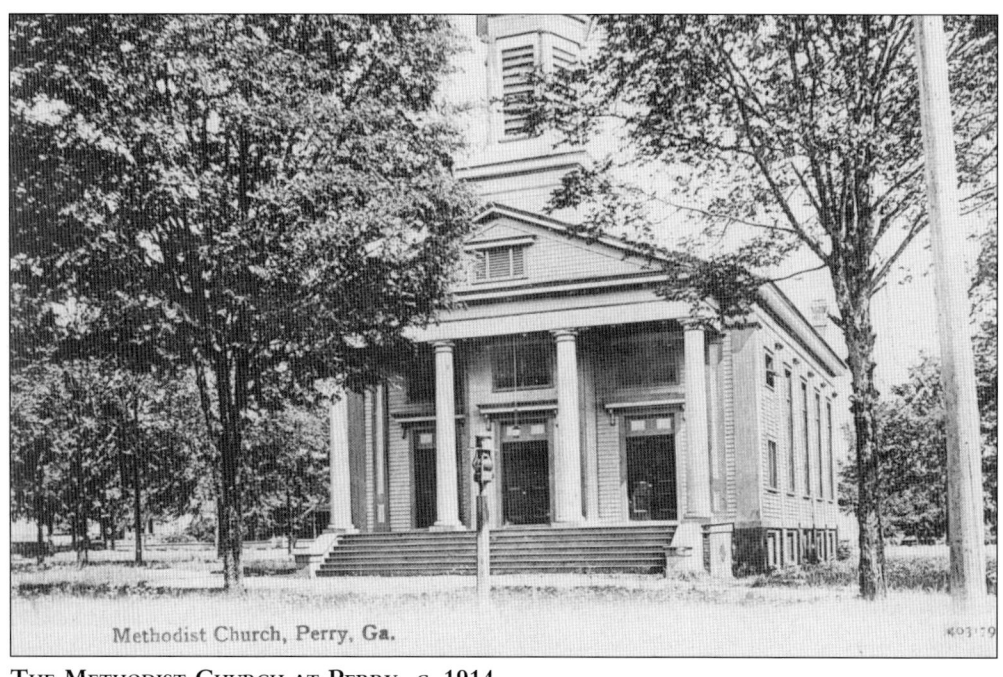

The Methodist Church at Perry, c. 1914.

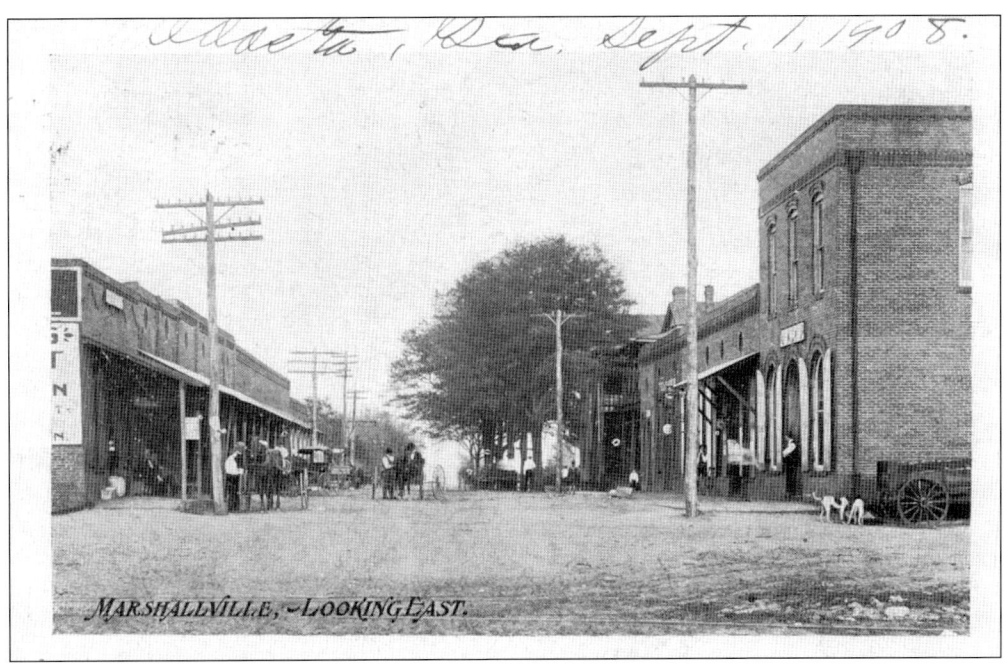

A Street Scene of Downtown Marshallville, c. 1908.

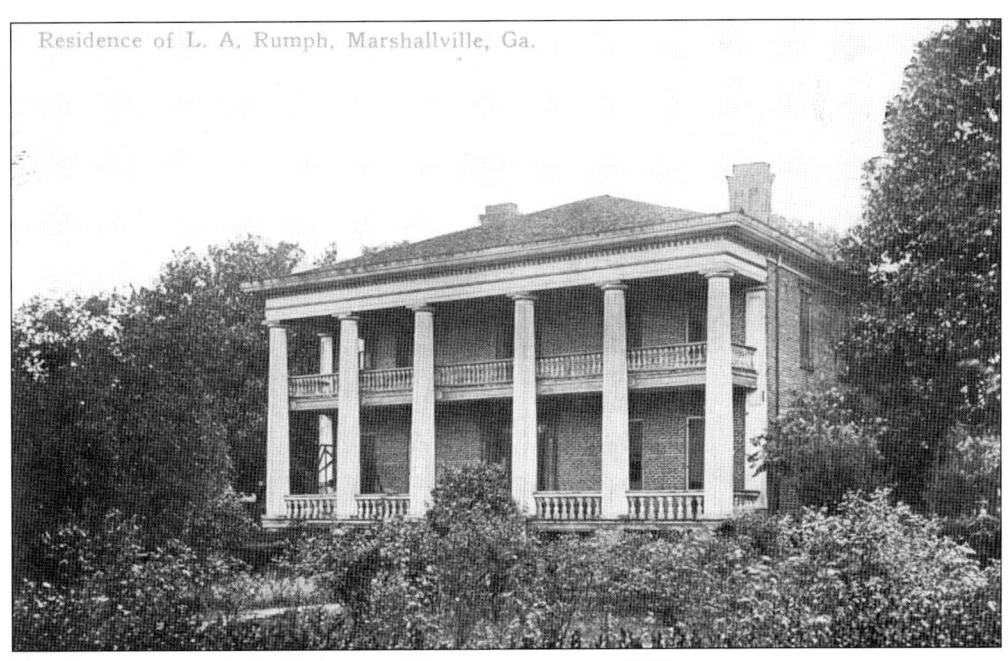

The Residence of L.A. Rumph at Marshallville, c. 1907.

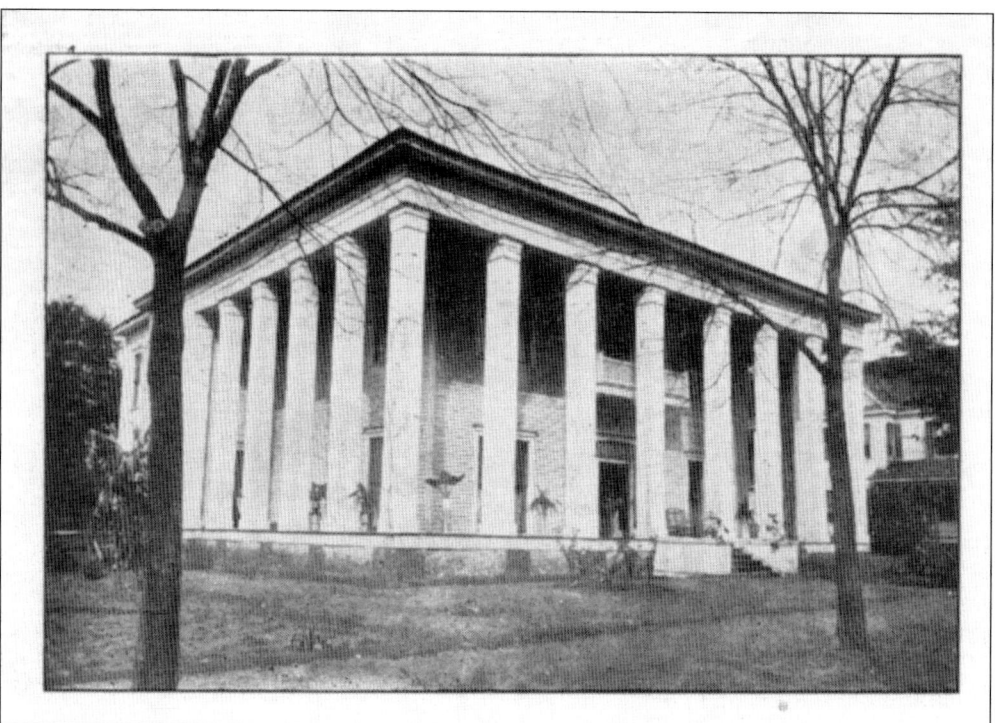

The Residence of James Harrison at Montezuma, c. 1906.

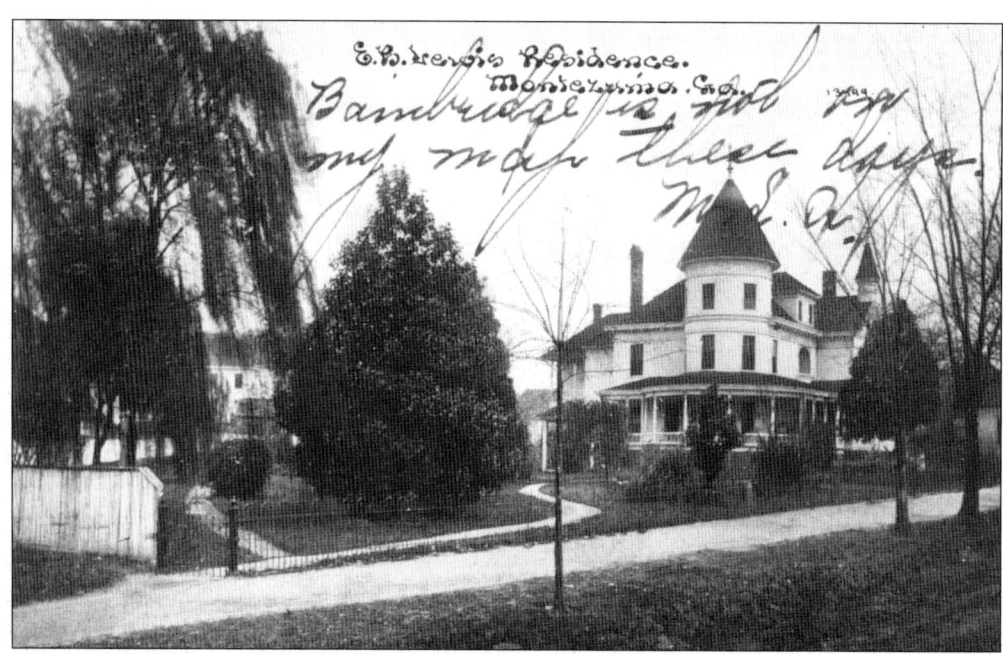

The Residence of E.B. Lewis, President of the Lewis Banking Company in Montezuma.

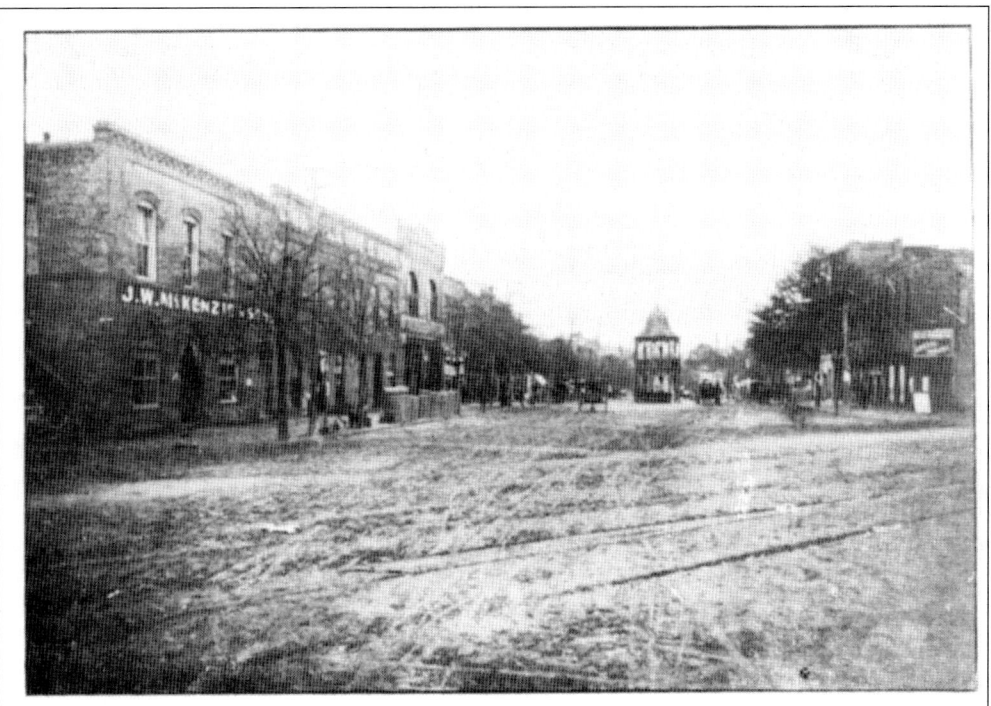

South Dooly Street, Montezuma, Ga.

SOUTH DOOLY STREET IN MONTEZUMA, ALMOST DESERTED IN THIS 1906 VIEW. J.W. McKenzie's cotton warehouse can be see on the corner, with a few bales of cotton sitting on the sidewalk.

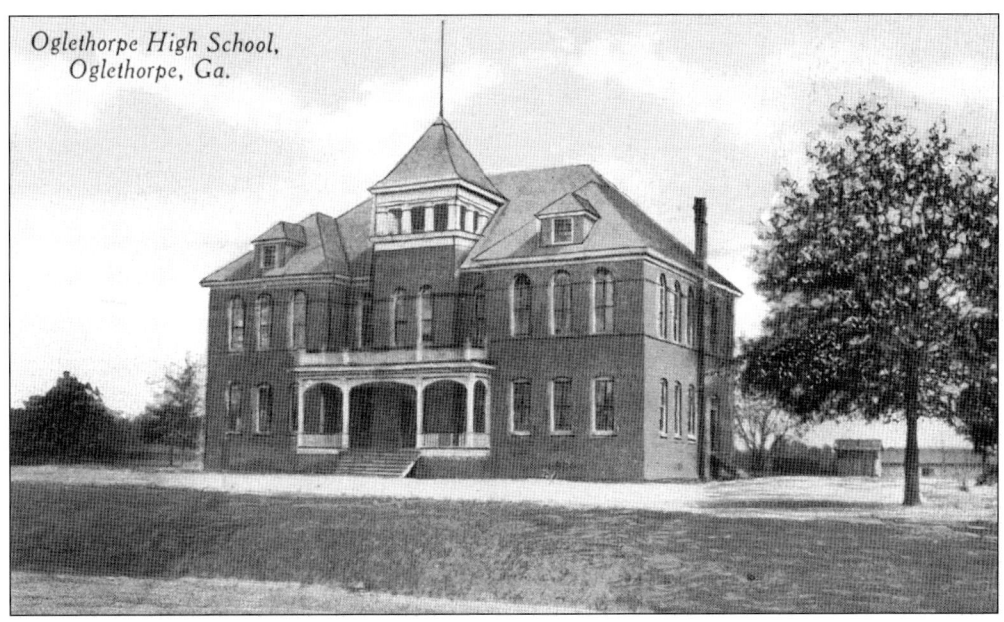

OGLETHORPE HIGH SCHOOL, C. 1910.

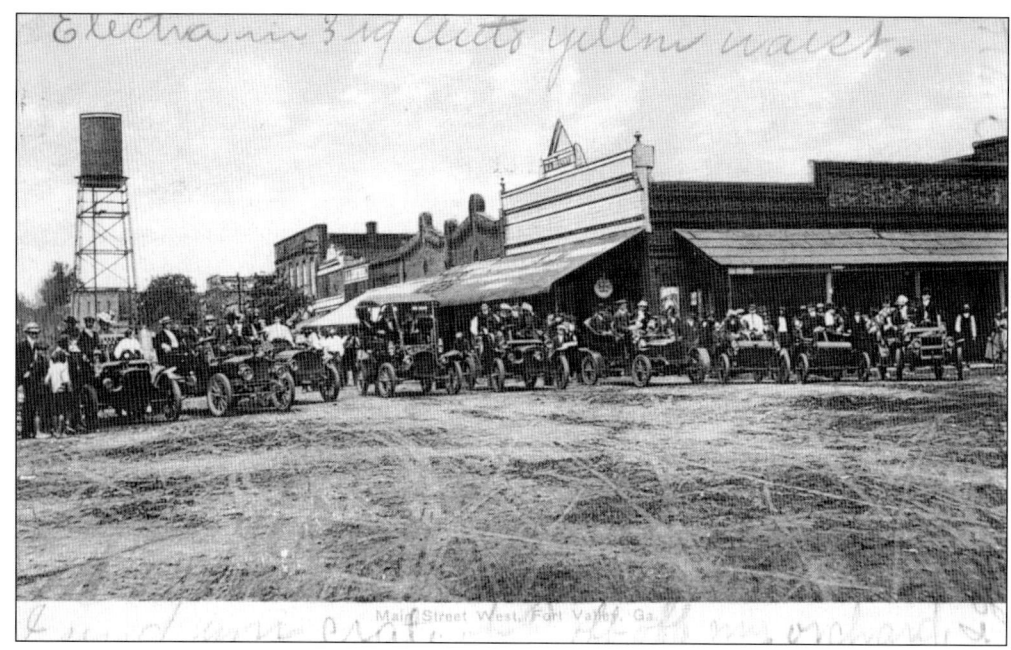

WEST MAIN STREET IN FORT VALLEY IN 1908. It must have been a special occasion for all these automobiles to be lined up. The sender wrote on the front: "Electra in 3rd auto [wearing a] yellow coat."

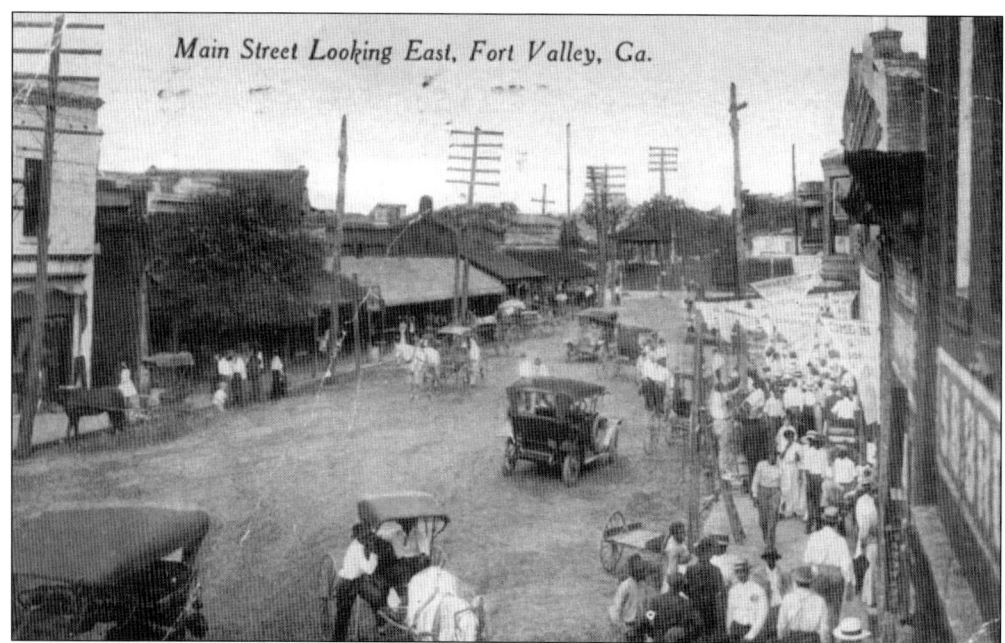

EAST MAIN STREET IN FORT VALLEY IN THE EARLY 1910S.

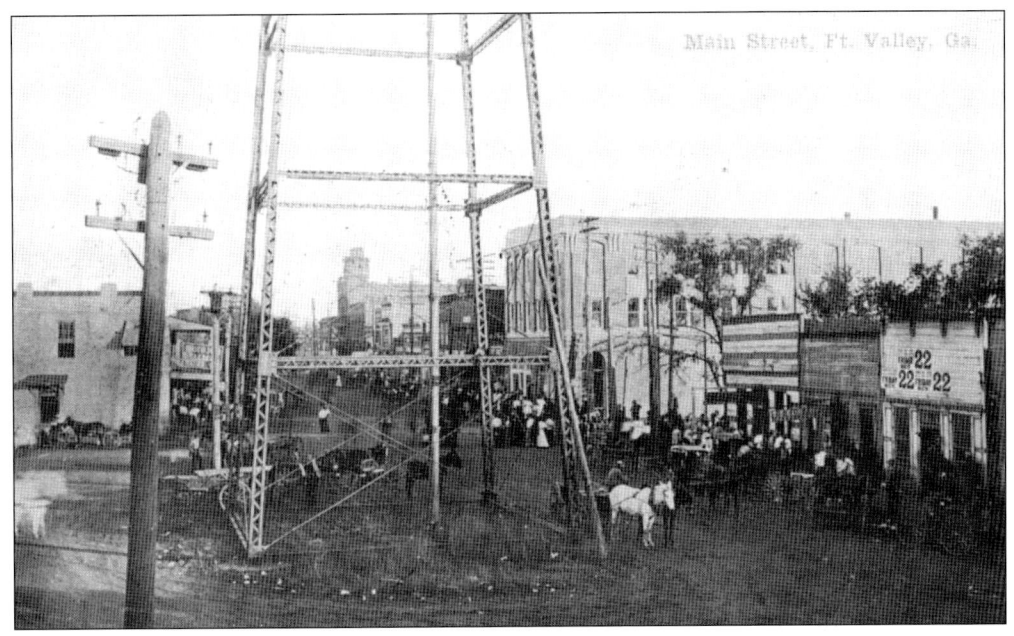
MAIN STREET IN FORT VALLEY, SHOWING THE BASE OF A HUGE WATER TOWER.

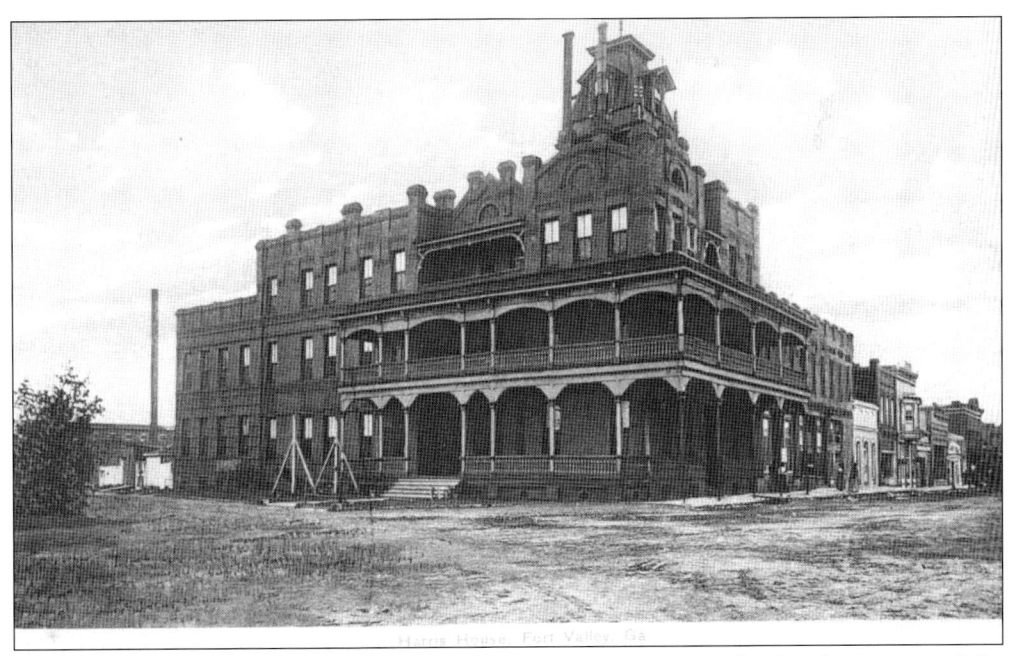
THE PALATIAL HARRIS HOUSE IN FORT VALLEY, C. 1908. The hotel was owned by W.H. Harris.

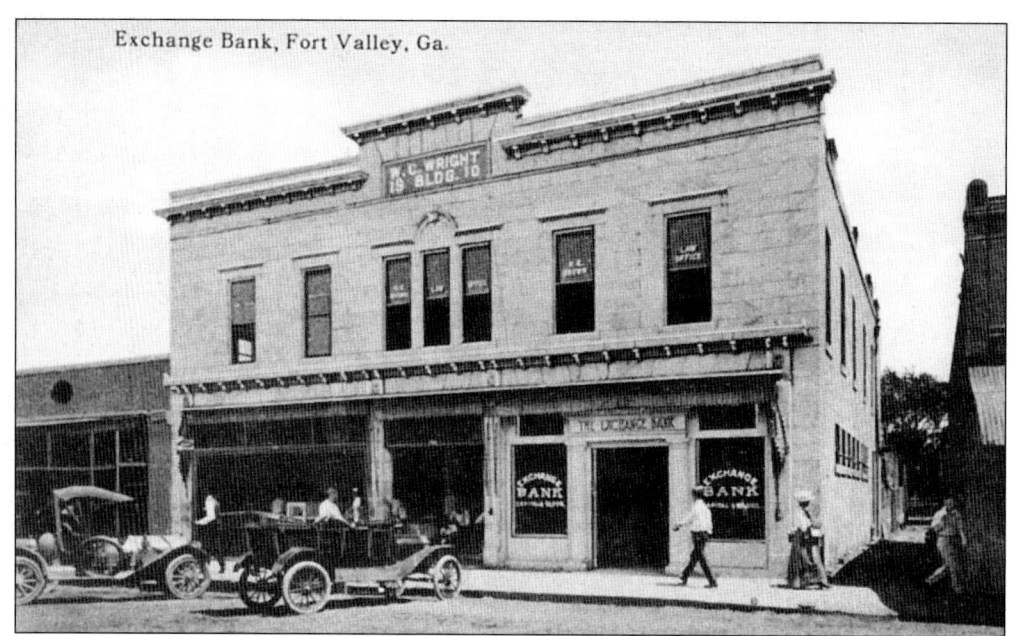

The Exchange Bank in Fort Valley, c. 1910.

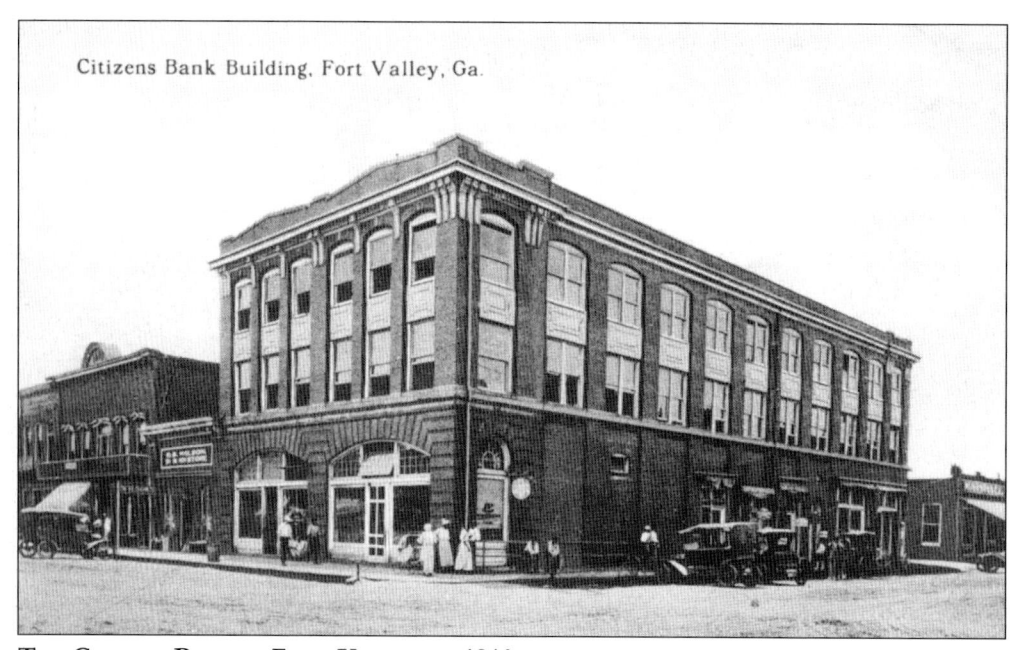

The Citizens Bank in Fort Valley, c. 1910.

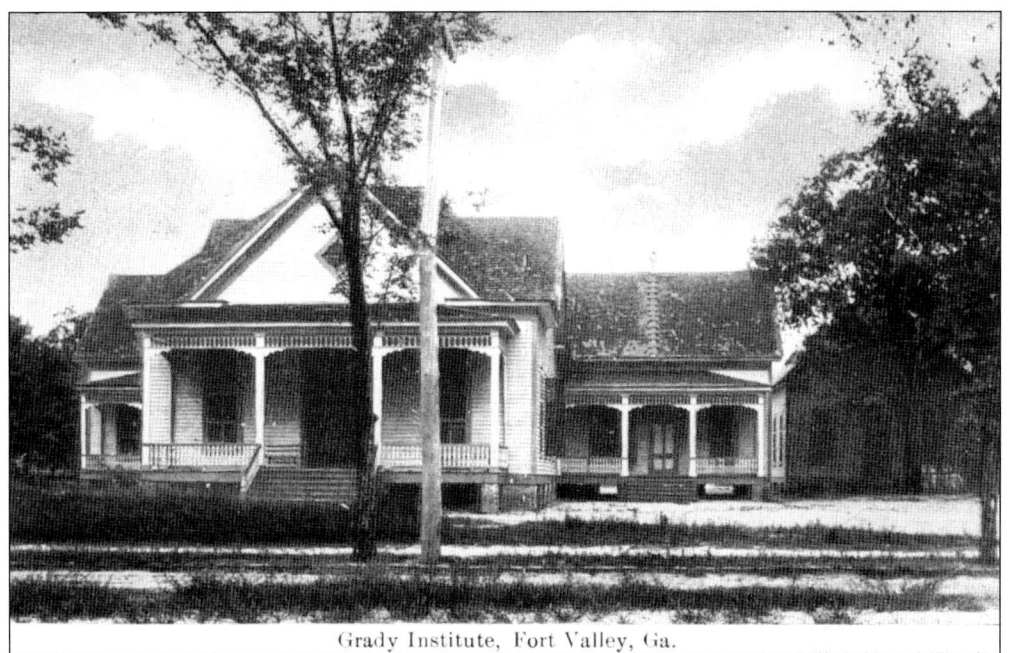

THE GRADY INSTITUTE IN FORT VALLEY. The card was postmarked 1910 and sent to Remington, Virginia. The message reads: "Hello Miss Eva. How are you getting along? I left Dawson about a week ago and came to Fort Valley Ga where I will be for a few weeks. Hope you are having a nice time in Old Va. Am just starting out this morning on my regular drive. Wish you could be with me; It would not be so lonesome. Frank."

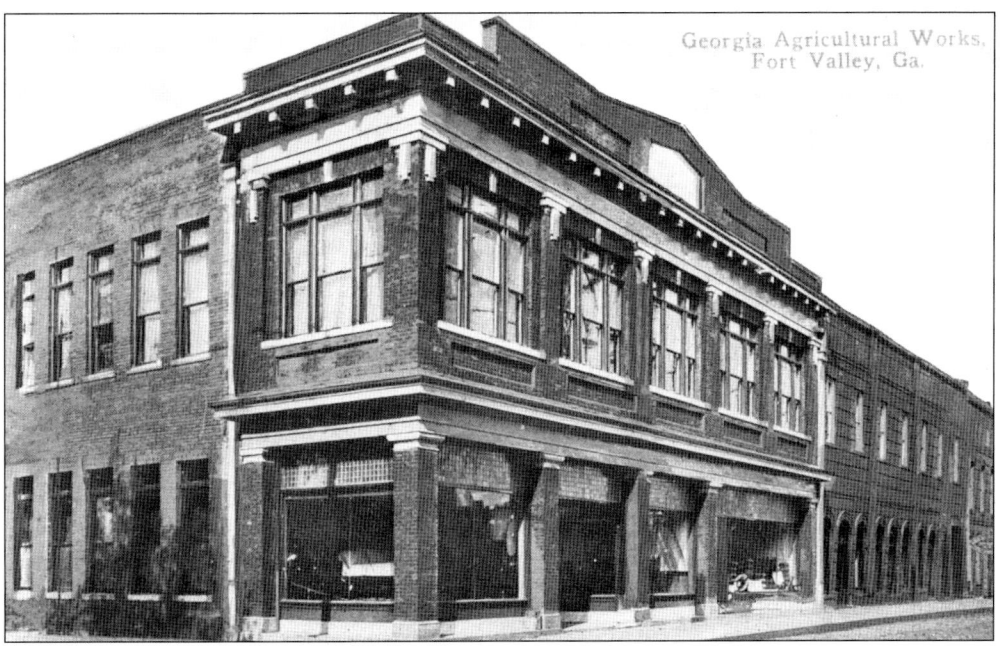

THE GEORGIA AGRICULTURAL WORKS IN FORT VALLEY. The company manufactured cotton gin machinery and dealt in buggies, wagons, farming implements, paints, and oils. They also served as the local undertaker!

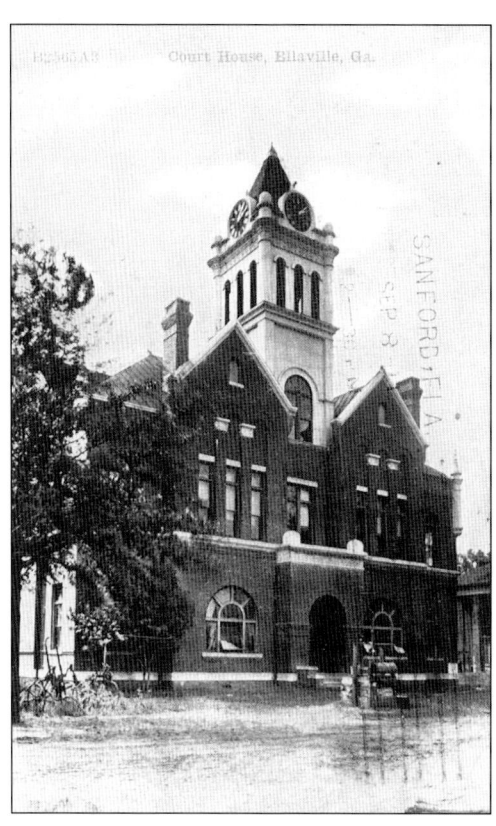

THE SCHLEY COUNTY COURTHOUSE IN ELLAVILLE. The courthouse was built in 1900 and is still being used.

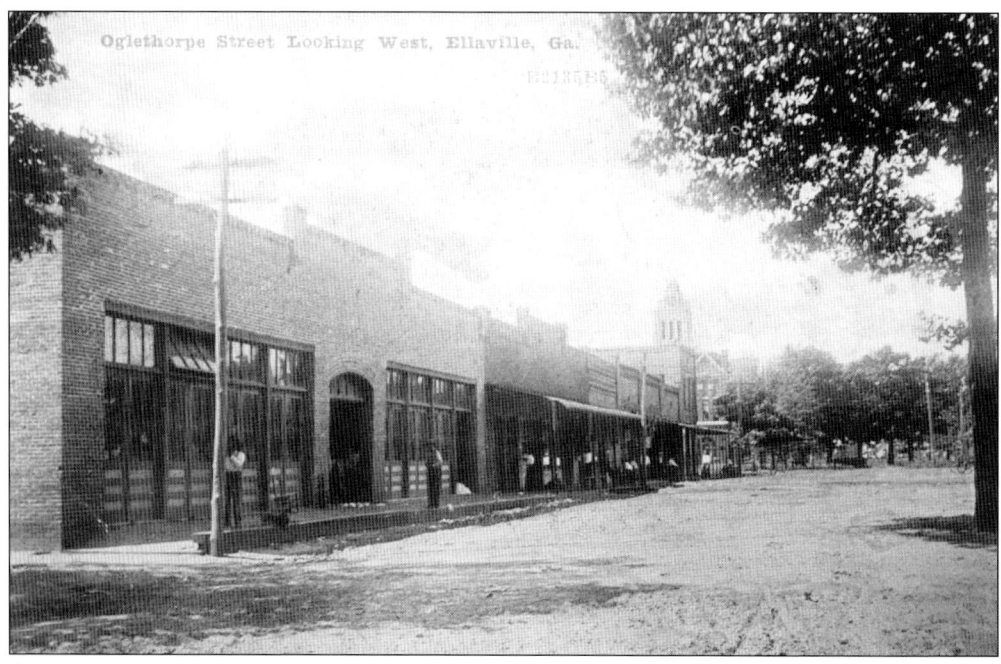

OGLETHORPE STREET LOOKING WEST IN ELLAVILLE, C. 1910.

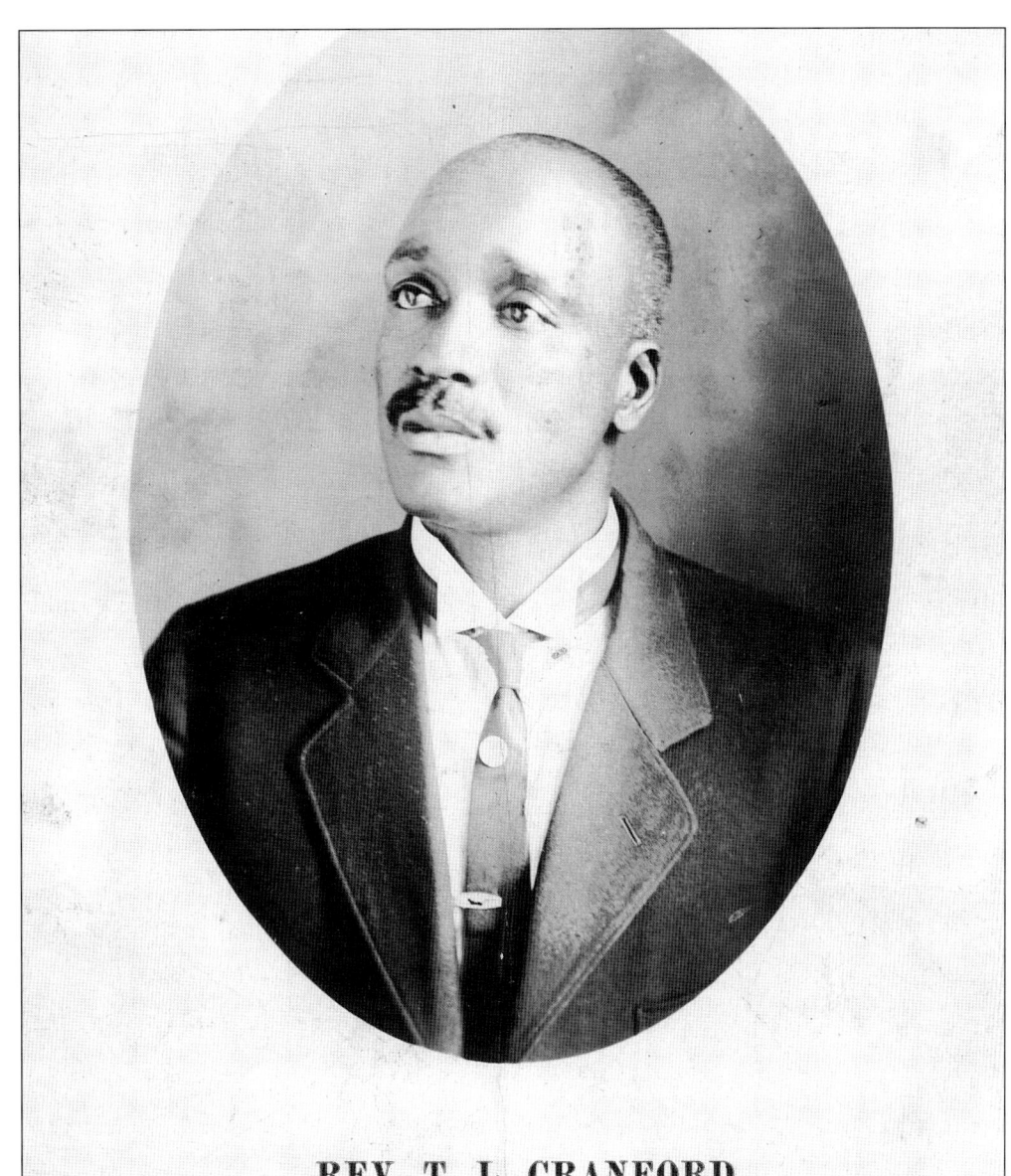

REV. T. L. CRANFORD

P. O. Box 283.   Talbotton, Ga.

Pastor of the First Baptist Church of Talbotton, Ga.; First Baptist Church, Waverly Hall, Ga.; Second Baptist Church, Molena, Ga.; First Baptist Church, Hollingville, Ga. Also President of the Mt. Carmel District Sunday School Convention.

THE REVEREND T.L. CRANFORD OF TALBOTTON. With a busy schedule, he probably preached at each of his four churches one Sunday a month.

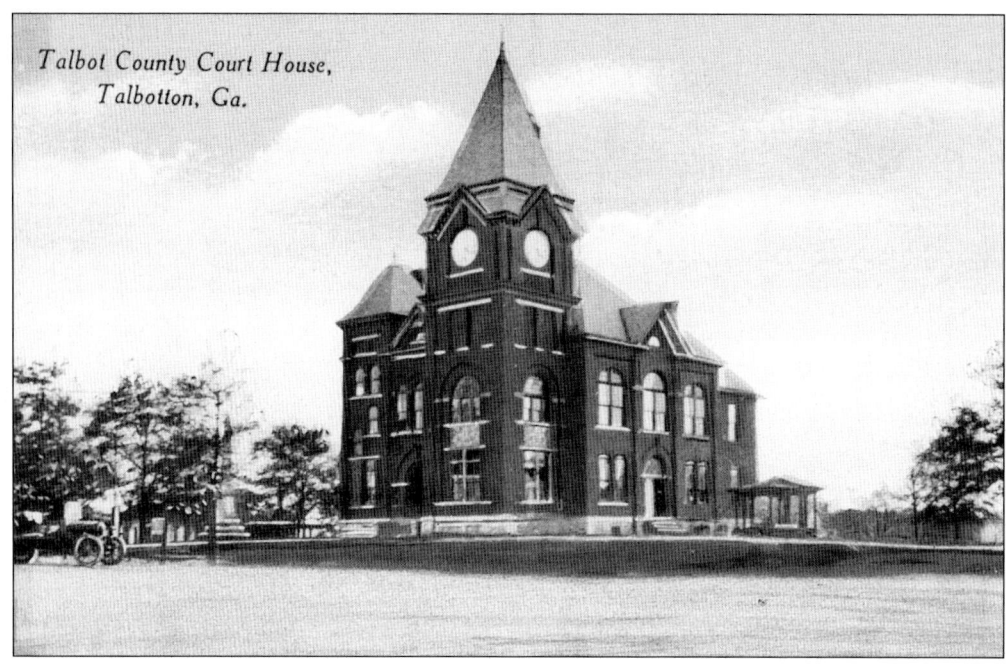

THE TALBOT COUNTY COURTHOUSE IN TALBOTTON. The courthouse was built in 1892 and still serves today.

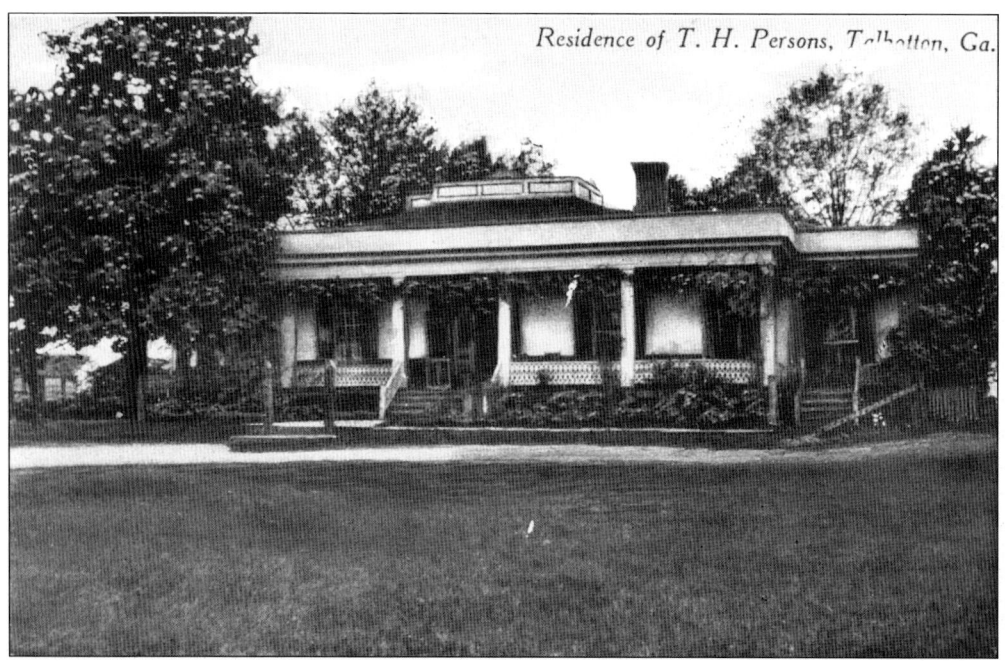

THE RESIDENCE OF T.H. PERSONS AT TALBOTTON, C. 1908.

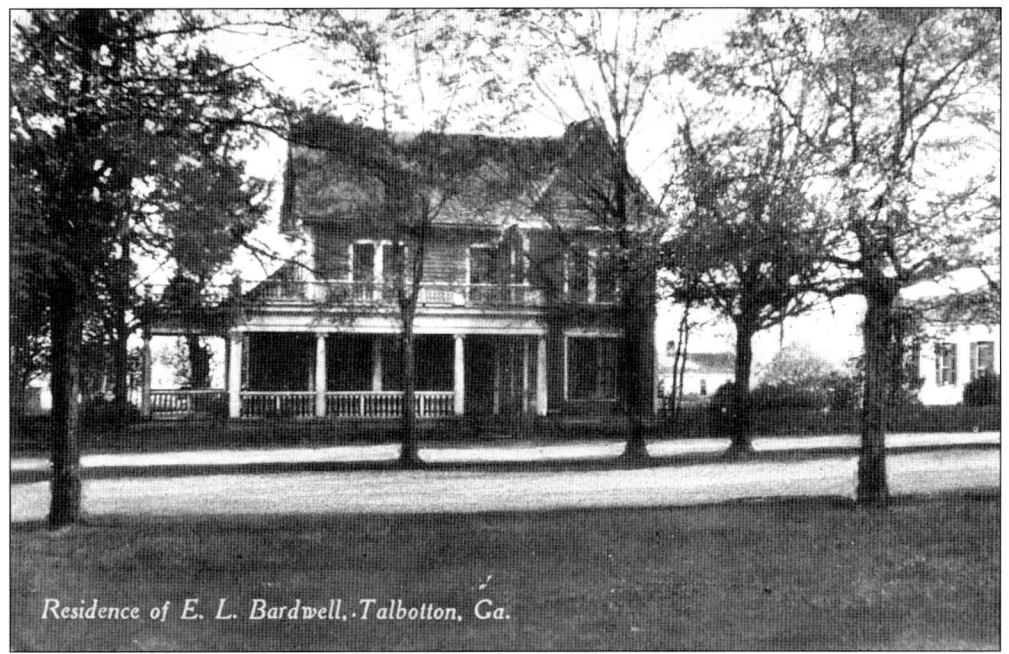

THE RESIDENCE OF E.L. BARDWELL, DRUGGIST AT TALBOTTON.

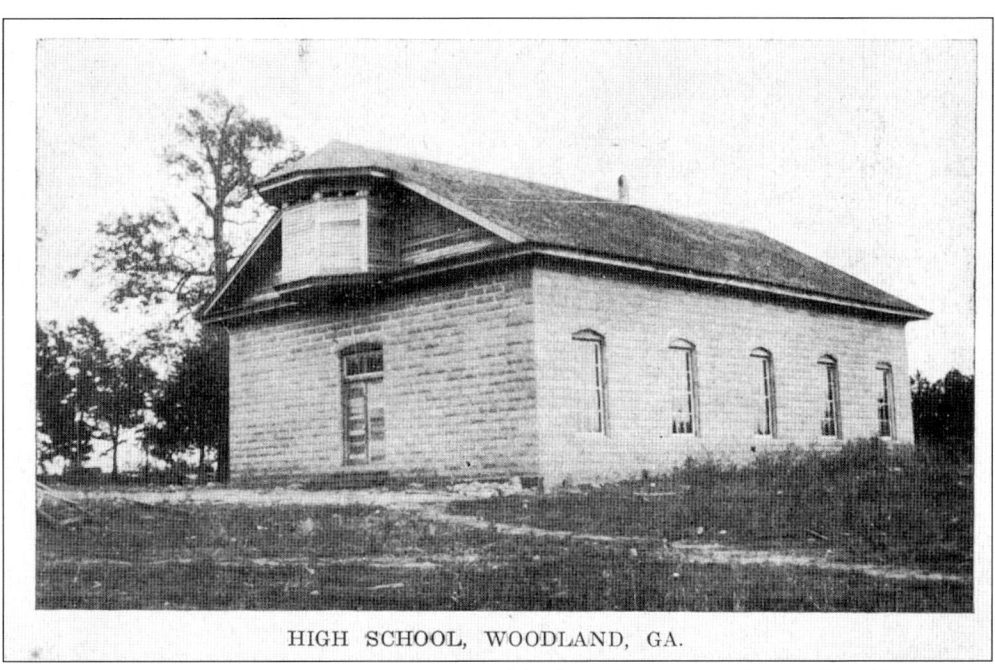

THE HIGH SCHOOL IN WOODLAND. The school looks to be a most substantial building in this 1908 view.

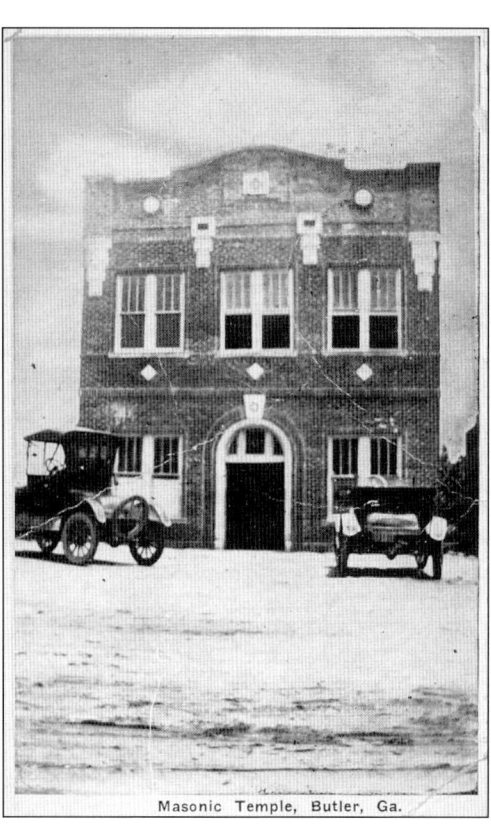

THE MASONIC TEMPLE AT BUTLER IN THE 1920s.

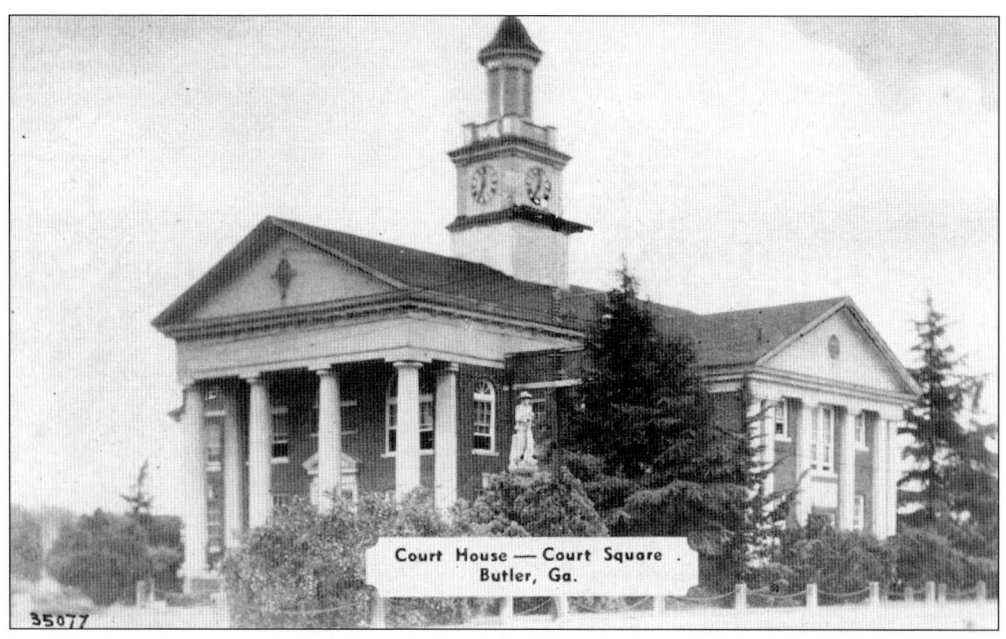

THE TAYLOR COUNTY COURTHOUSE IN BUTLER. The original courthouse was built in 1852 but was torn down in 1935 and this building was constructed.

Six
Harris, Meriwether, and Troup Counties

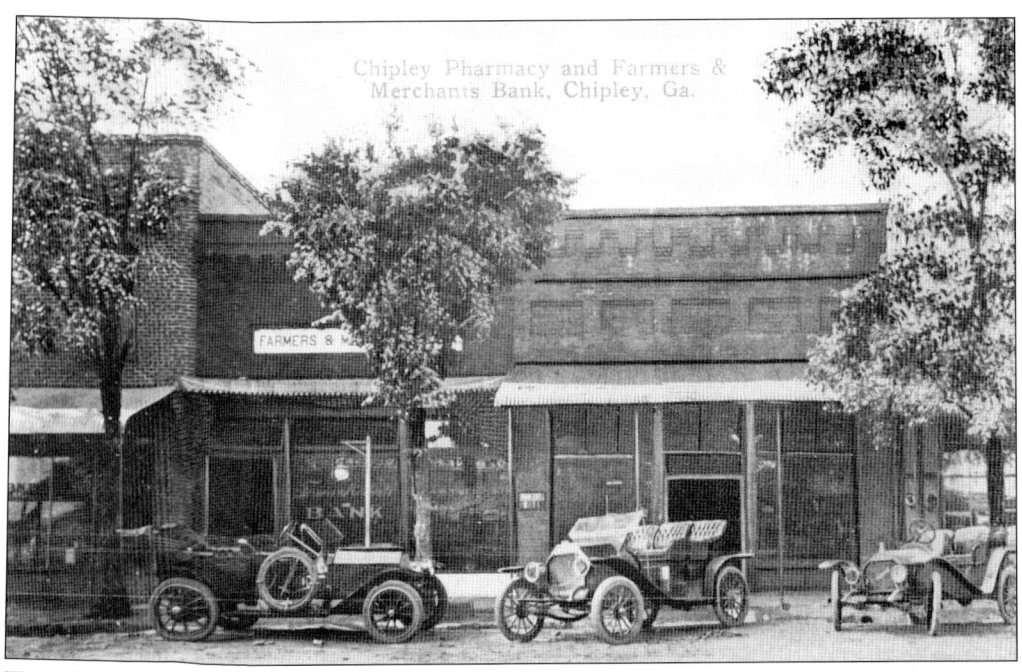

The Chipley Pharmacy and Farmers & Merchants Bank of Chipley, c. 1910.

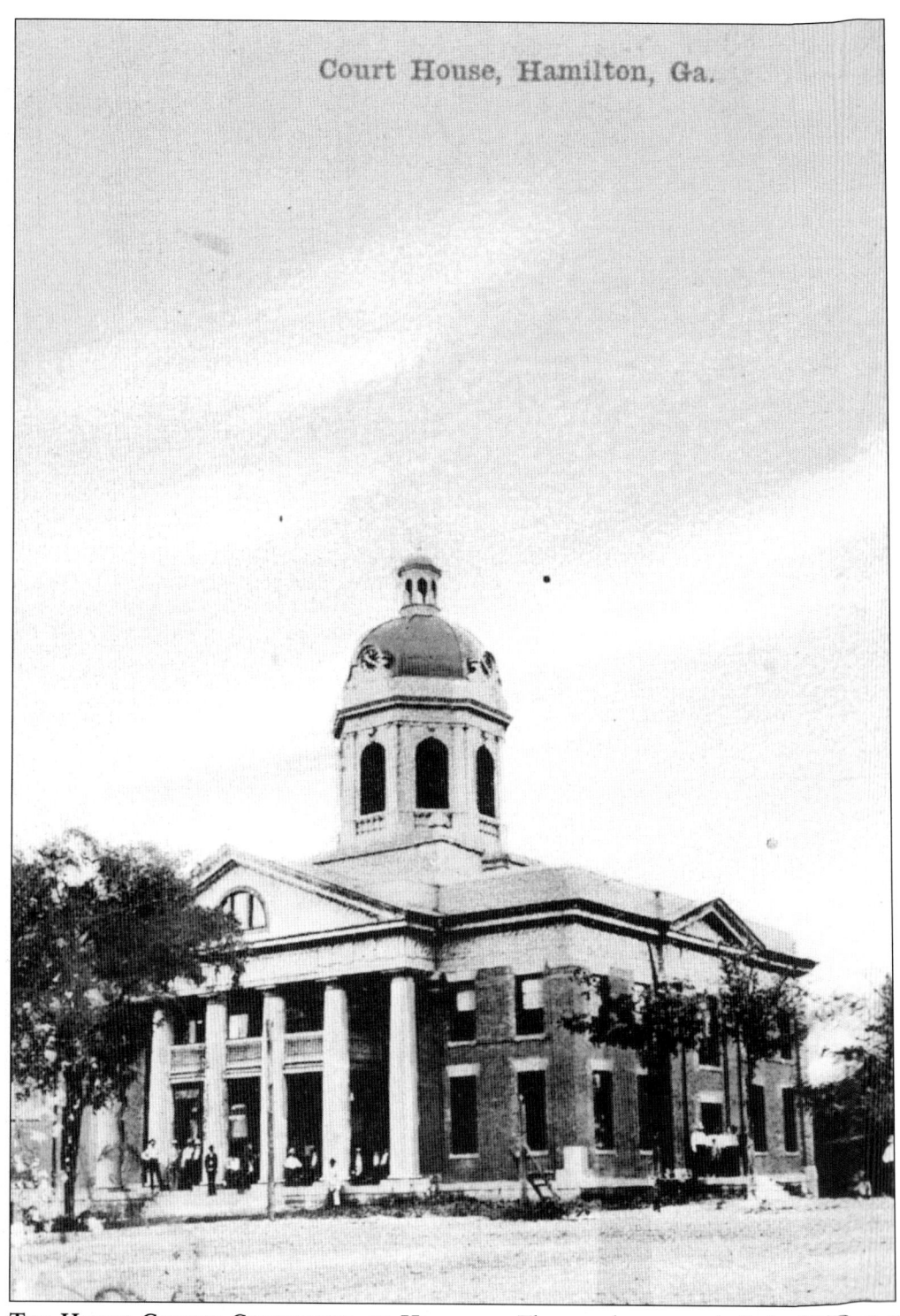

THE HARRIS COUNTY COURTHOUSE AT HAMILTON. The courthouse was built in 1908 at a cost of $35,000. Plans were drawn by Ed C. Hosford and the construction was by the Mutual Construction Company.

THE BAPTIST CHURCH AT
HAMILTON, C. 1908.

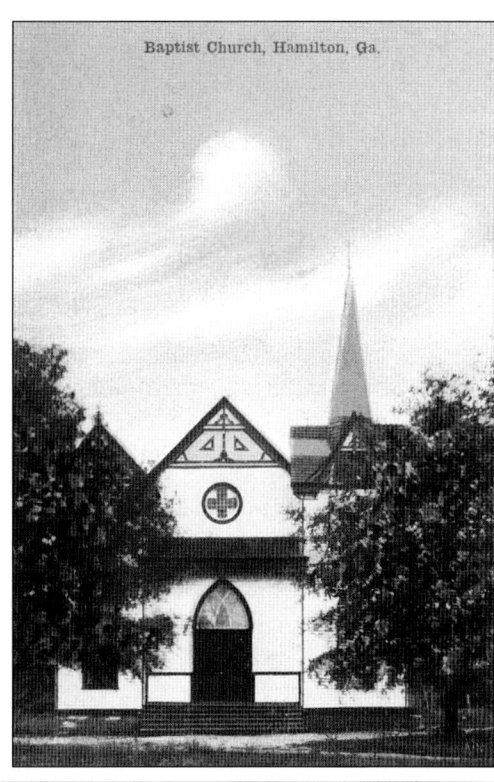

THE METHODIST CHURCH AT
HAMILTON, C. 1908.

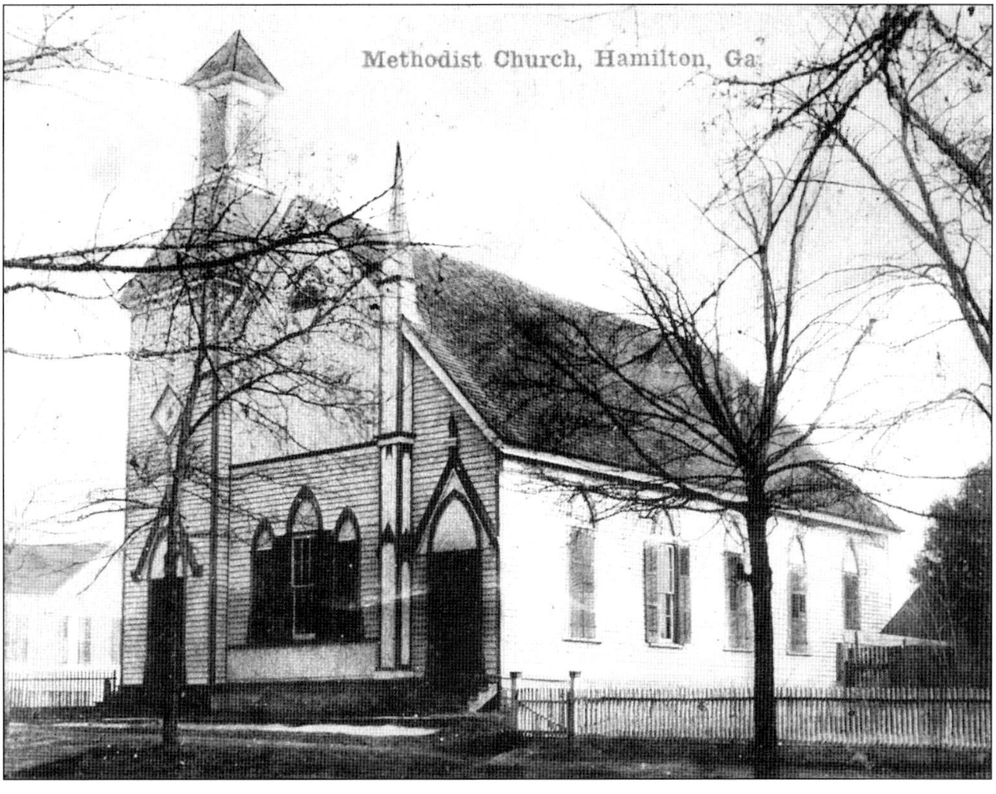

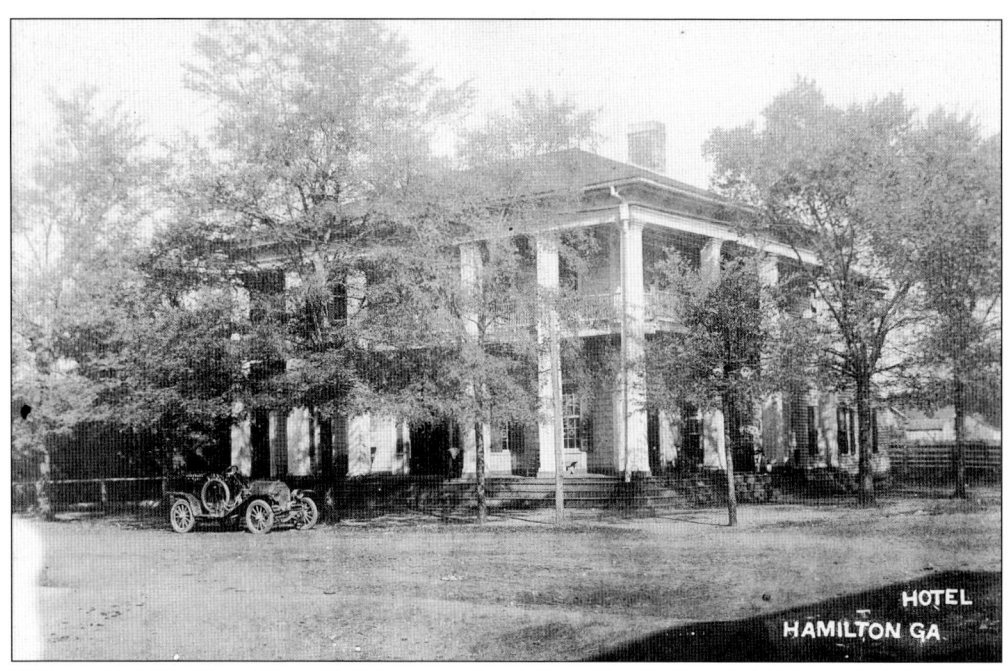

A Real-Photo Post Card View of the Hotel at Hamilton, c. 1910.

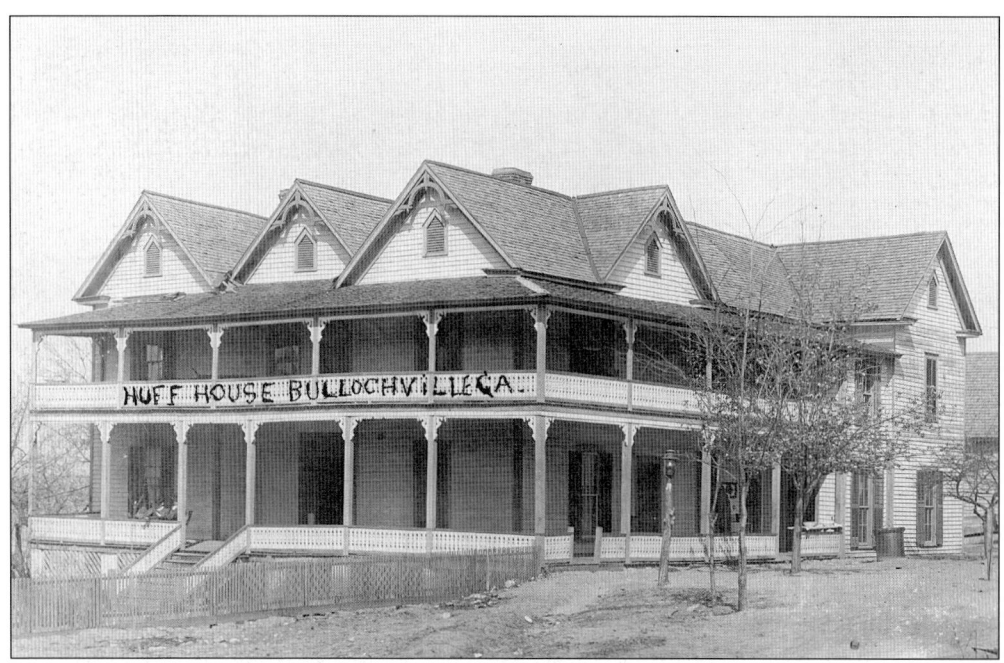

The Huff House in Bullochville. The house was operated by Mrs. C. Huff. The name of Bullochville was changed to Warm Springs on August 6, 1924.

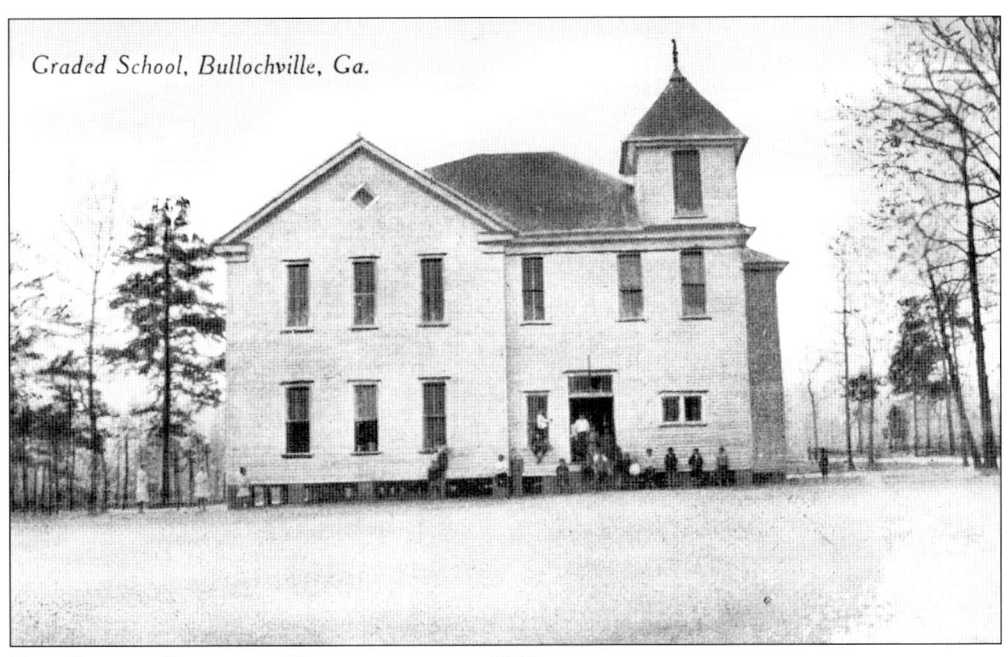

THE GRADED SCHOOL AT BULLOCHVILLE, C. 1910.

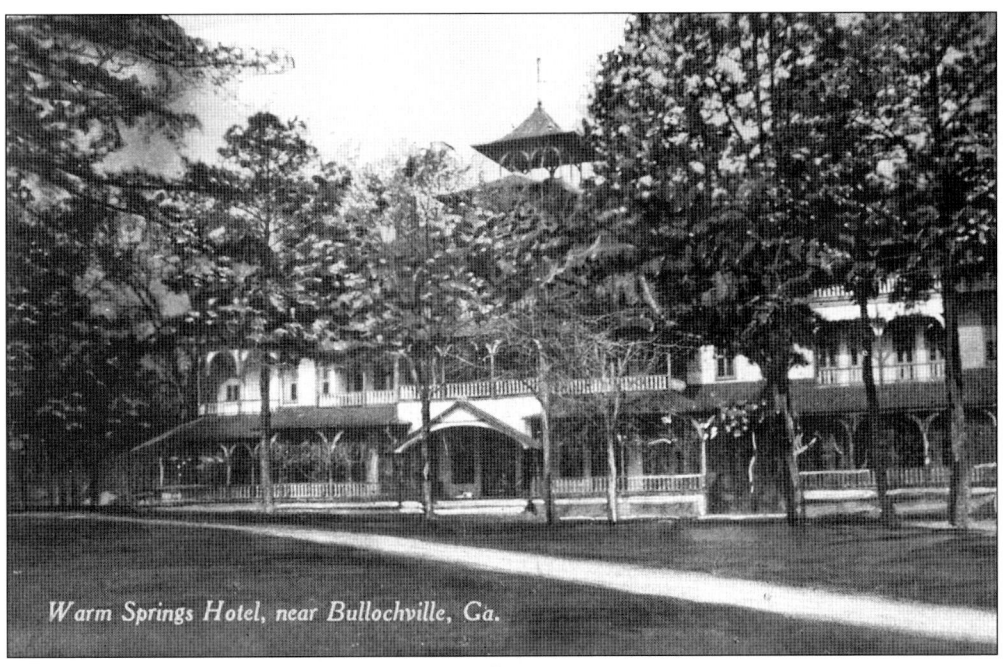

THE IMMENSE WARM SPRINGS HOTEL, NEAR BULLOCHVILLE.

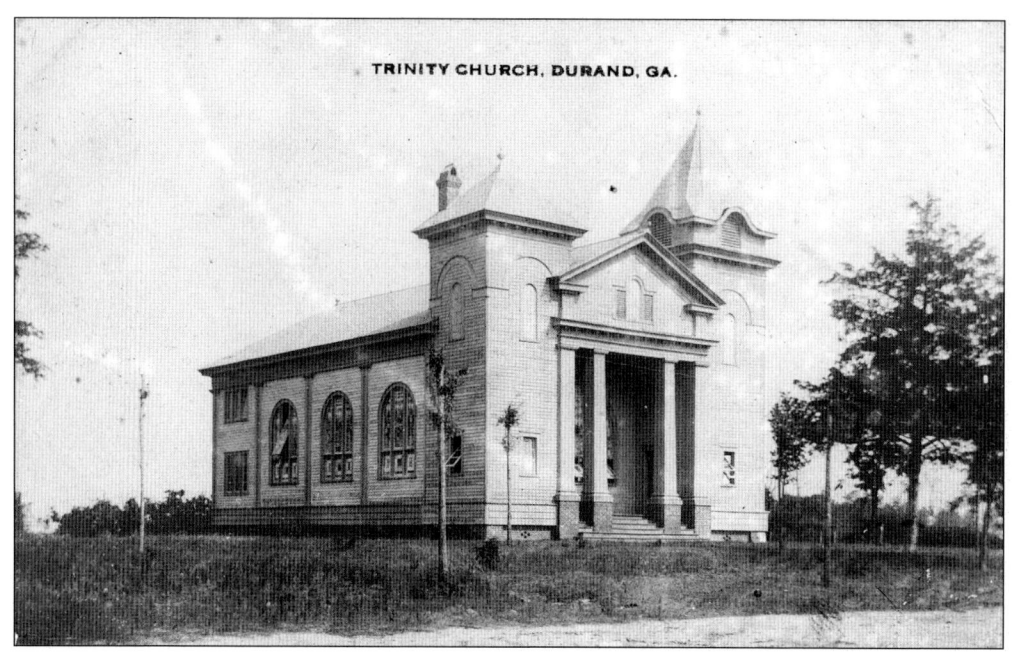

THE TRINITY CHURCH AT DURAND. The name of the community was previously Stinson.

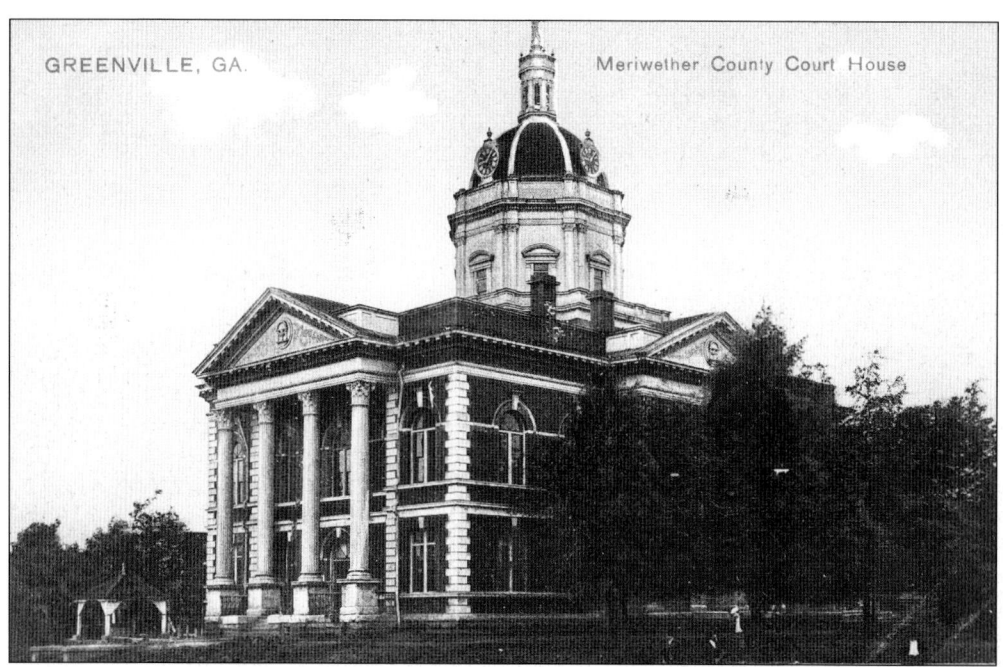

THE MERIWETHER COUNTY COURTHOUSE IN GREENVILLE. The courthouse was built in 1903.

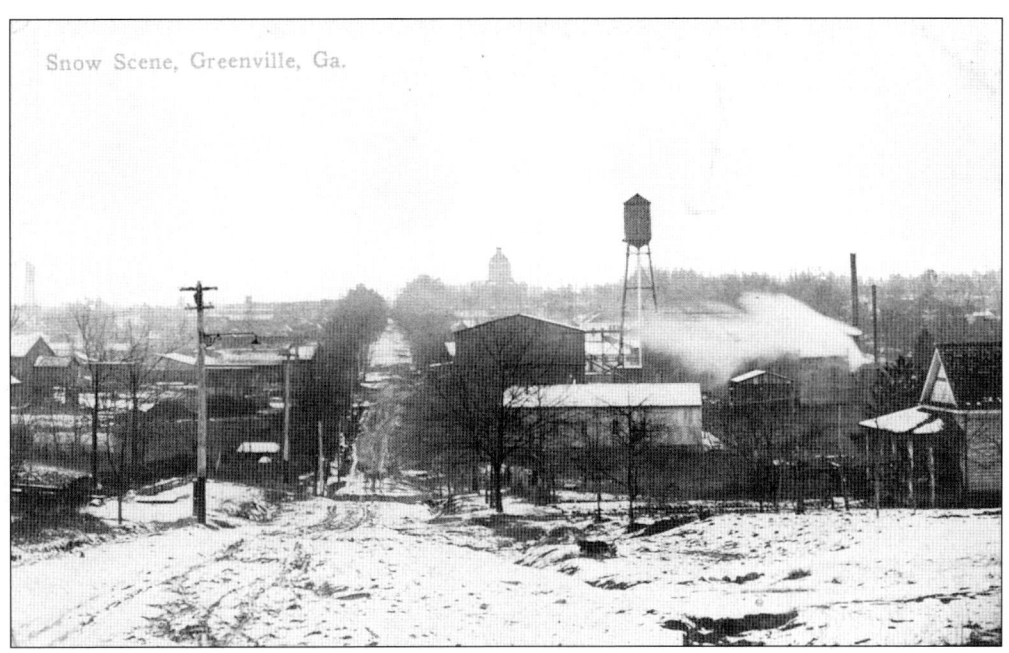

A SNOW SCENE IN GREENVILLE, C. 1912, LOOKING DOWN THE MAIN STREET.

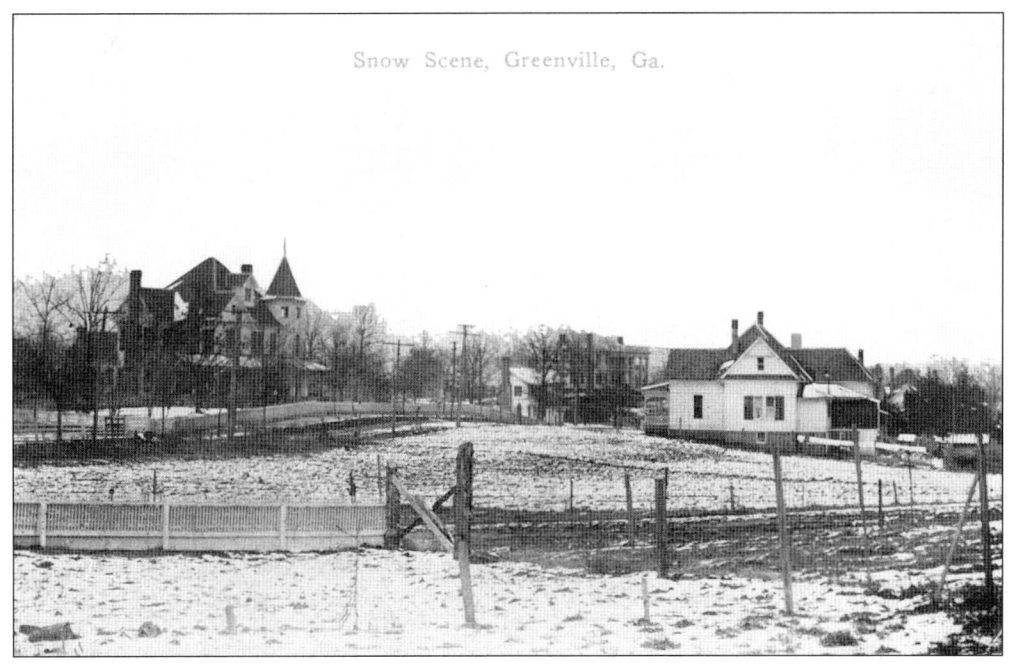

ANOTHER VIEW OF SNOW-COVERED GREENVILLE, C. 1912, SHOWING SOME OF THE RESIDENTIAL AREA.

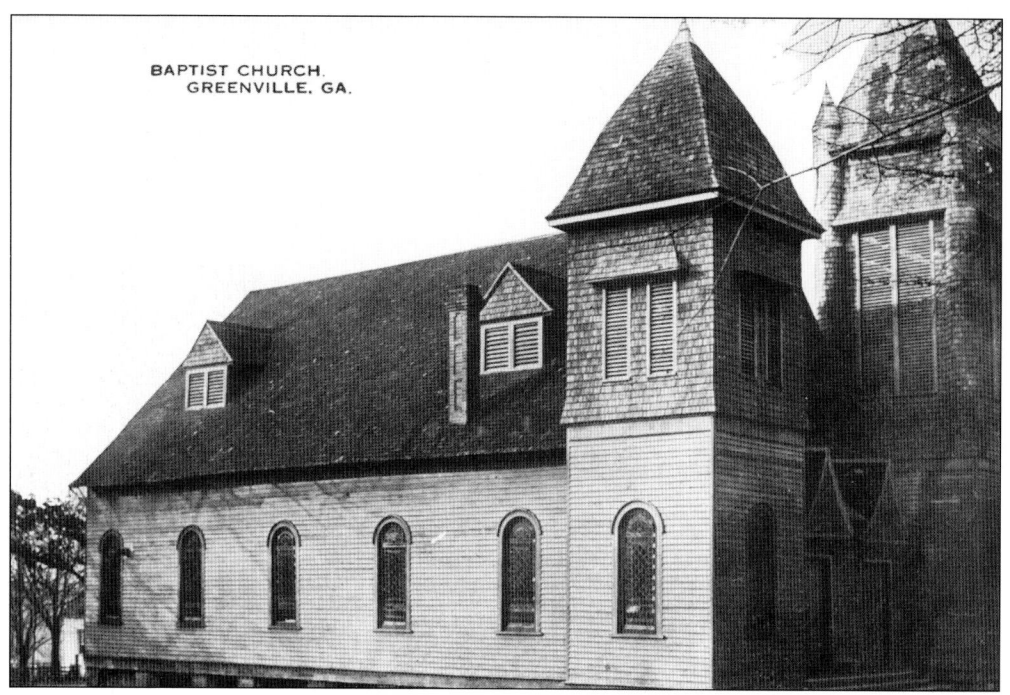

The Baptist Church in Greenville, c. 1916.

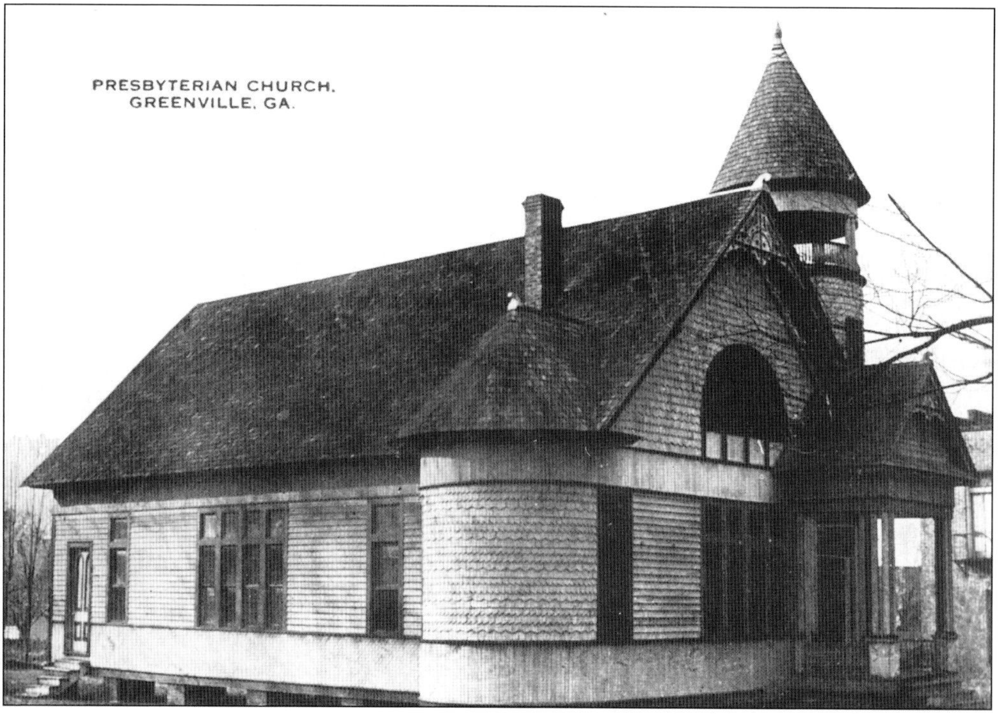

The Presbyterian Church in Greenville, c. 1916.

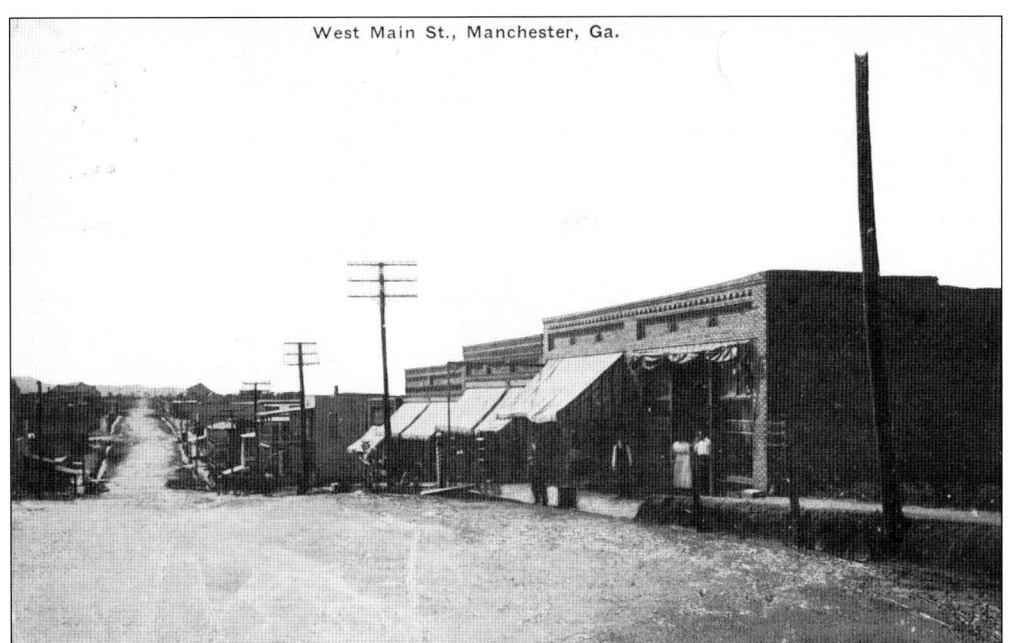

WEST MAIN STREET IN MANCHESTER. This card was postmarked on April 27, 1912, and was mailed to Lakeview, Indiana. The message reads in part: "I am at this place at present. Am running the wrecker for the A.B. & A. [Atlanta, Birmingham, & Atlantic Railroad] but don't think will stay long. Say, that girl that you are writing to down here is going to be married Sunday. It was a surprise to me. Why don't you write me, I think you owe me a letter. We are having lots of rain but it is a nice place. From an old Friend L.E. Eberhart."

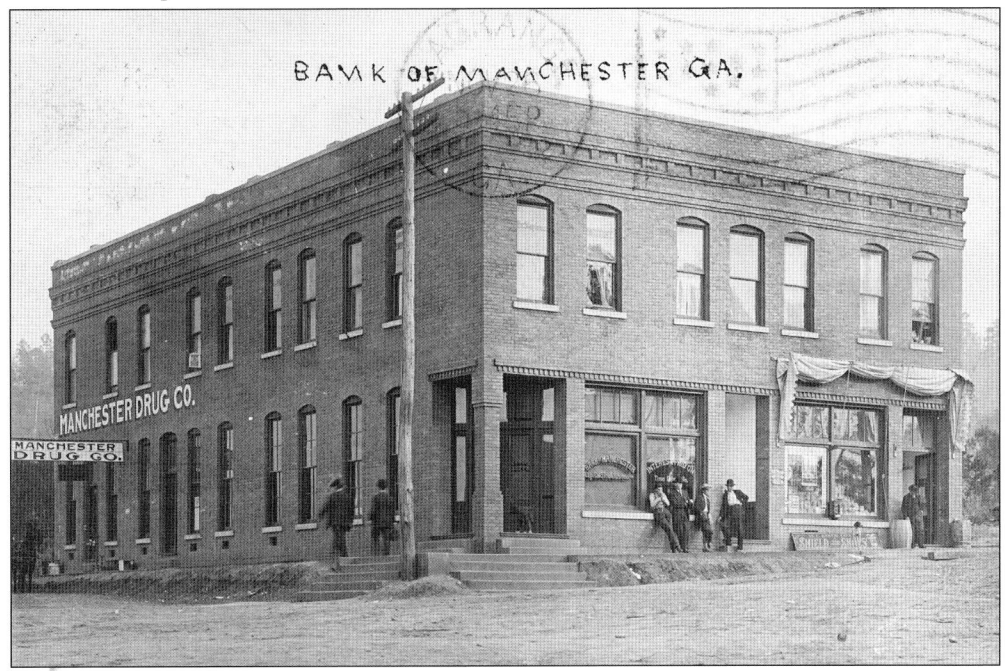

A REAL-PHOTO VIEW OF THE BANK OF MANCHESTER AND THE MANCHESTER DRUG COMPANY, MAILED ON NOVEMBER 26, 1912.

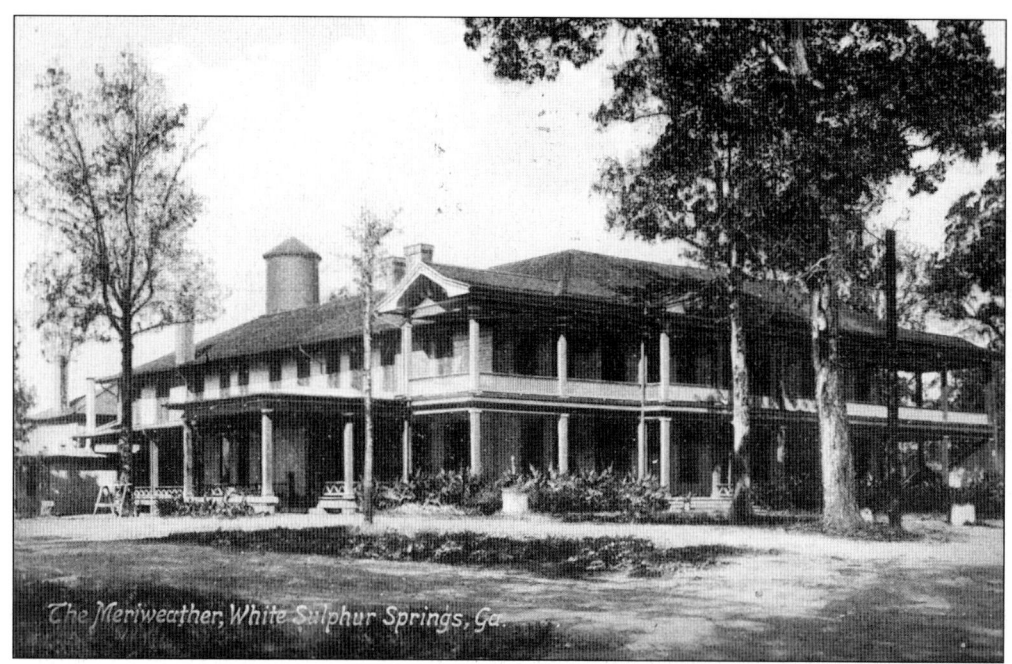

The Hotel Meriwether at White Sulphur Springs in Meriwether County. There also was a White Sulphur Springs in Hall County near Gainesville, but it was never as popular.

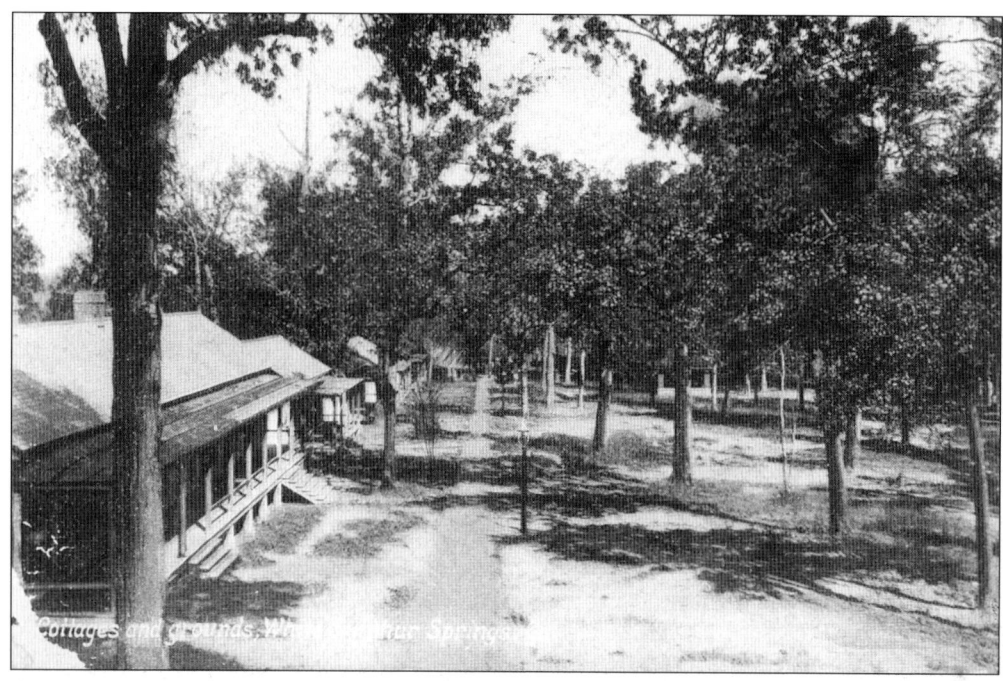

Cottages for Guests at White Sulphur Springs Who Preferred not to Stay in the Hotel.

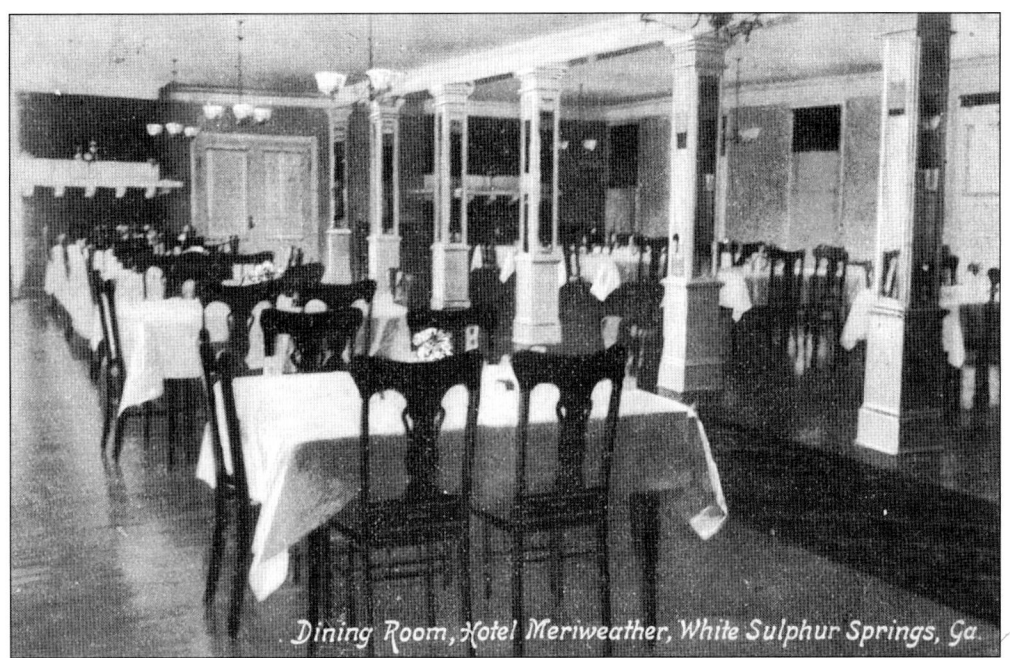

An Interior View of the Dining Room at the Hotel Meriwether at White Sulphur Springs.

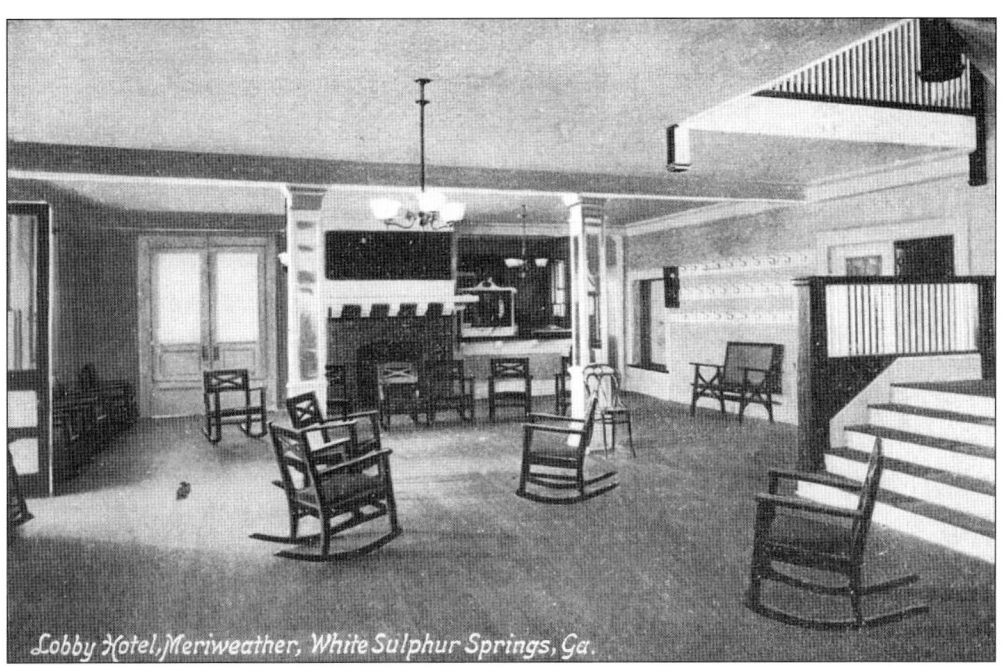

The Lobby at the Hotel Meriwether at White Sulphur Springs.

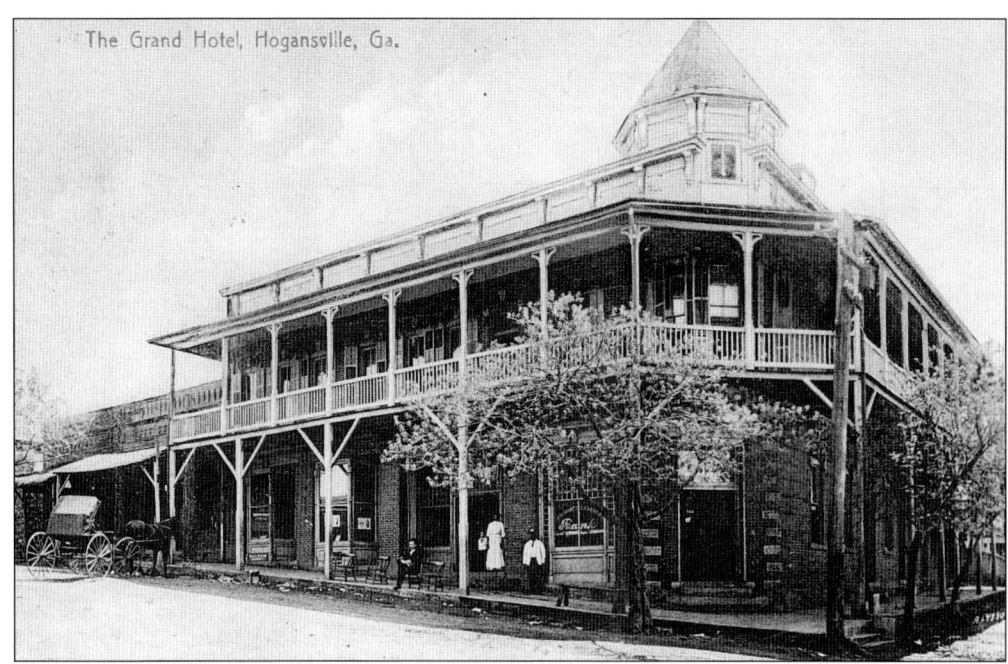

THE GRAND HOTEL AT HOGANSVILLE IN 1910. The hotel was indeed grand. The Merchants and Farmers Bank occupied the corner office with the catercornered doorway.

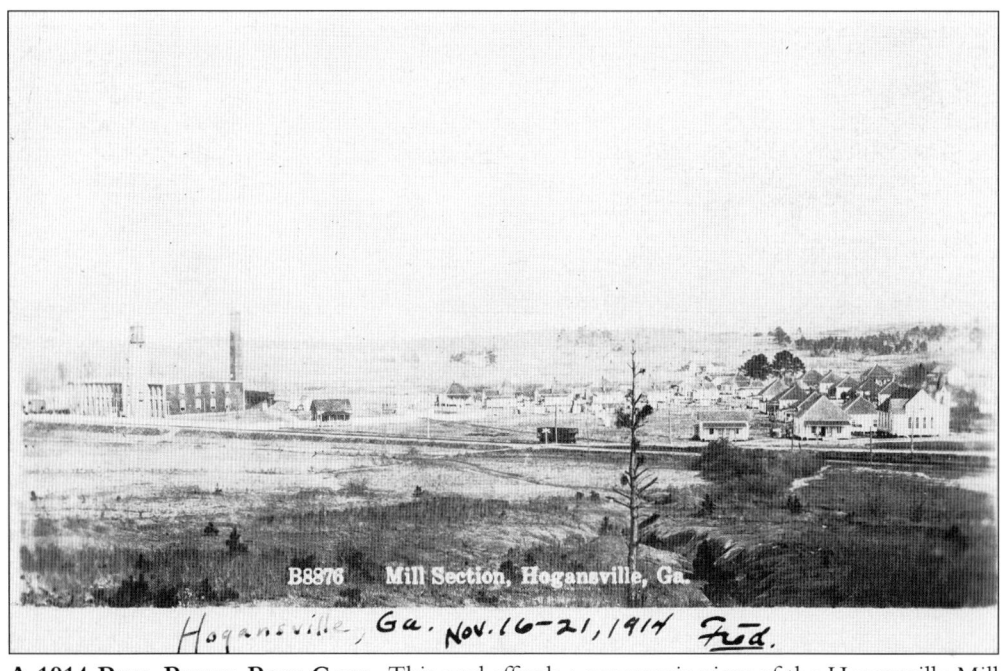

A 1914 REAL-PHOTO POST CARD. This card affords a panoramic view of the Hogansville Mill and the workers' houses.

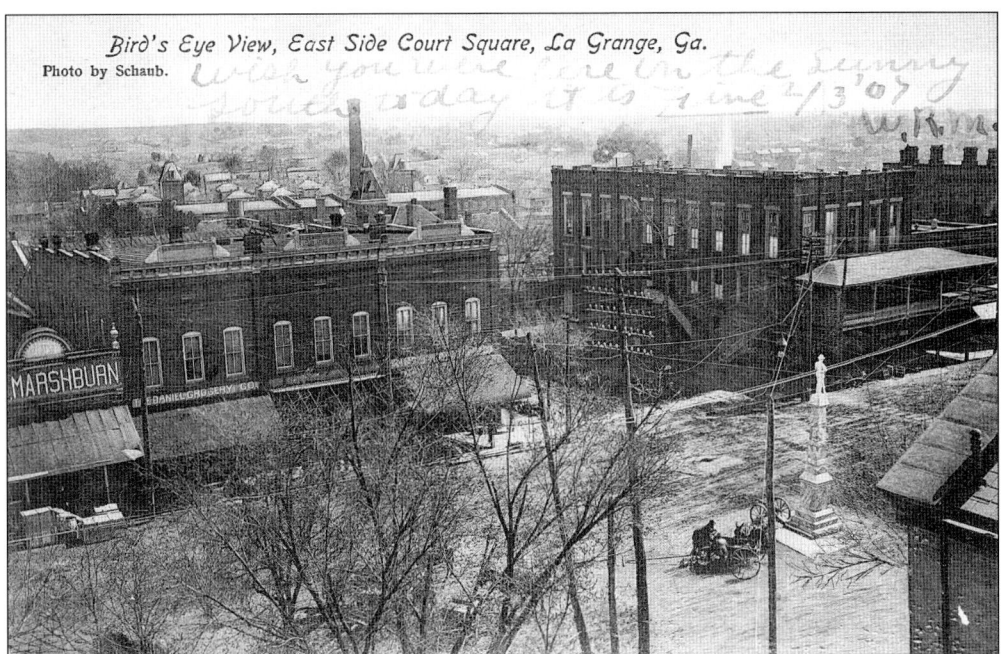

A BIRD'S-EYE VIEW OF THE EAST SIDE OF THE COURTHOUSE SQUARE IN LAGRANGE, c. 1906. The Confederate Monument seen in the middle of the square was unveiled October 30, 1902. When the courthouse burned and was rebuilt, the monument was moved to that location on Ridley Avenue in 1943. The need for more parking space at the courthouse forced another move in 1976 and the monument was placed in Confederate Park on Highway 29.

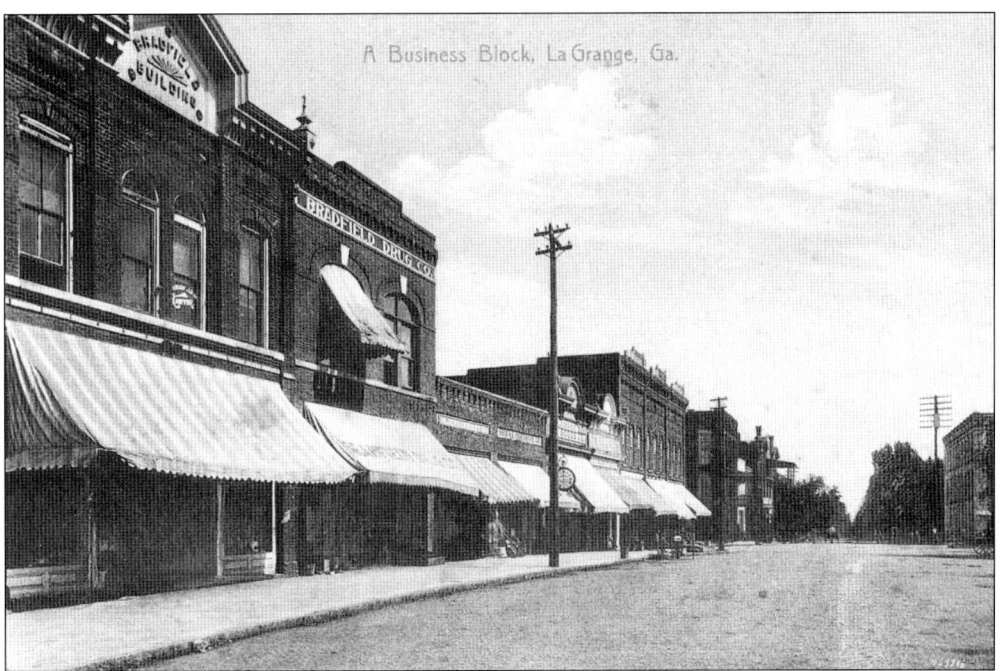

A BUSINESS BLOCK IN LAGRANGE, c. 1910.

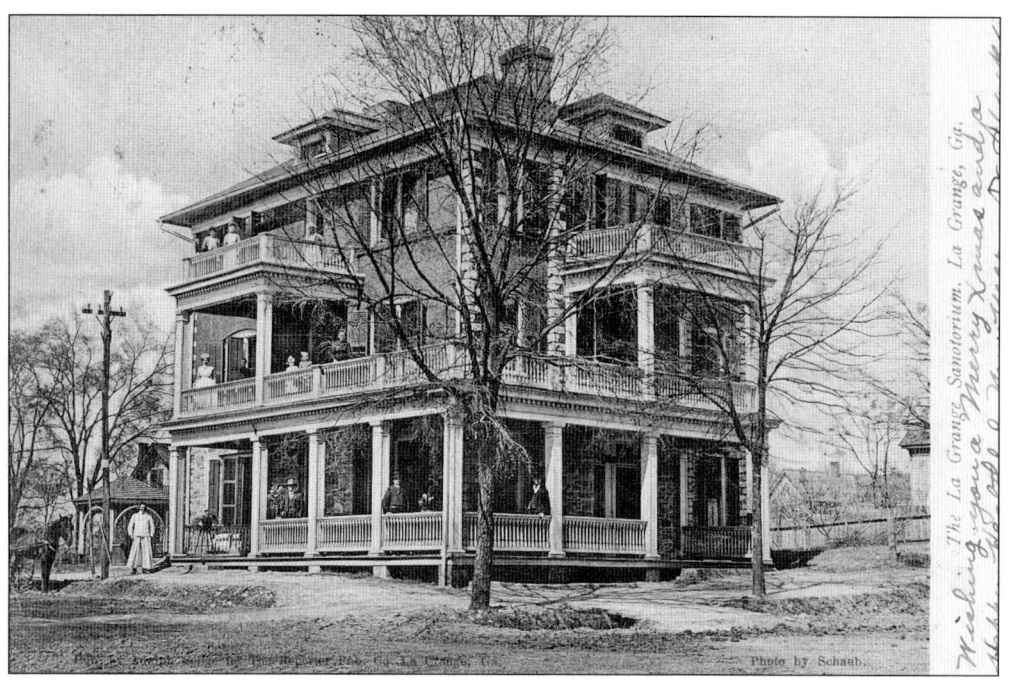

THE LAGRANGE SANATORIUM, C. 1907.

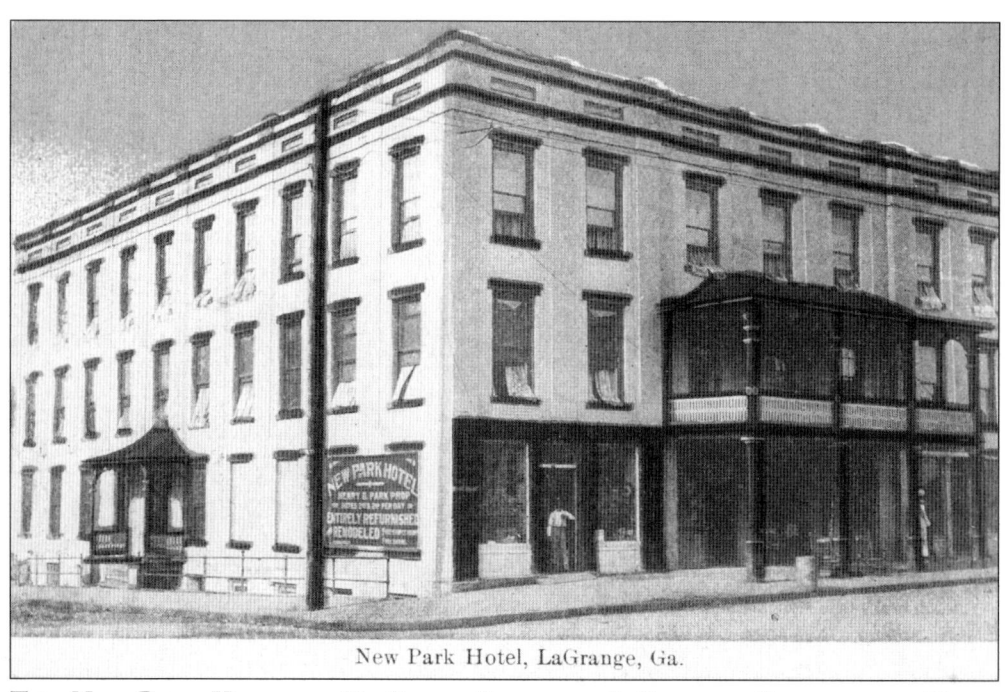

THE NEW PARK HOTEL AT 35 COURT STREET IN LAGRANGE, OPERATED BY HENRY B. PARK.

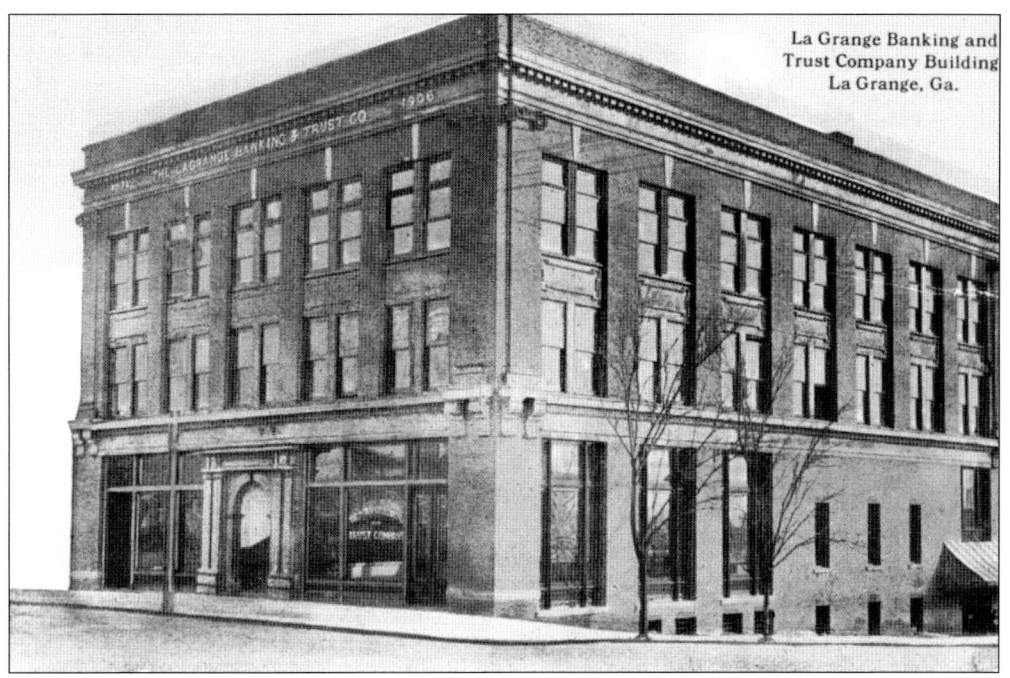

THE LAGRANGE BANKING AND TRUST COMPANY BUILDING IN LAGRANGE, LOCATED AT 29 COURT SQUARE.

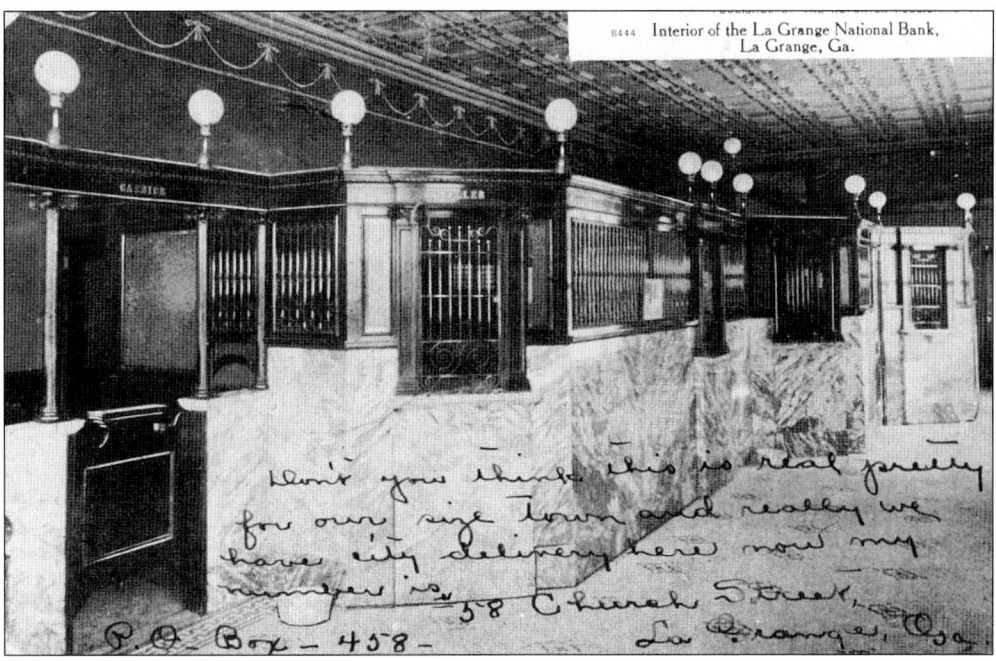

AN INTERIOR VIEW OF THE LAGRANGE BANKING AND TRUST COMPANY, C. 1907.

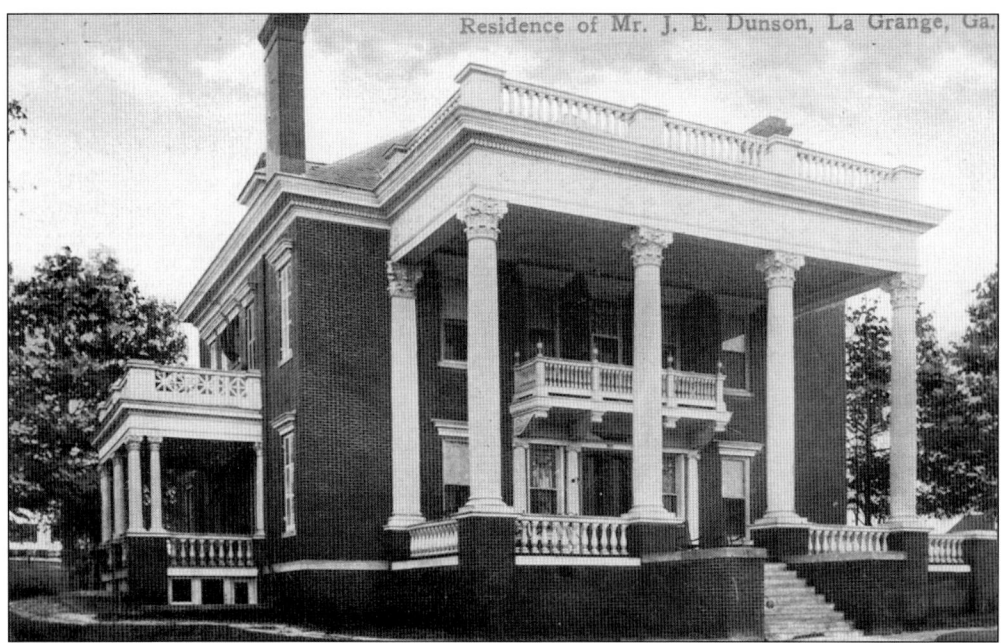

THE RESIDENCE OF MR. J.E. DUNSON OF LAGRANGE. Dunson operated a general merchandise store and dealt in livestock and vehicles.

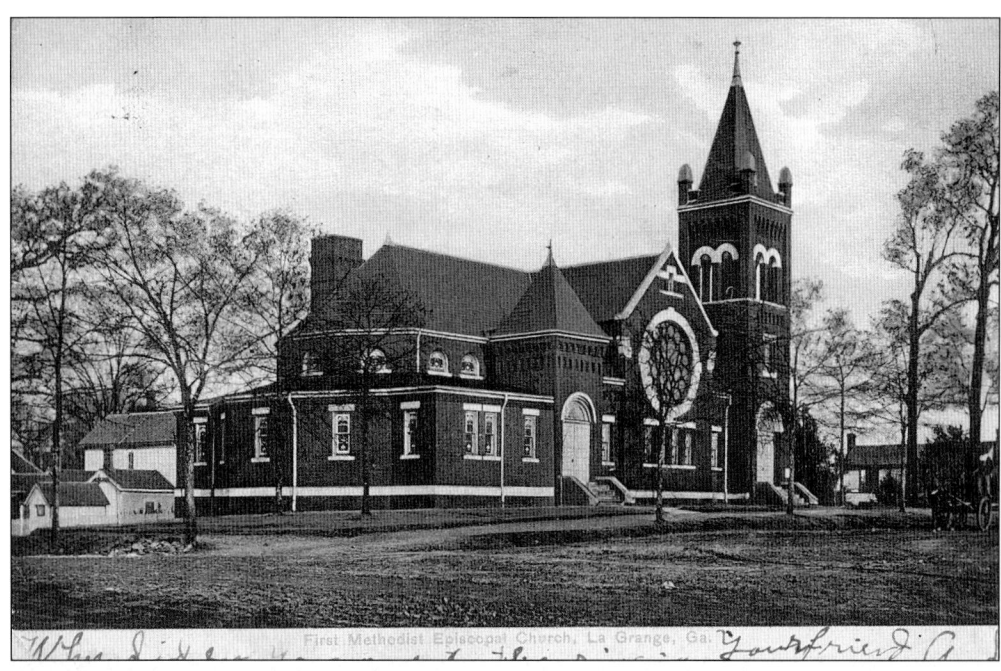

THE FIRST METHODIST EPISCOPAL CHURCH IN LAGRANGE. This card was mailed from Homer to Ashland on June 30, 1908, with the following message: "Why didn't you come to the singing? Your friend, A.D."

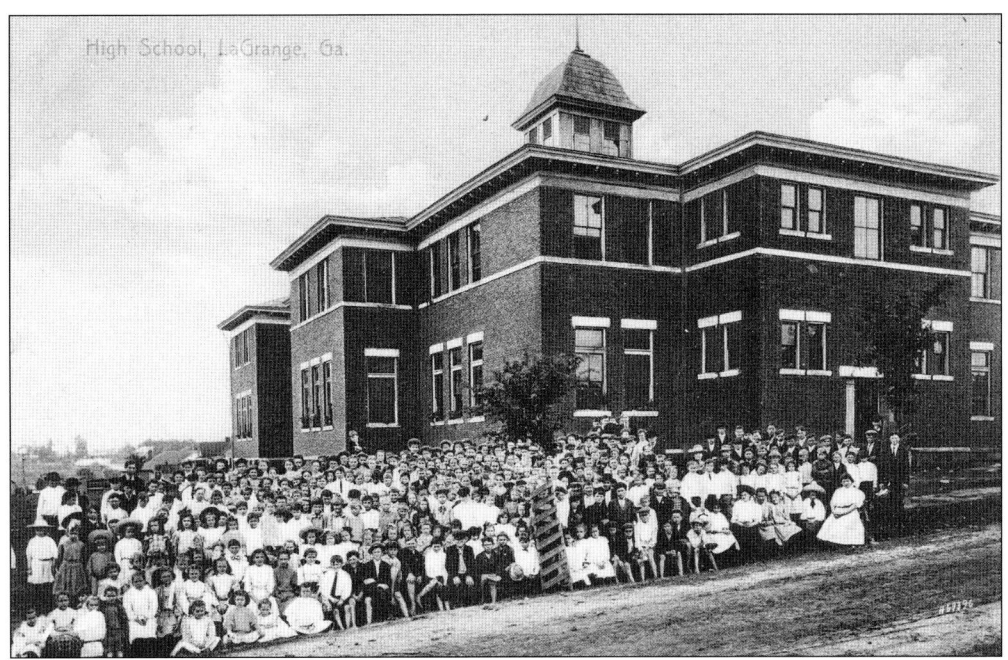

A Large Student Body and the Teachers Pose outside the LaGrange High School, c. 1910..

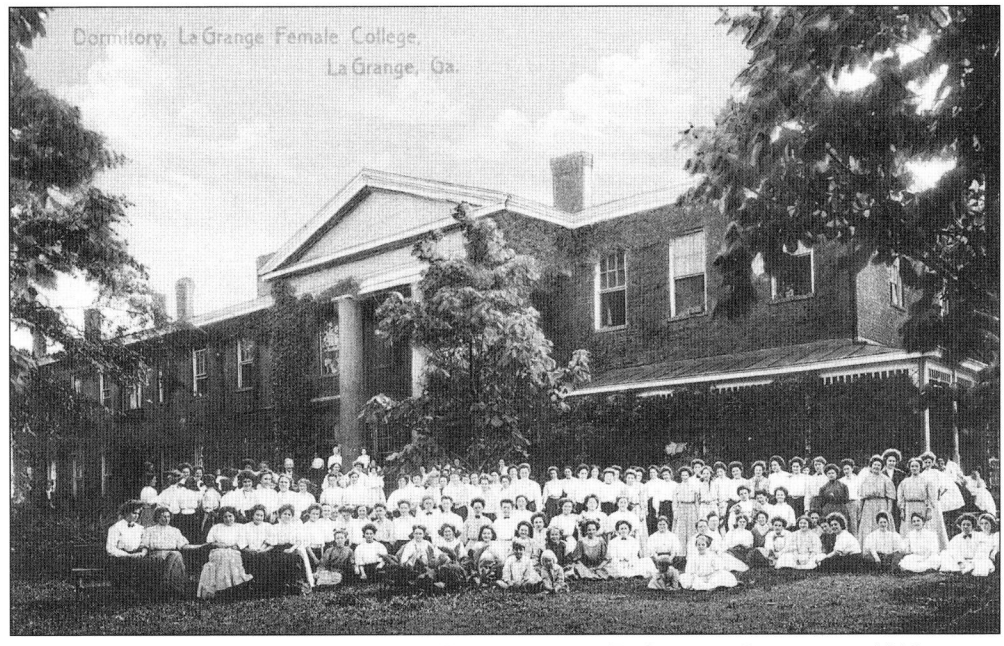

The Young Ladies Who Lived in the Dormitory at LaGrange College, c. 1910.

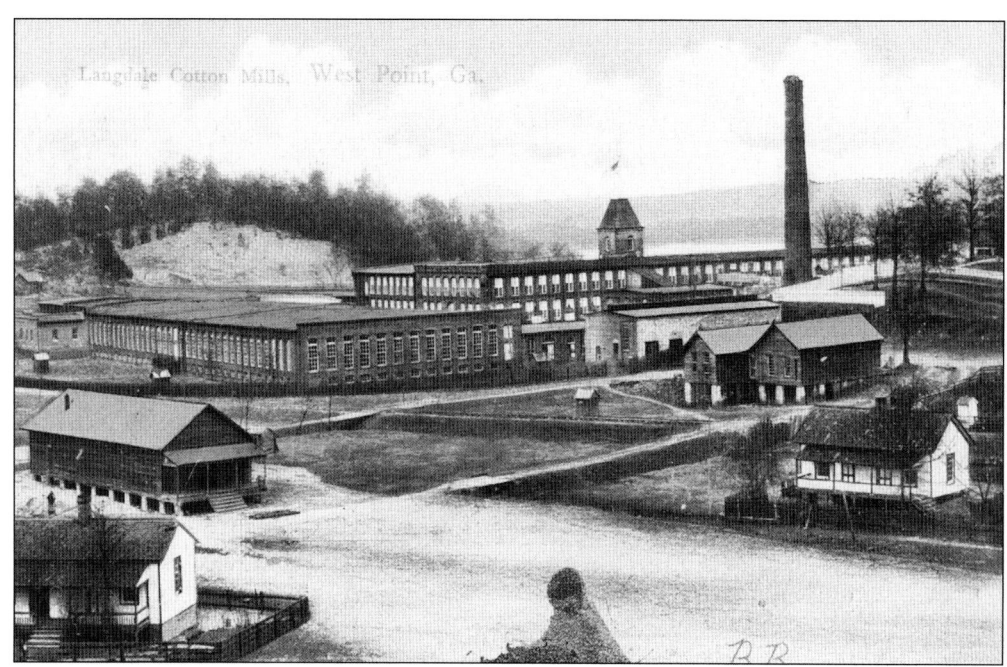

THE LANGDALE COTTON MILLS AT LAGRANGE. The mills provided many jobs for people in the community.

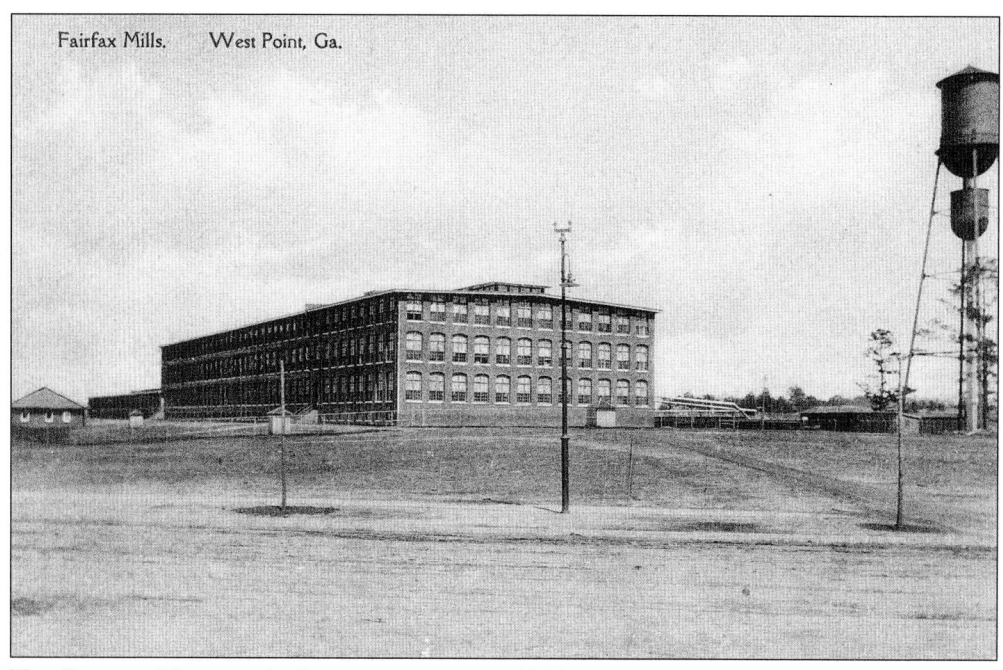

THE FAIRFAX MILLS AT LAGRANGE IN THE MID-1910S.

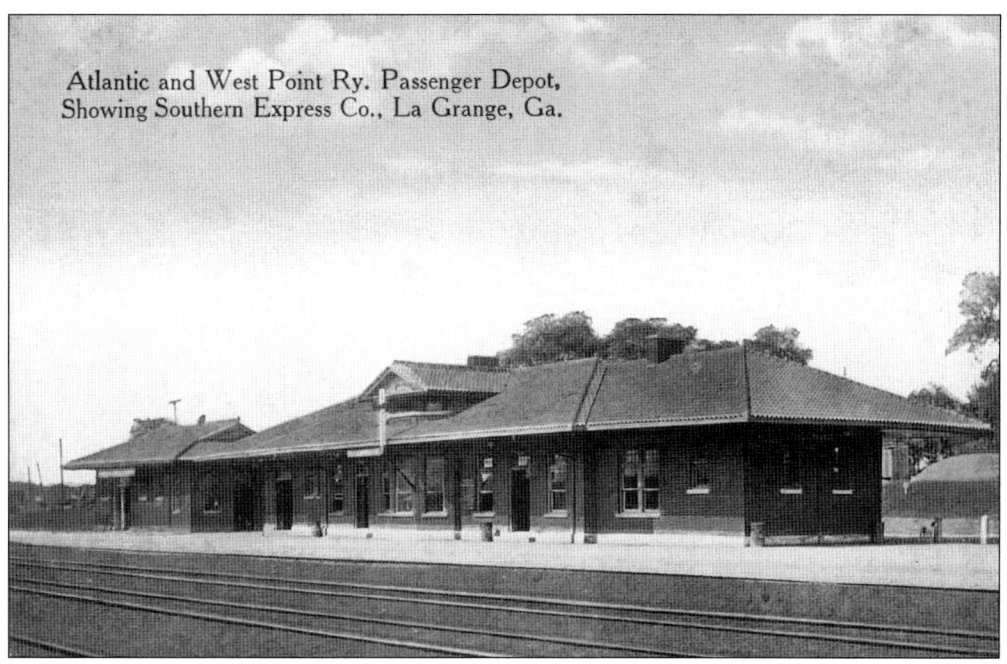

A Picture of the Atlanta and West Point Railroad Passenger Depot at LaGrange, along with the offices of the Southern Express Company.

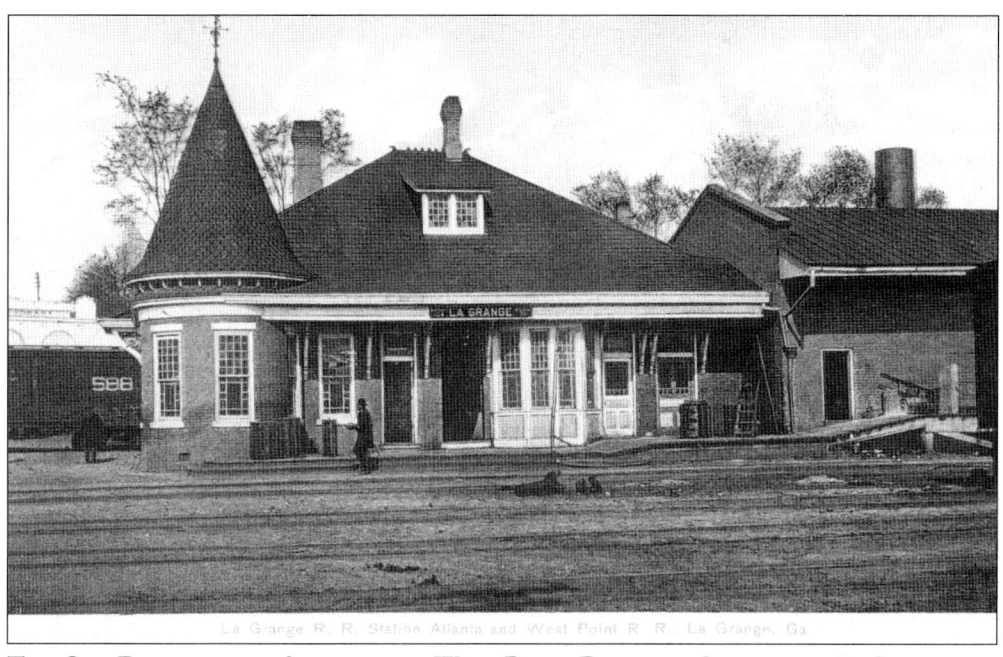

The Old Depot of the Atlanta and West Point Railroad Company at LaGrange.

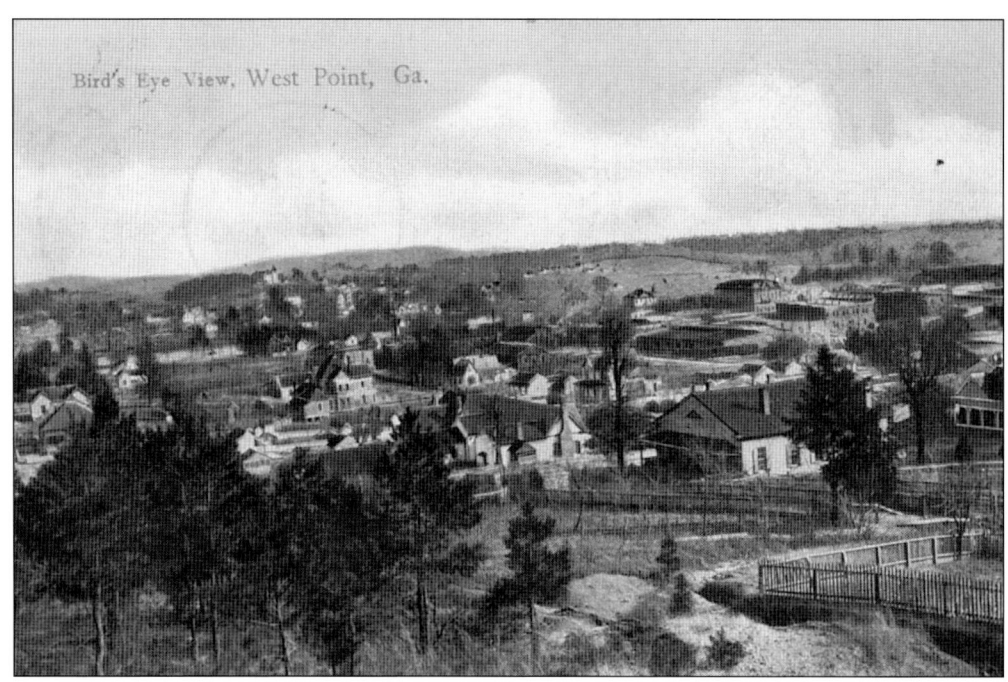

A Bird's-eye View of West Point, c. 1909..

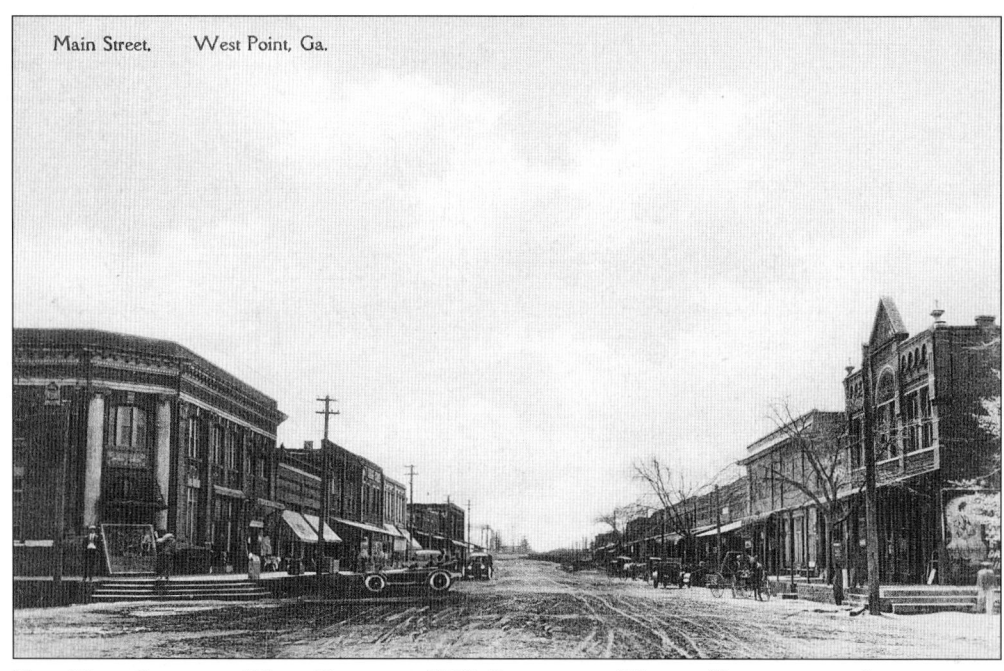

The Main Street in West Point, c. 1912, Showing a Mix of Buggies and Automobiles on the Street.

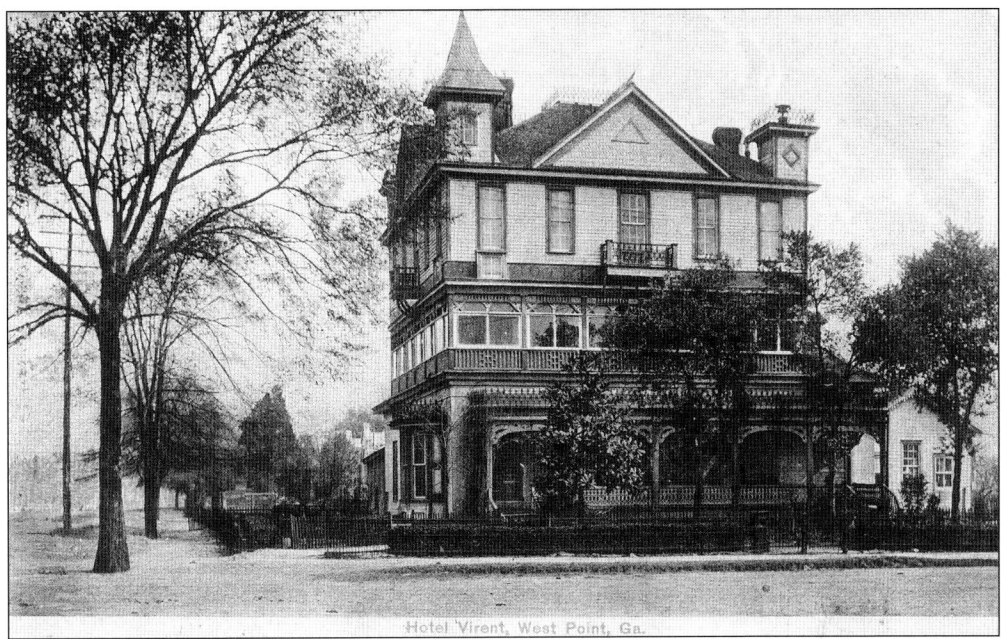

THE HOTEL VIRENT, LOCATED ON BRIDGE STREET IN WEST POINT AND OWNED BY D.H. WILLIAMS. The message gives some insight into how serious the post card collecting hobby had become by the time this card was mailed to Basic City, Virginia, on March 23, 1908. The message states in part: "Your pretty card received. I expect to have some views from Montgomery Ala soon. I have about 200 cards, received most of them this year. Got 48 last week. Don't you think the P Card exchange is a good thing? John."

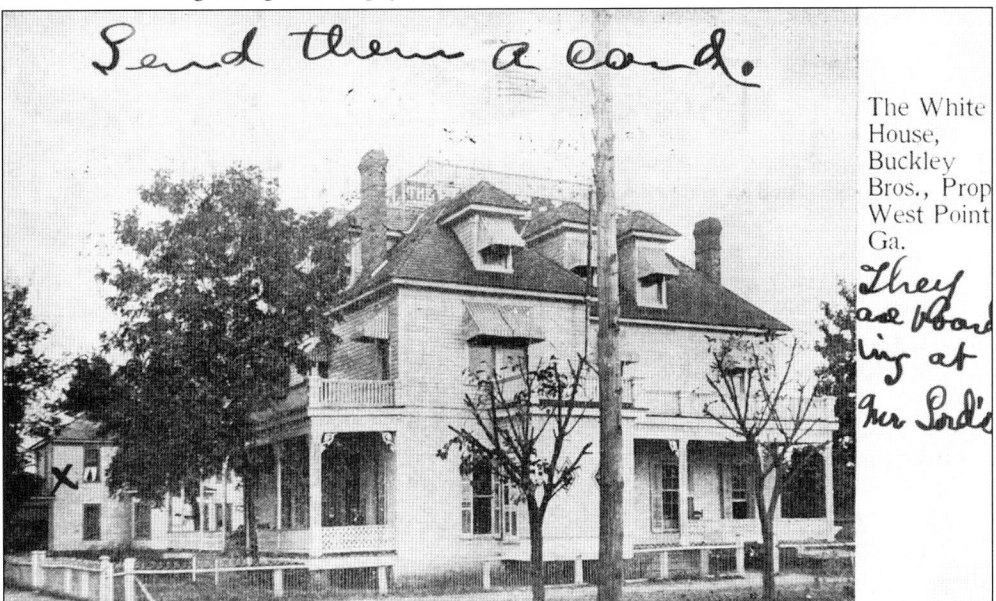

THE BUCKLEY HOUSE ON RAILROAD AVENUE IN WEST POINT, OWNED BY THE BUCKLEY BROTHERS. The card was mailed to Macon on January 27, 1909, and carried the following message: "Mamie Blunt Noland & Dunson Johnson ran away and married last night. What do you think of that? Send them a card. They are boarding at Mr. Lord's."

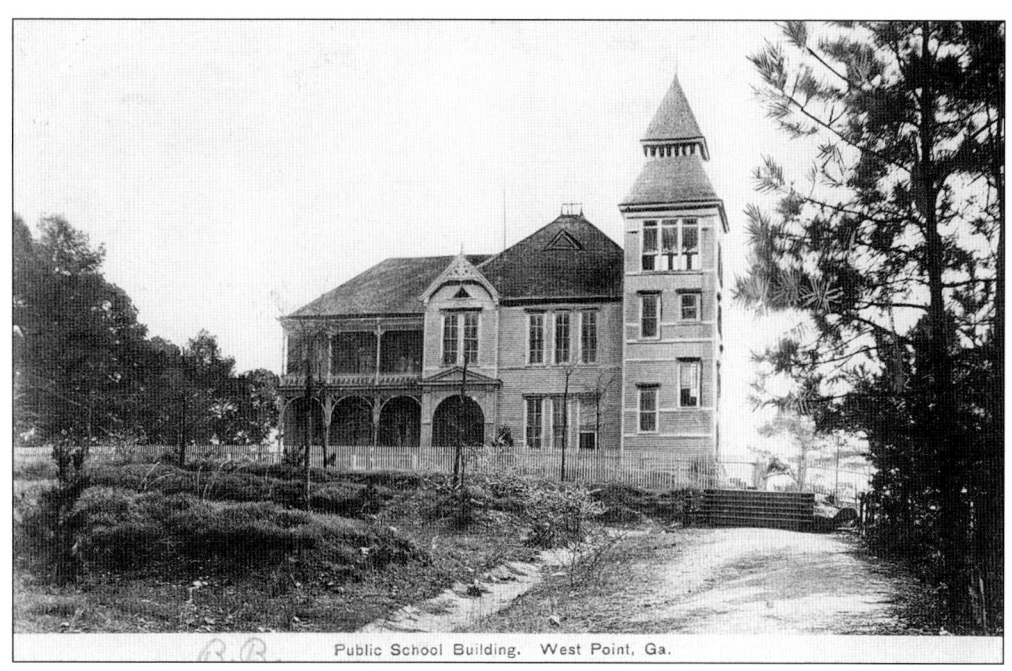

The Public School Building at West Point, c.1908.

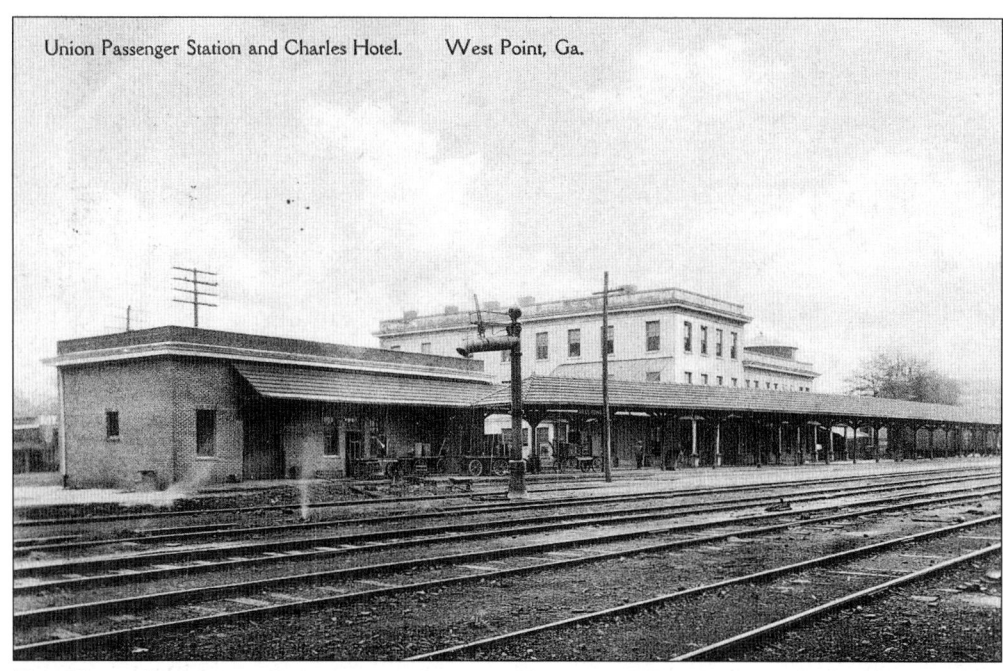

The Union Passenger Station and Charles Hotel in West Point. The hotel was owned by J.W. Williams.

Seven

Lamar, Pike, Upson, Monroe, and Spalding Counties

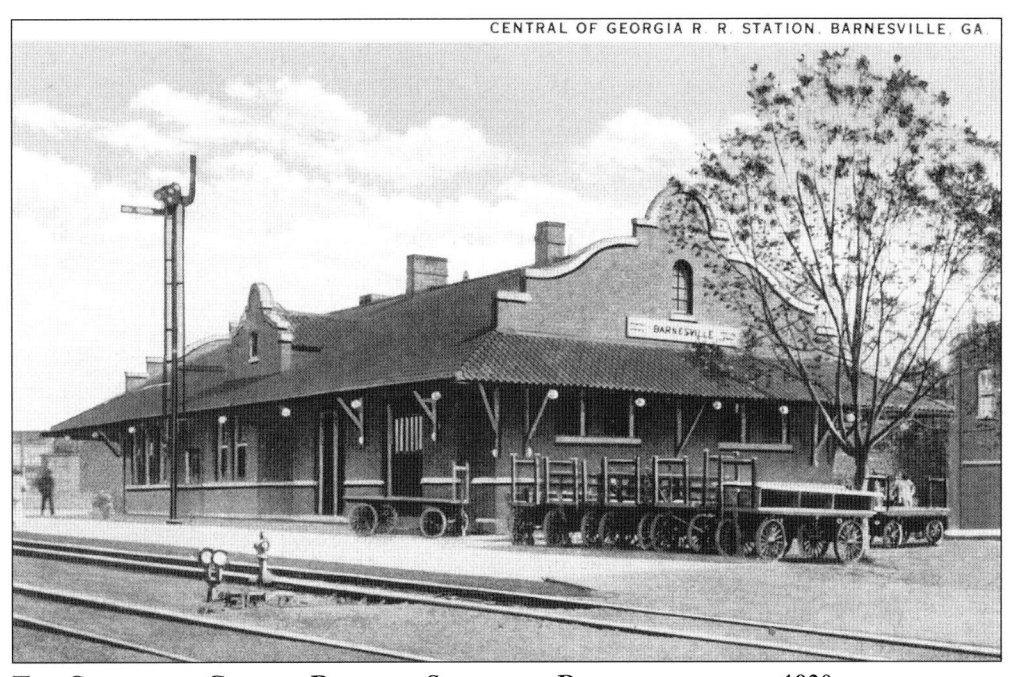
The Central of Georgia Railroad Station at Barnesville in the 1920s.

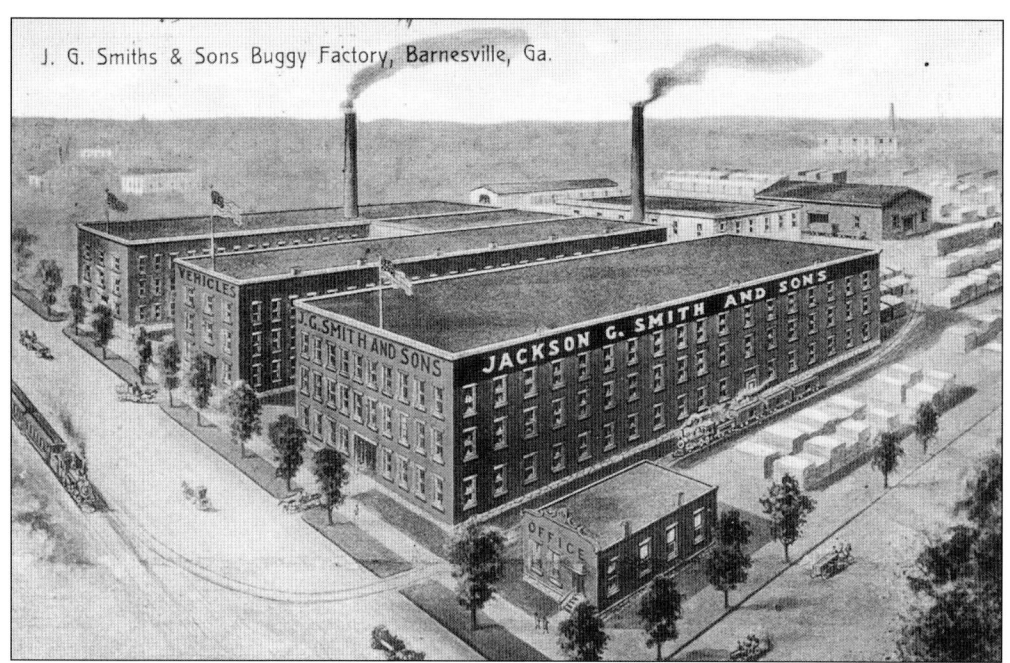

J.G. SMITH & SONS' BUGGY FACTORY ON FORSYTH STREET IN BARNESVILLE, C.1912.

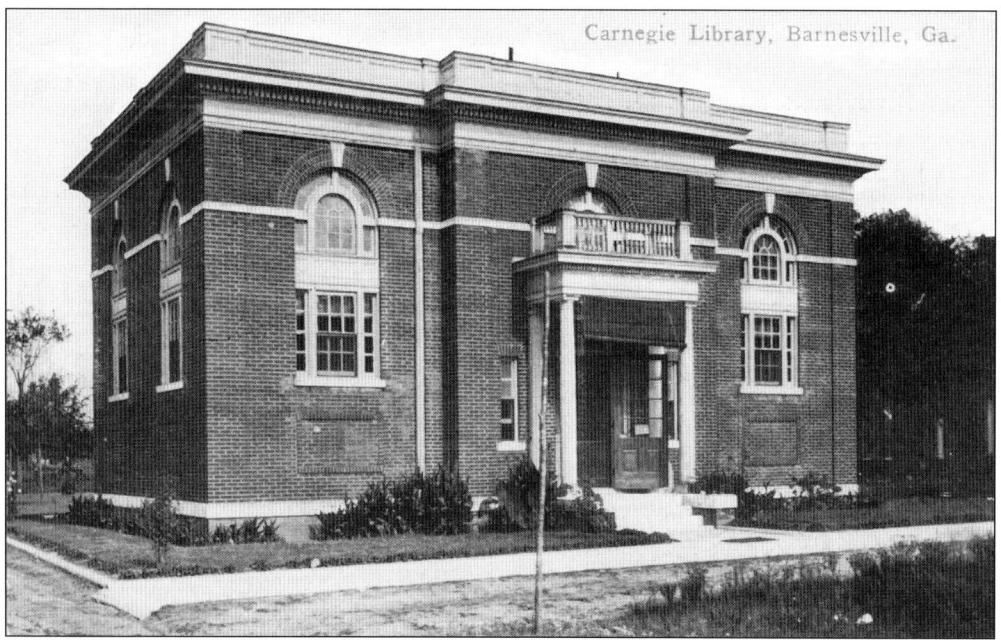

THE CARNEGIE LIBRARY IN BARNESVILLE. This card was mailed to Warner, New Hampshire, on January 10, 1917, with the following message: "This is a progressive place with a military school, an agricultural college, nice homes, plenty of red clay roads, this Library, & a fine Scotch Cong'l. minister & wife. Yours, M.L. Daniels."

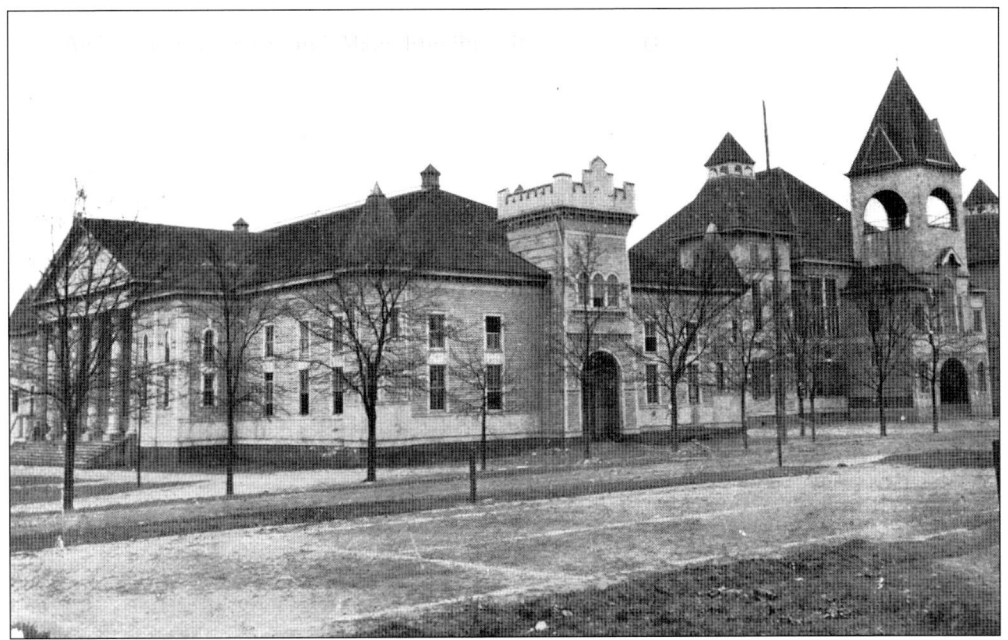
THE AUDITORIUM, ARMORY, AND MAIN BUILDING OF GORDON INSTITUTE AT BARNESVILLE, C.1912.

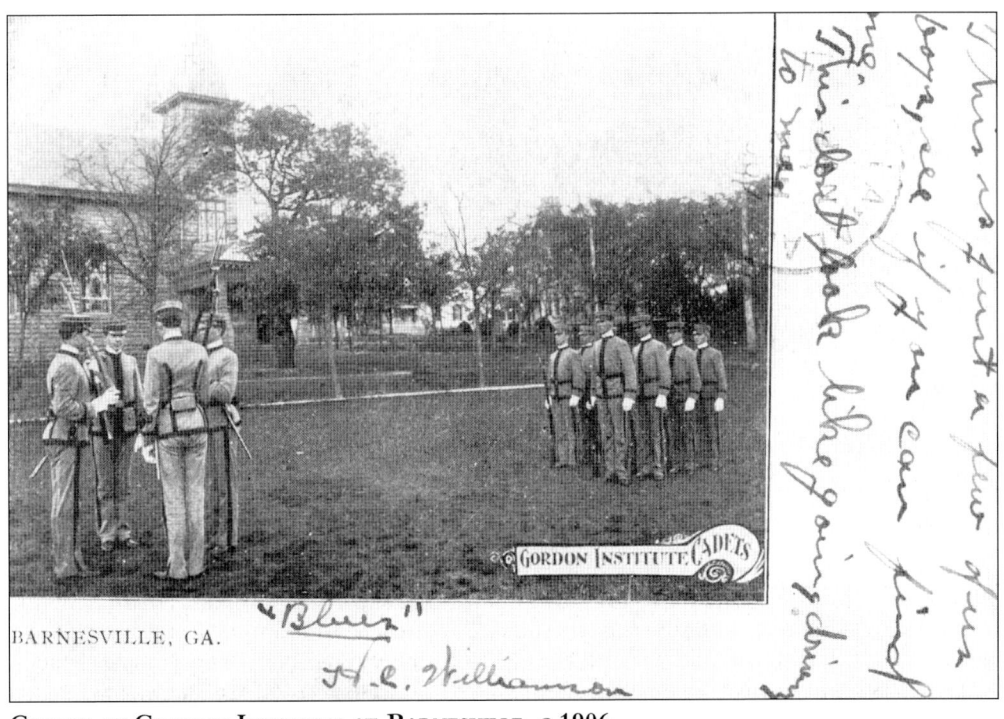
CADETS AT GORDON INSTITUTE AT BARNESVILLE, C.1906.

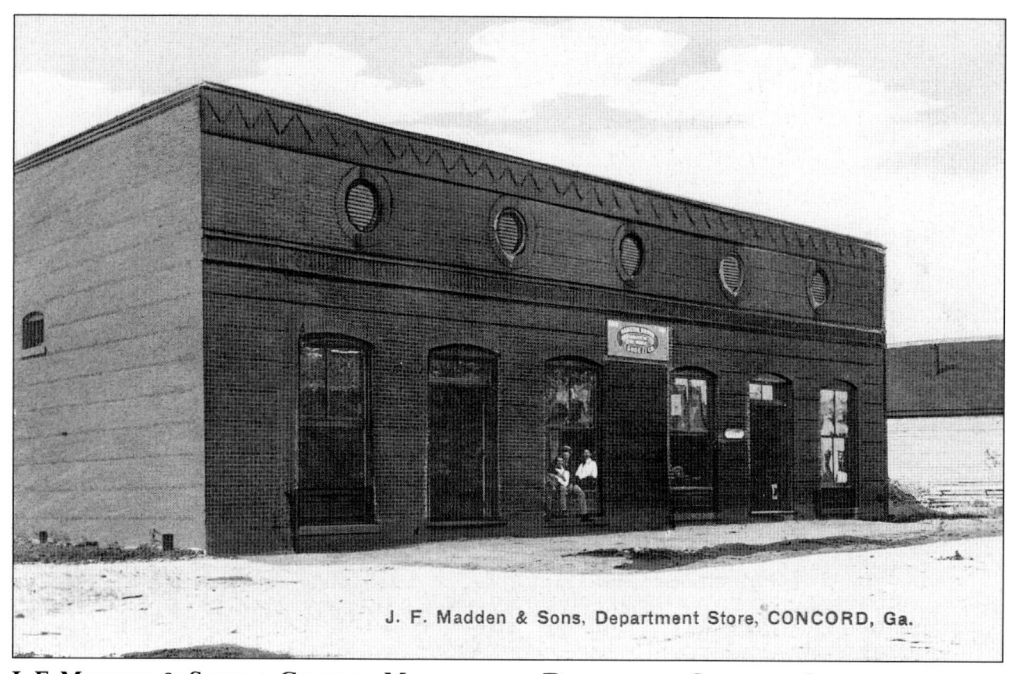

J. F. Madden & Sons, a General Merchandise Department Store in Concord.

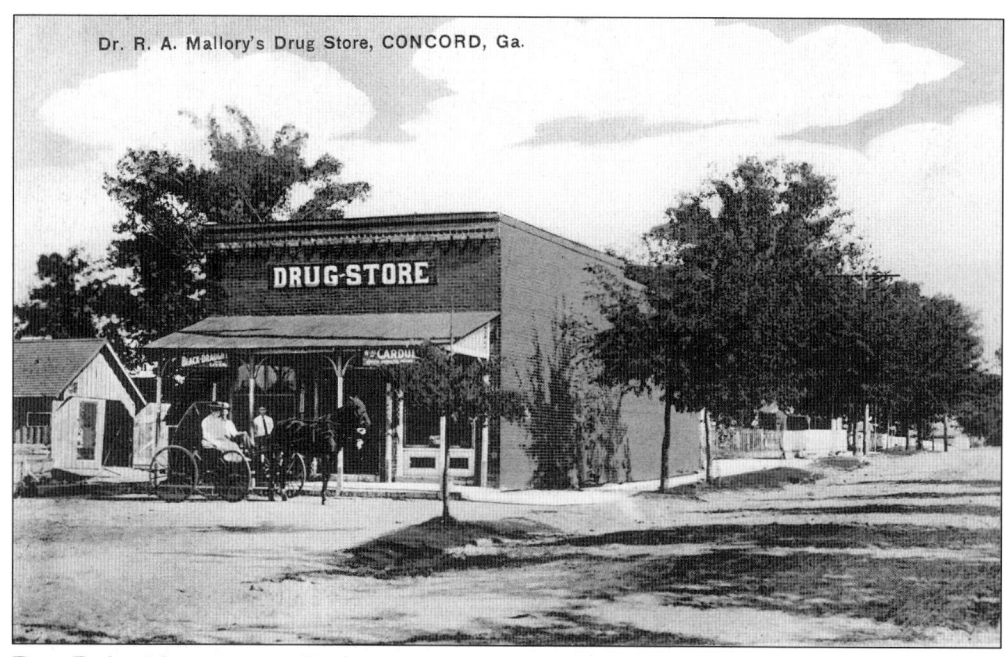

Dr. R.A. Mallory, a Physician Who also Operated the Town Drug Store in Concord.

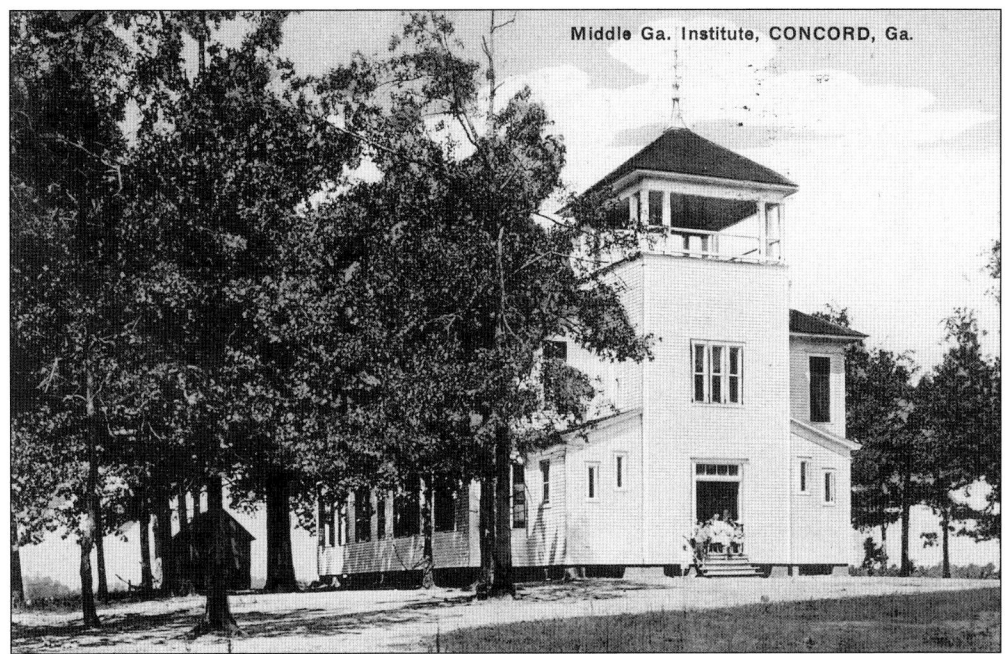

MIDDLE GEORGIA INSTITUTE IN CONCORD IN 1910.

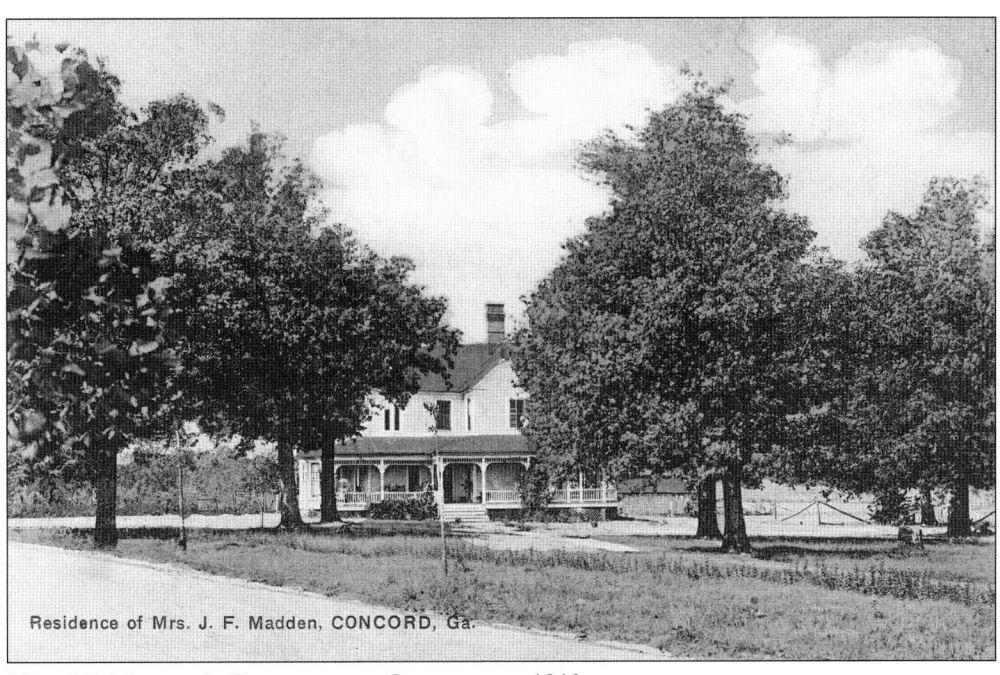

MRS. J.F. MADDEN'S RESIDENCE IN CONCORD IN 1910.

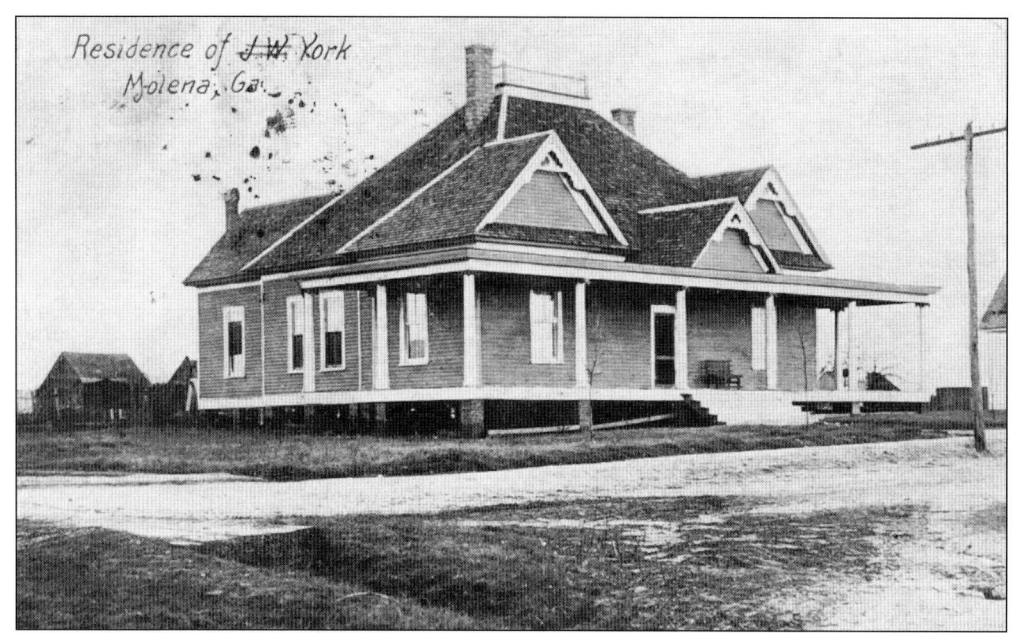

A Post Card Showing J.W. York's Home in Molena. The card was mailed to Woodbury, Georgia, on January 31, 1914. The message states: "Hello: Your card rec'd OK. glad to hear from you. why did you think I was mad? Why certainly not. good bye Maud."

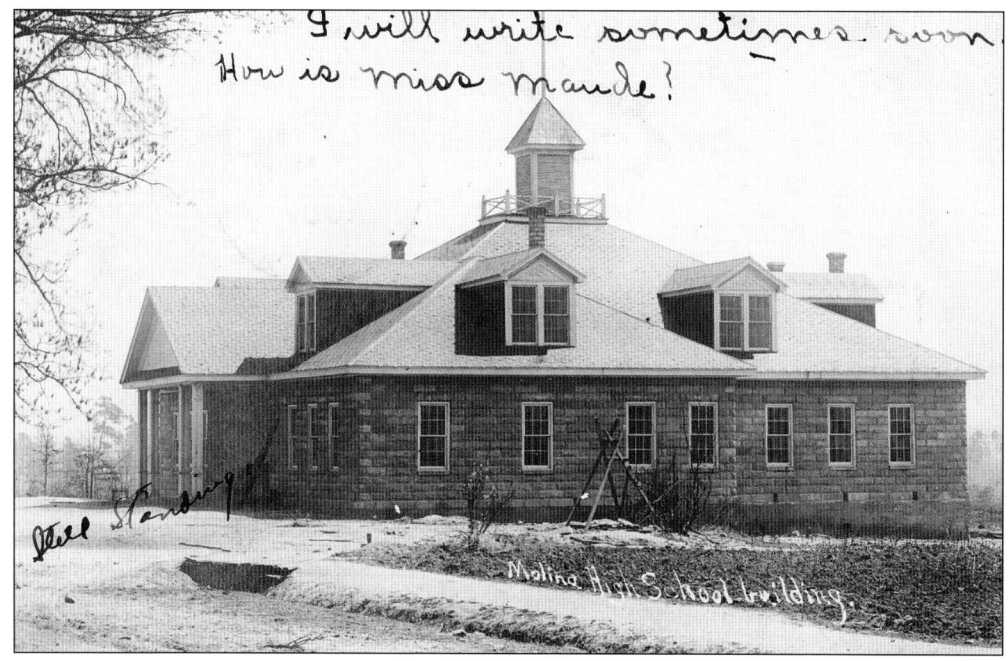

A 1907 Real-photo Post Card Showing the High School Building in Molena.

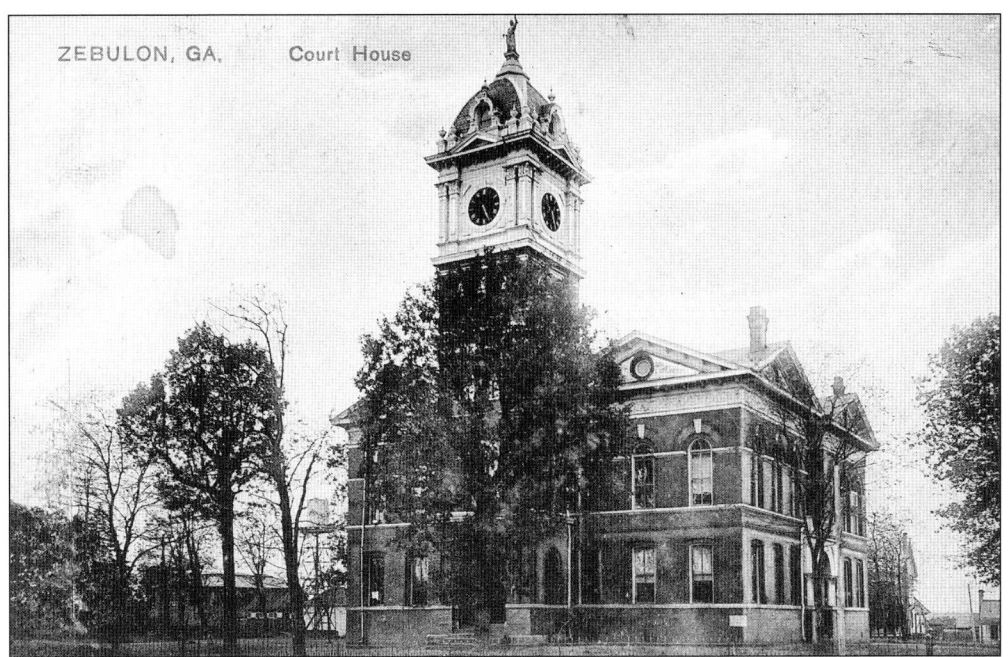

THE PIKE COUNTY COURTHOUSE IN ZEBULON, BUILT IN 1895 AT A COST OF $18,200. The plans were made by Bloucke & Stewart and the building was put up by Arthur Marshall.

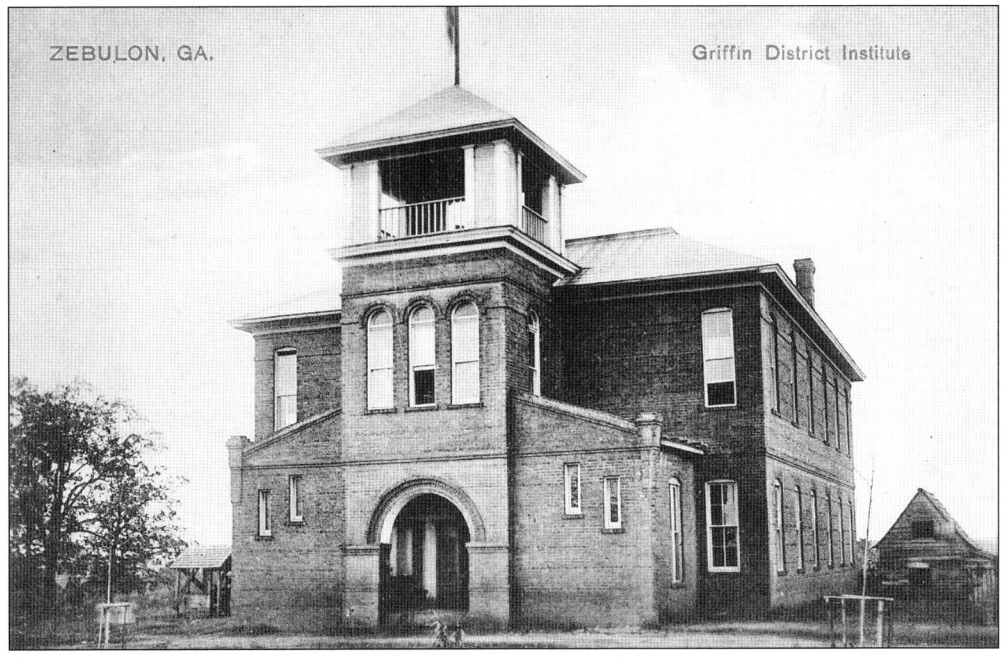

THE GRIFFIN DISTRICT INSTITUTE IN ZEBULON, C. 1908.

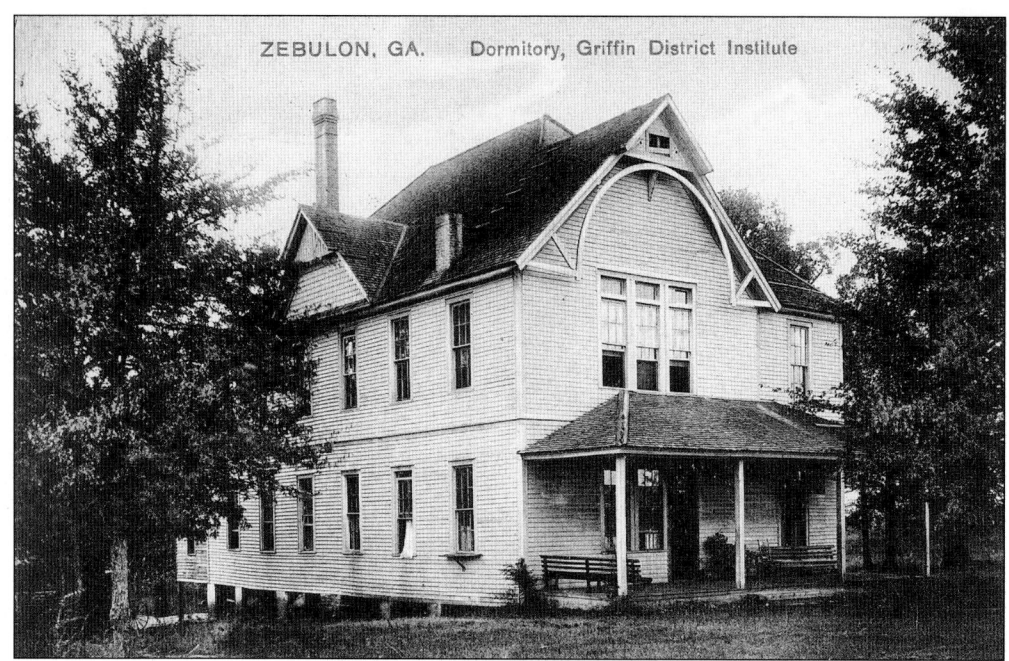
The Dormitory at the Griffin District Institute in Zebulon, c. 1908.

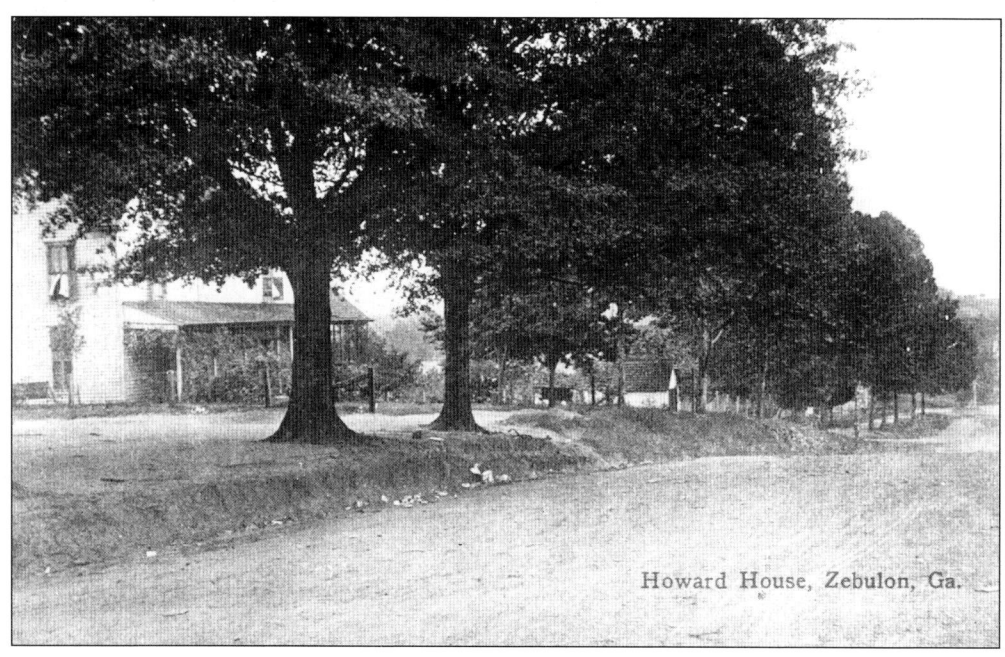
The Howard House Hotel in Zebulon, c. 1916.

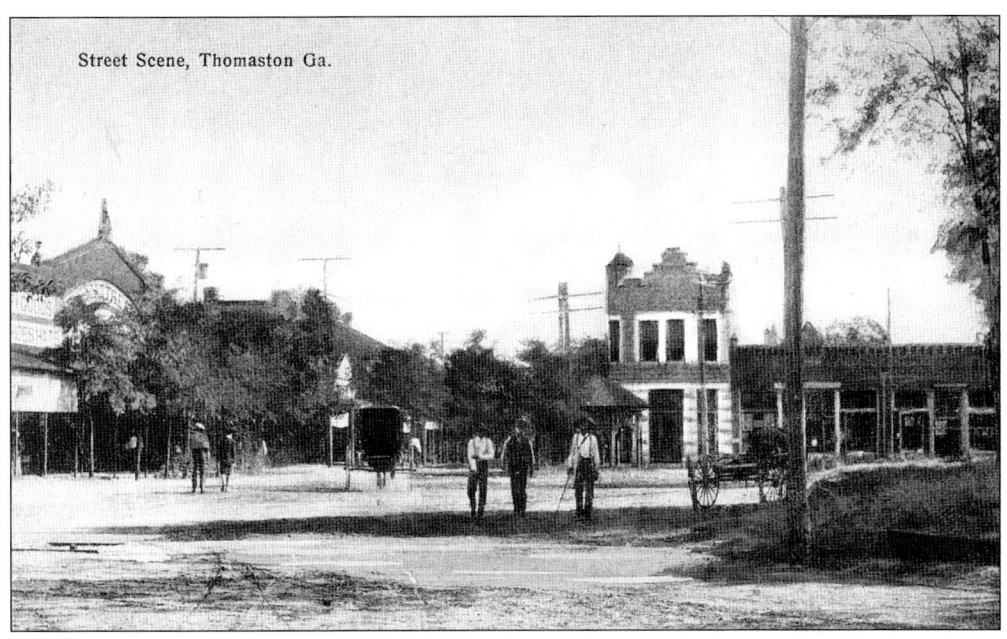

A Pleasant Street Scene in Thomaston, c. 1907.

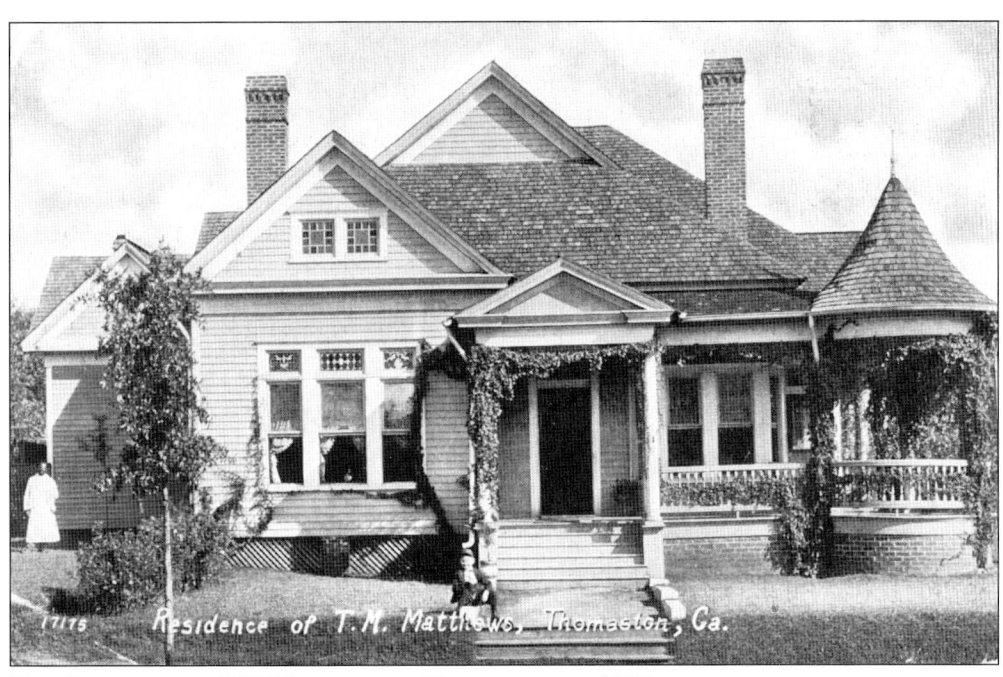

The Residence of T.N. Matthews in Thomaston, c. 1907.

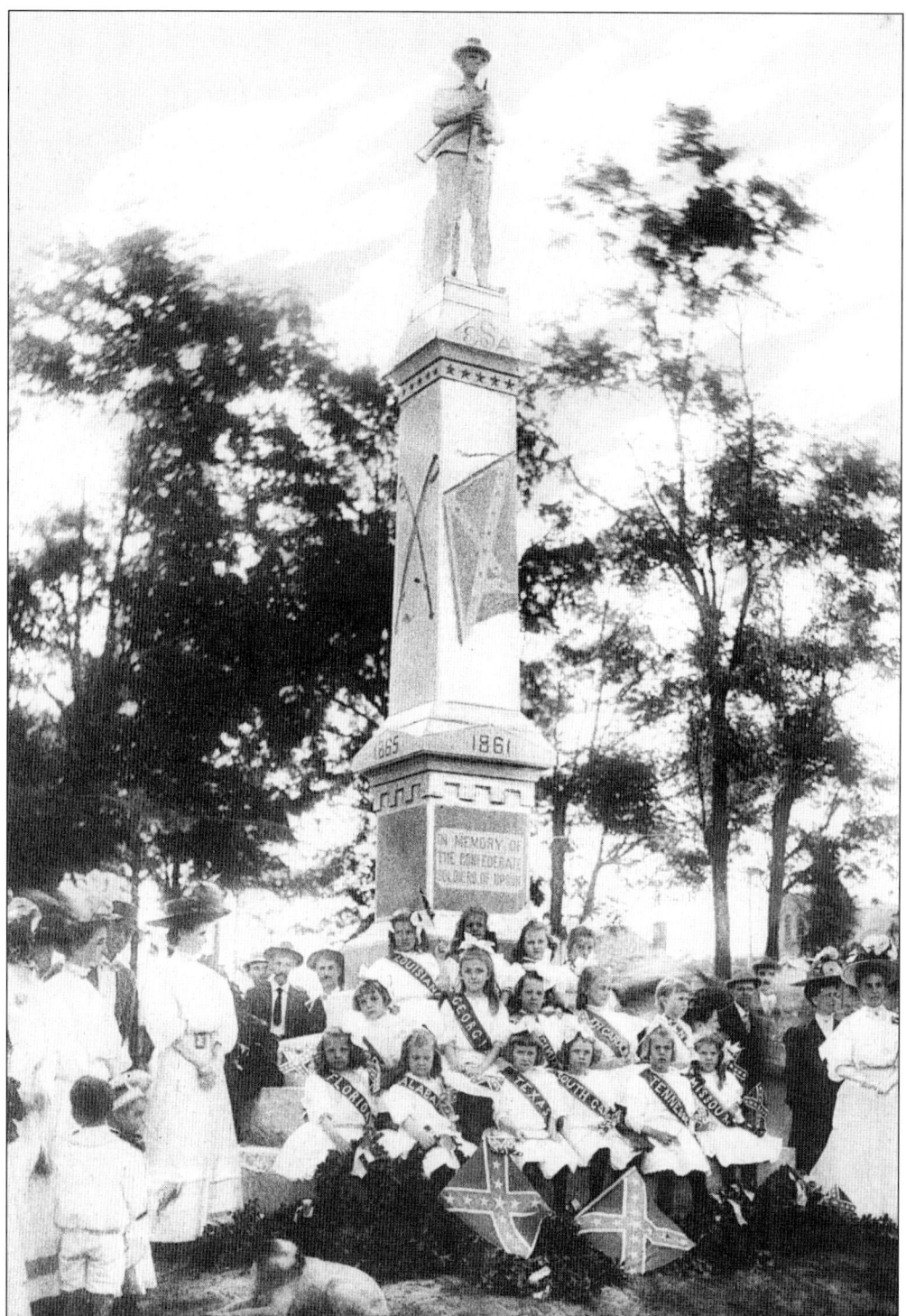

THE CONFEDERATE MONUMENT IN THOMASTON. The monument was dedicated May 2, 1908. It had taken the United Daughters of the Confederacy five years to raise the $1,300 that the McNeel Mable Company charged for the monument.

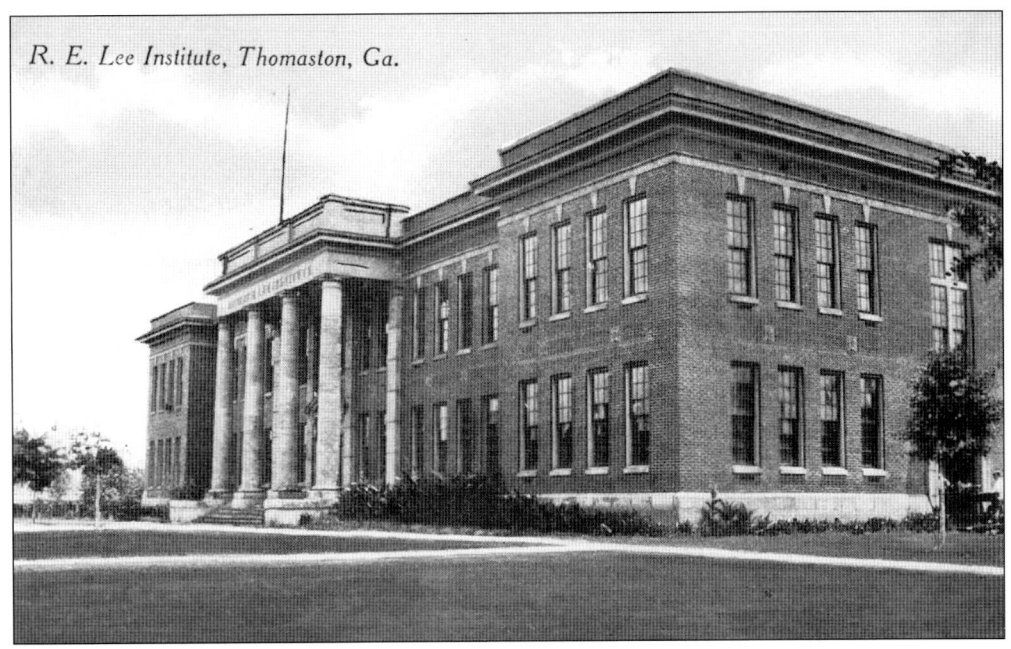

THE ROBERT E. LEE INSTITUTE IN THOMASTON, C. 1908.

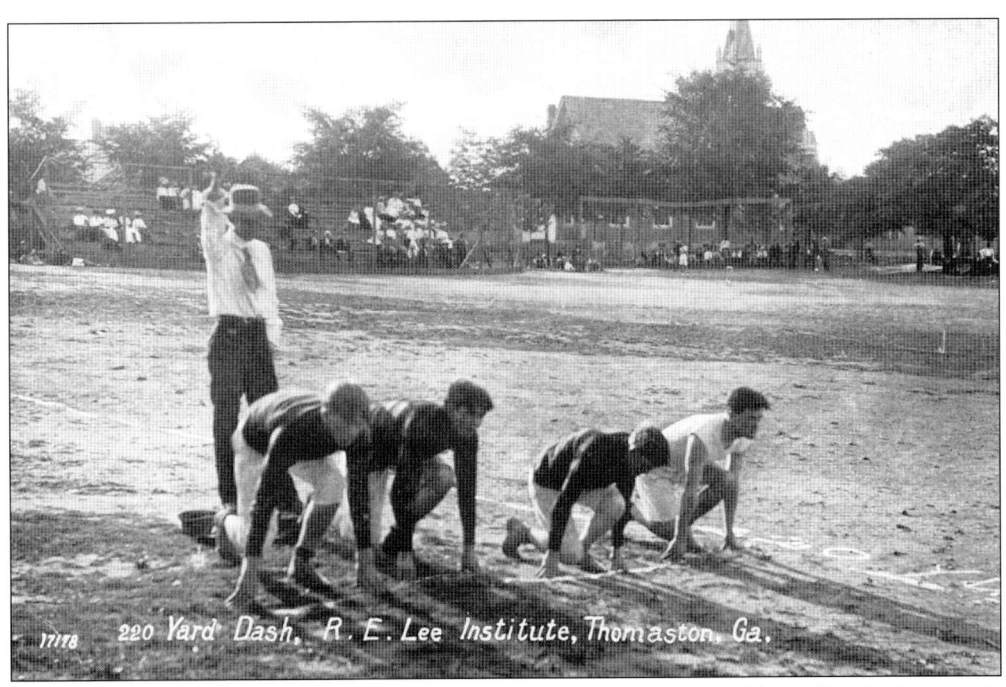

COMPETITORS IN THE 220-YARD DASH. The runners are preparing to blast off at the Robert E. Lee Institute at Thomaston, c. 1907.

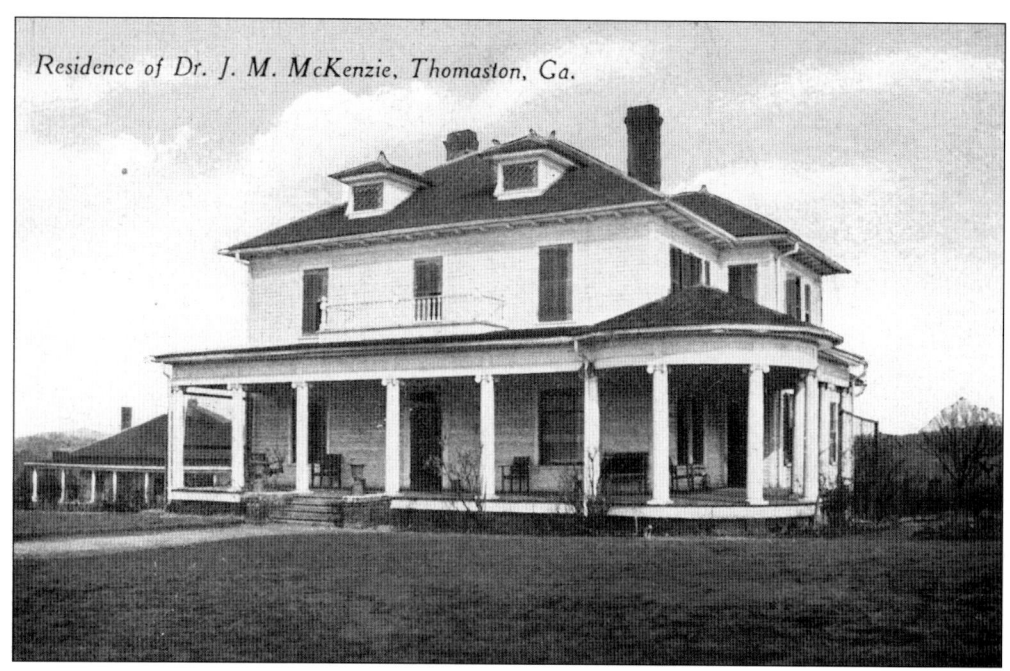

THE RESIDENCE OF DR. J.M. MCKENZIE IN THOMASTON, C. 1915.

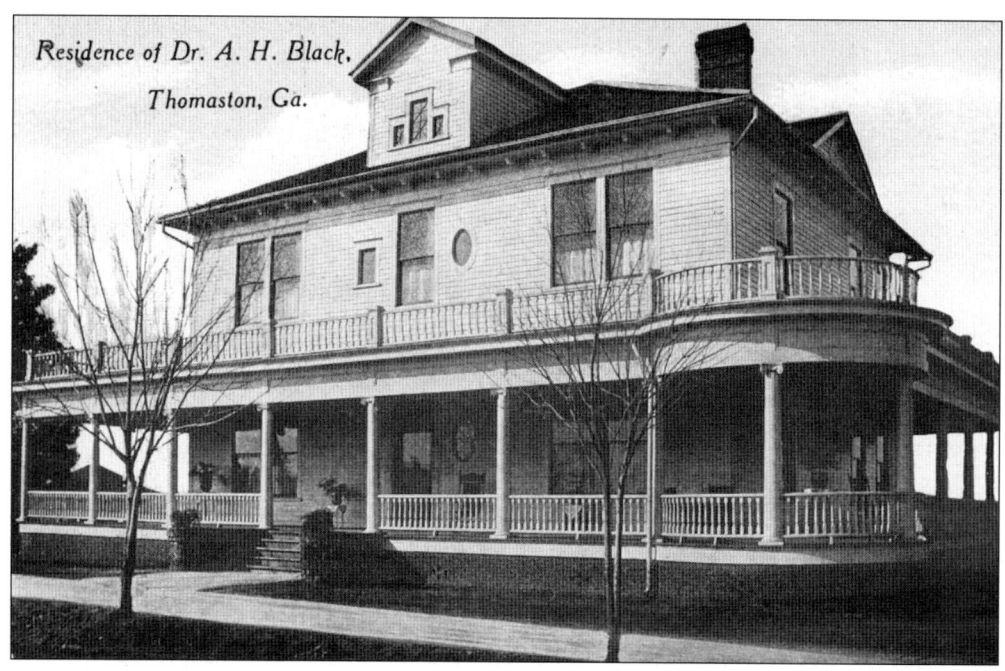

THE RESIDENCE OF DR. A.H. BLACK IN THOMASTON, C. 1915.

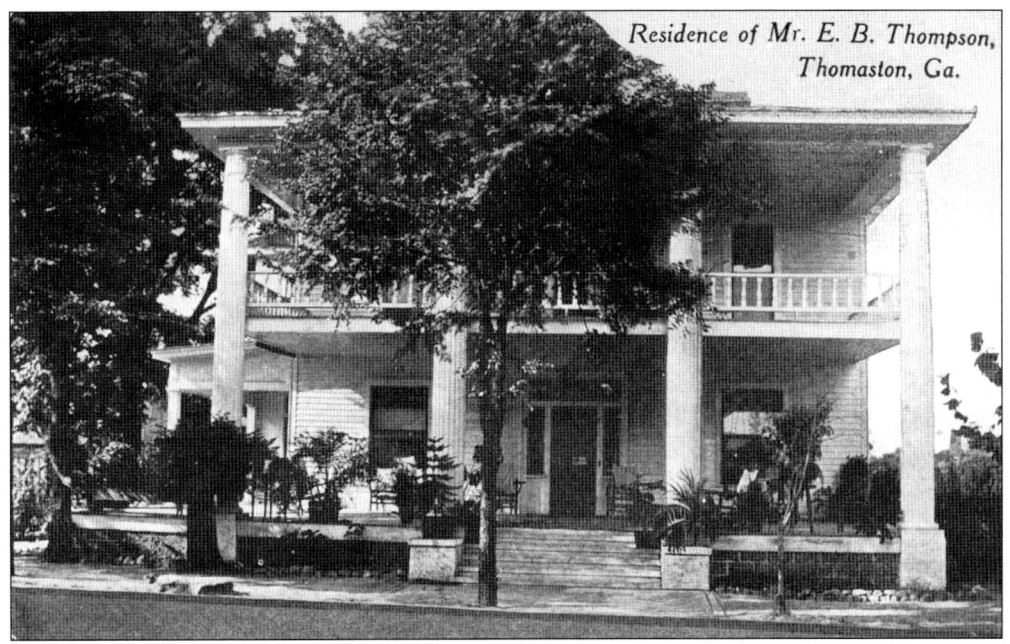

THE RESIDENCE OF MR. E.B. THOMPSON IN THOMASTON, C. 1915.

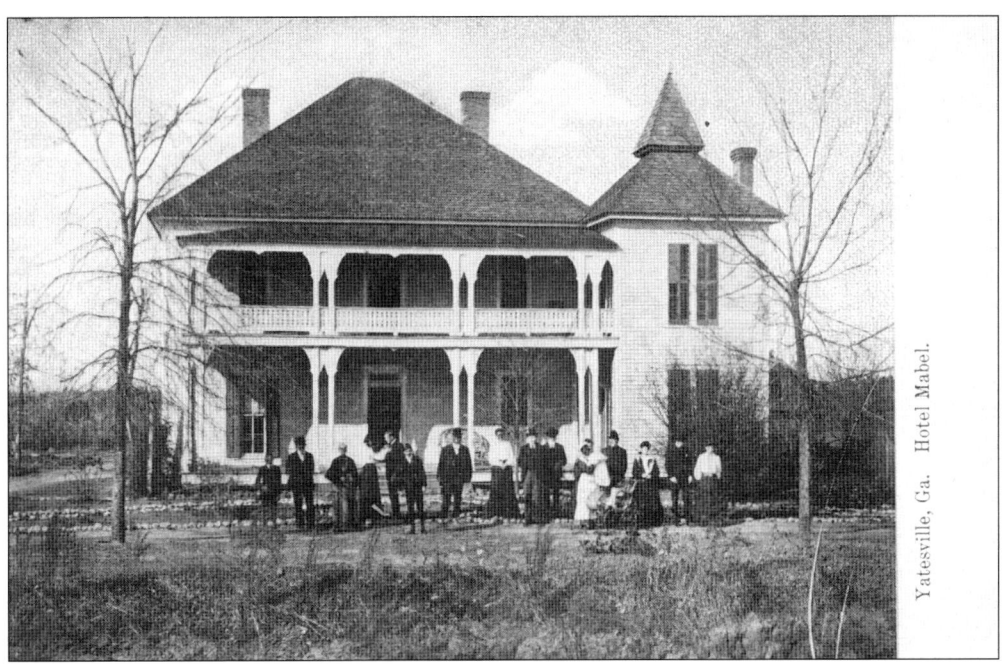

THE HOTEL MABEL IN YATESVILLE, C. 1908. The hotel was operated by Mrs. Della Waters.

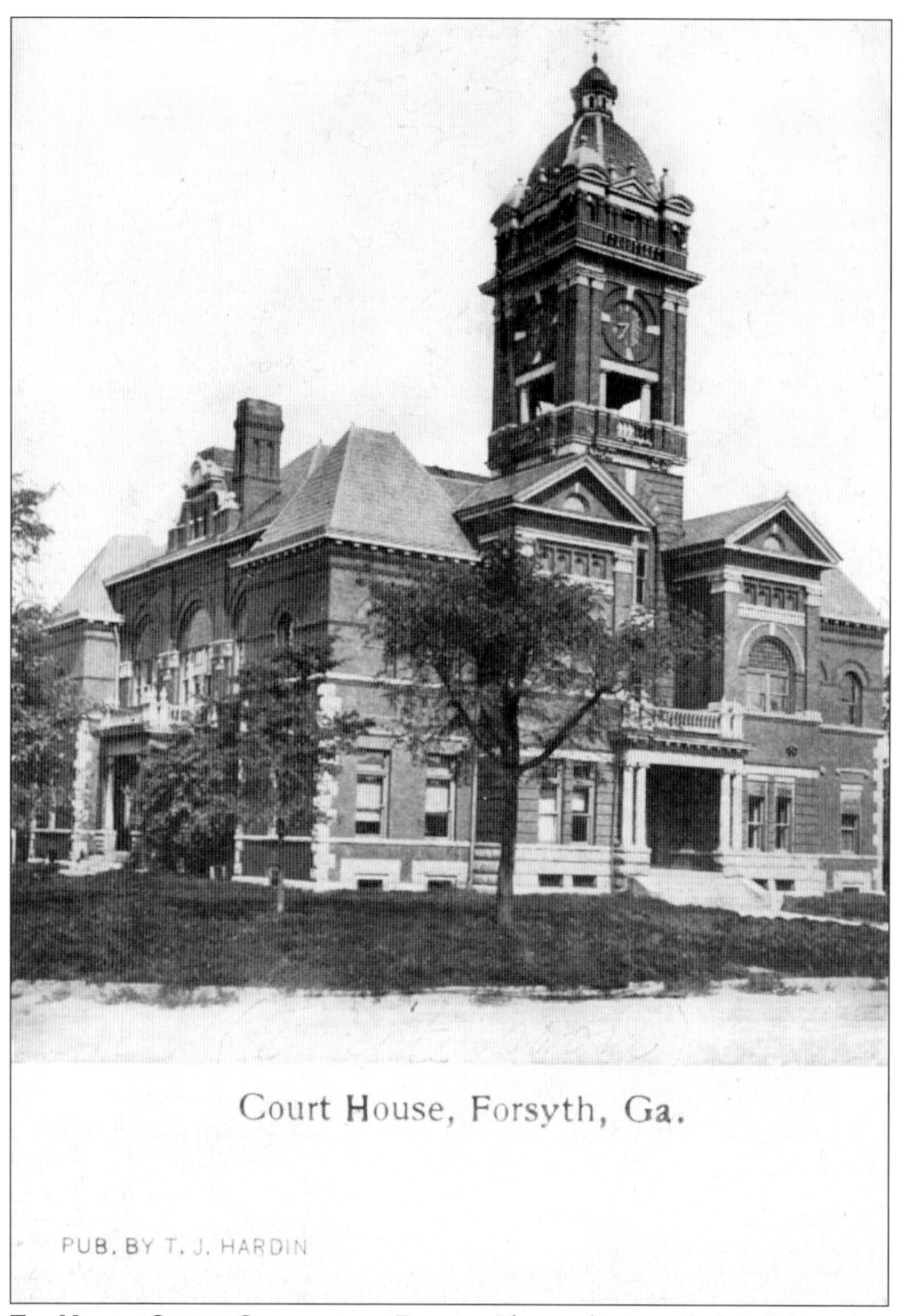

THE MONROE COUNTY COURTHOUSE IN FORSYTH. The courthouse was built in 1896 at a cost of nearly $30,000. Bruce & Morgan designed the building, which was built by the Knoxville Construction Co.

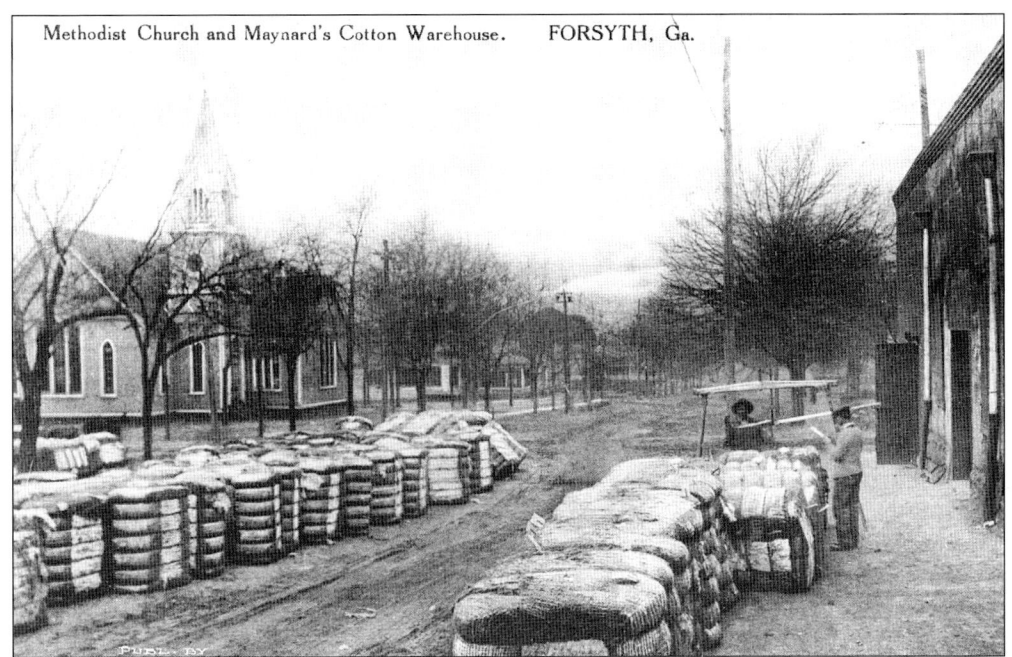

A Street Scene in Forsyth Showing the Methodist Church and Maynard's Cotton Warehouse.

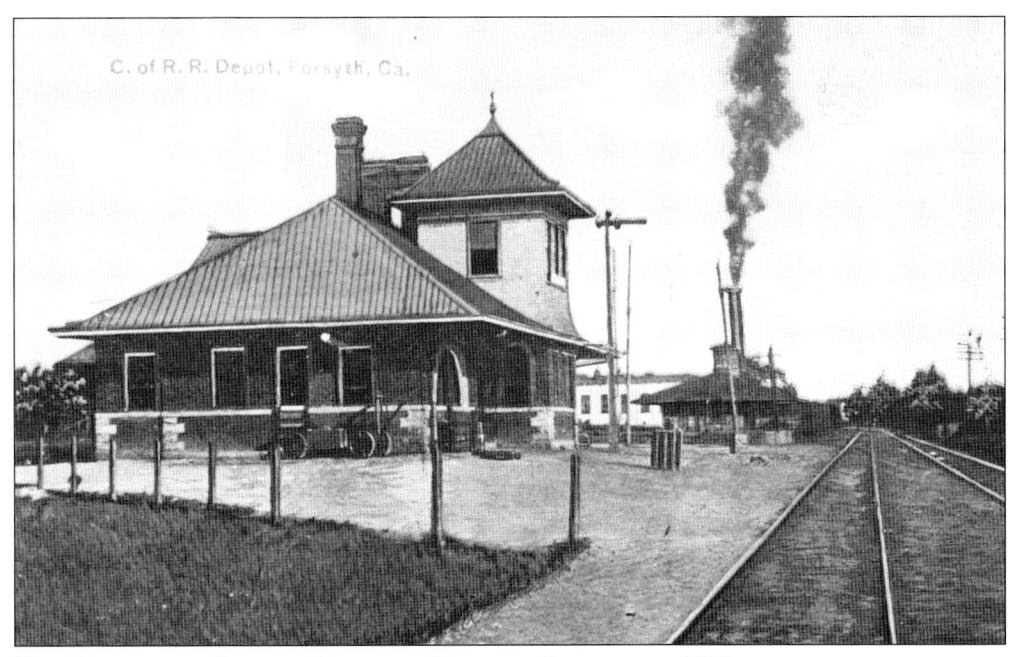

The Central of Georgia Railroad Depot in Forsyth, c. 1912.

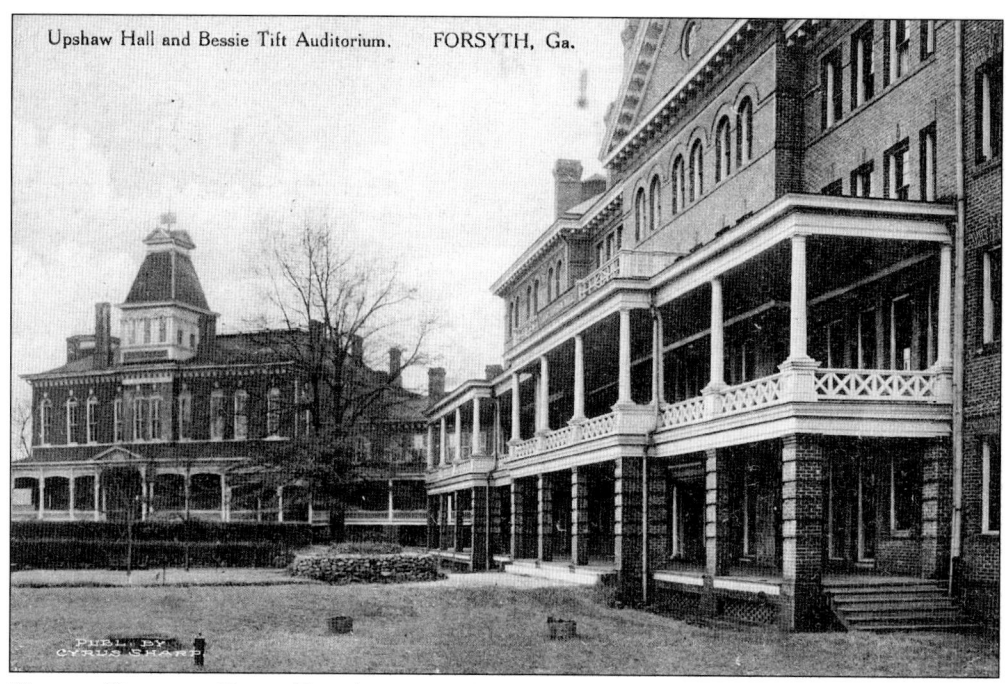

Upshaw Hall and Bessie Tift Auditorium at Bessie Tift College in Forsyth, c. 1914..

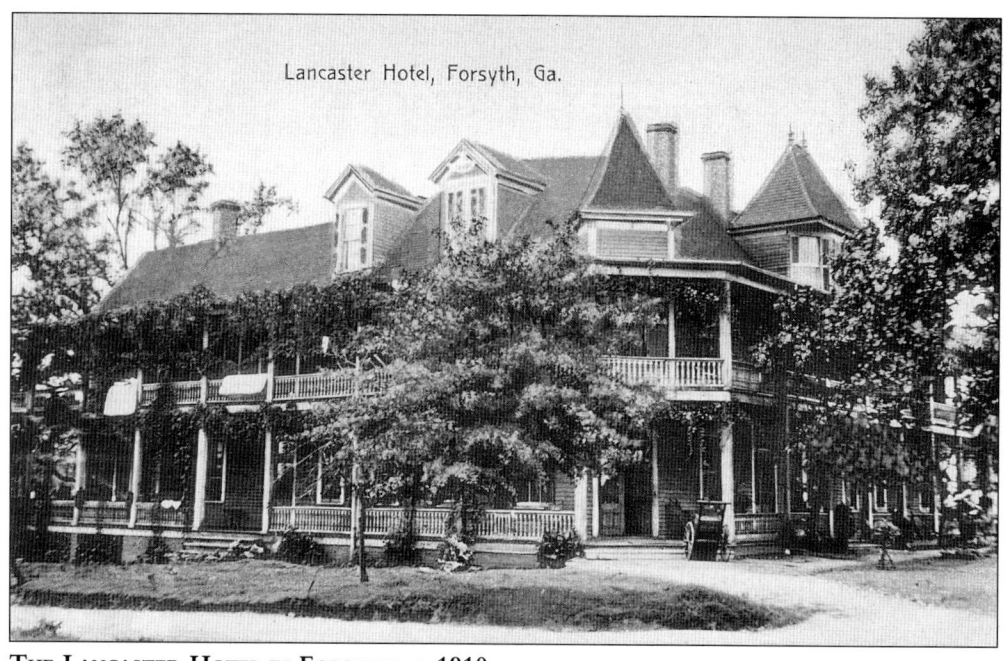

The Lancaster Hotel in Forsyth, c. 1910.

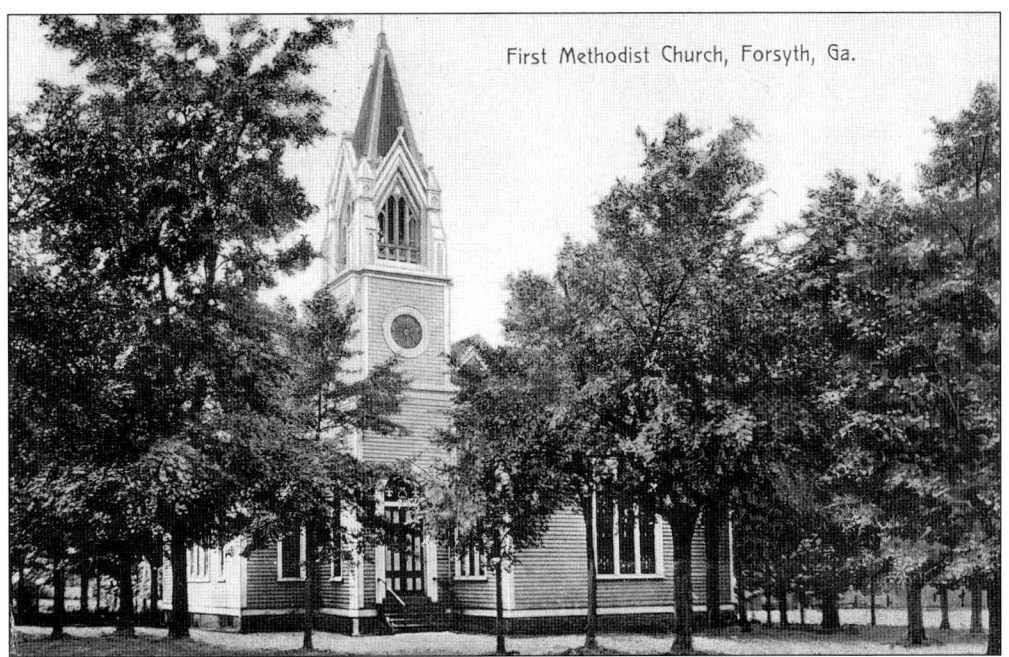

First Methodist Church in Forsyth, c. 1910..

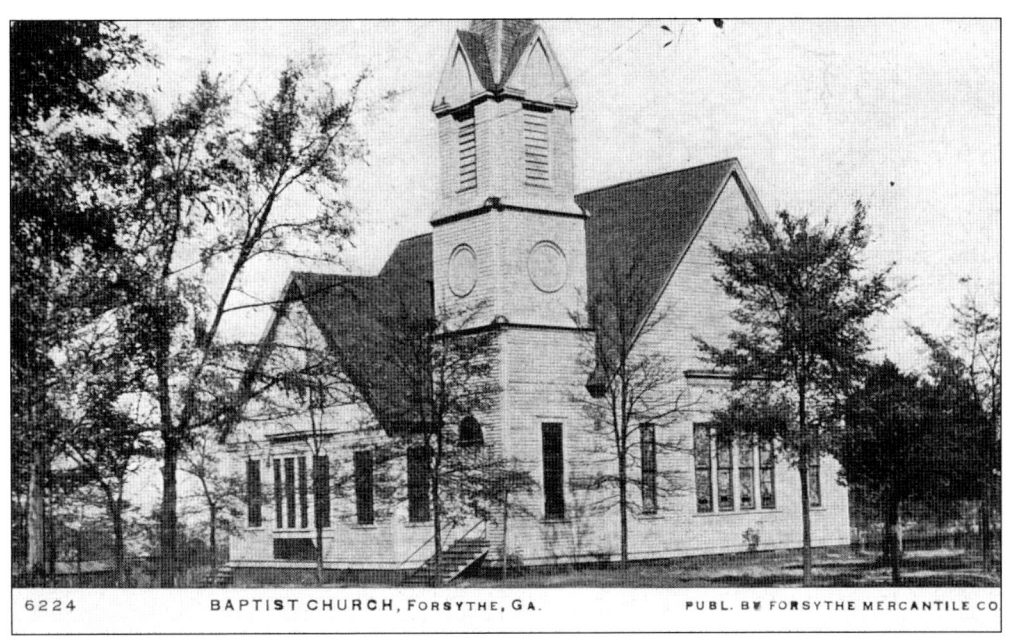

The Baptist Church in Forsyth, c. 1908..

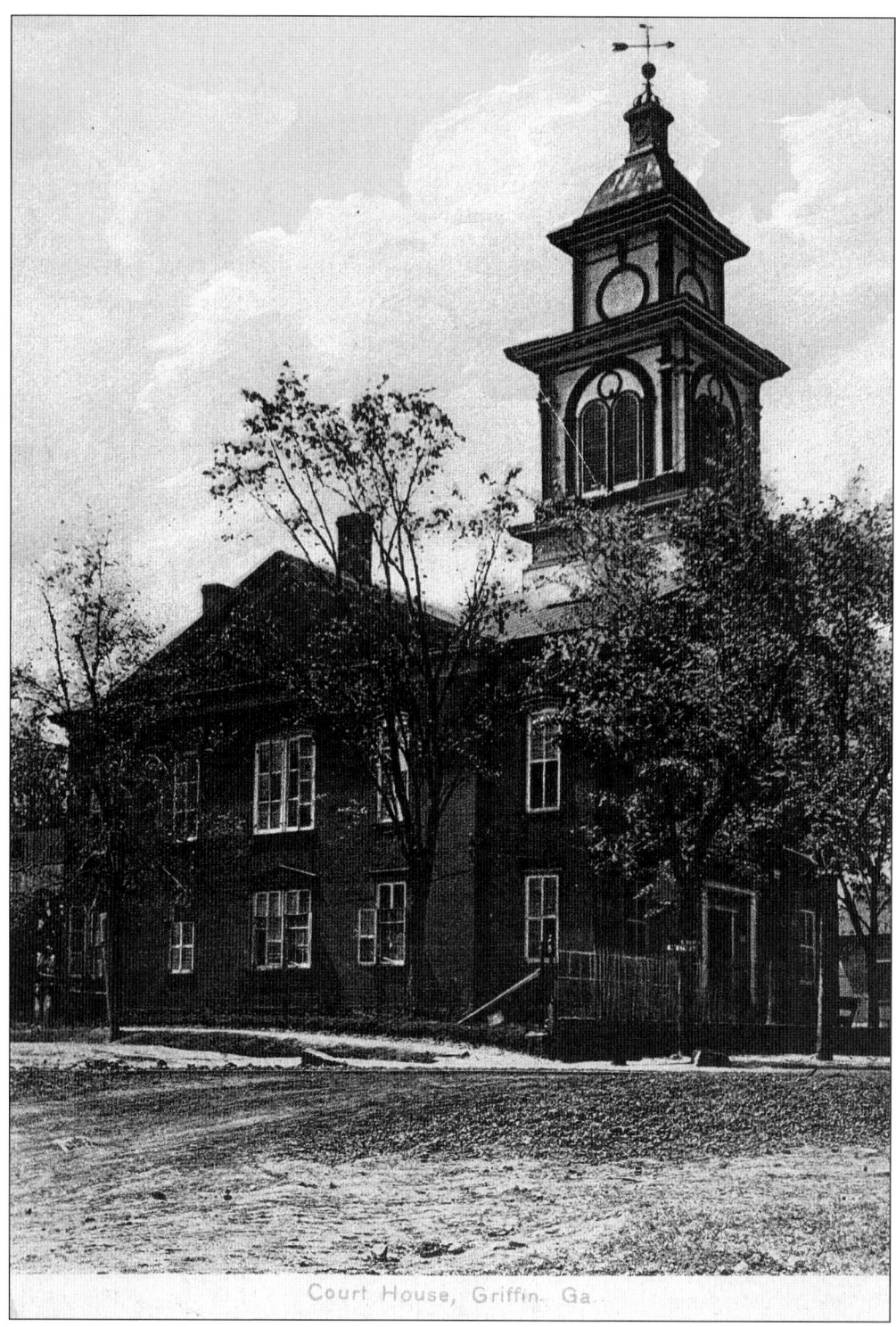

THE SPALDING COUNTY COURTHOUSE IN GRIFFIN, BUILT IN 1859. In 1910, the clock tower was removed, the building was converted to the county jail, and a new courthouse was built.

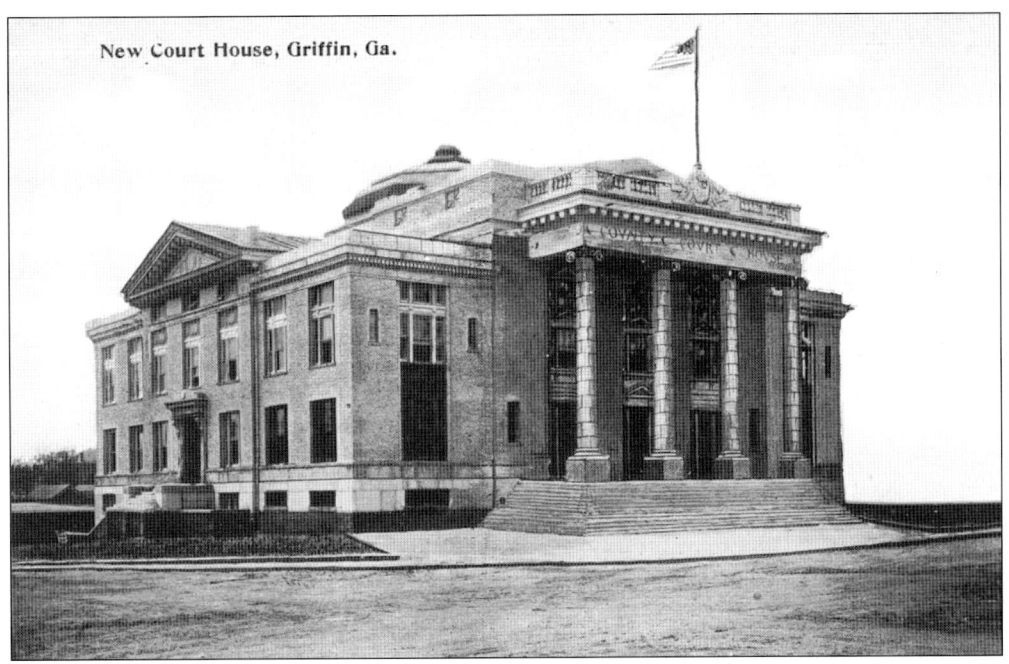

THE "NEW" SPALDING COUNTY COURTHOUSE IN FRIFFIN, BUILT IN 1911.

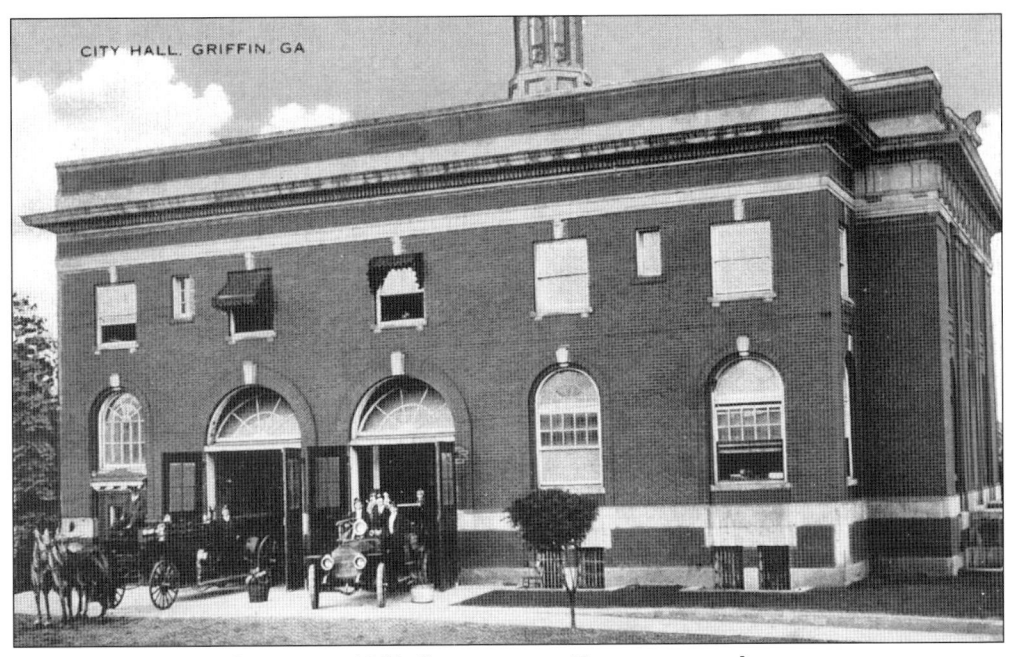

THE CITY HALL IN GRIFFIN, C. 1917, SHOWING THE FIRE-FIGHTING APPARATUS.

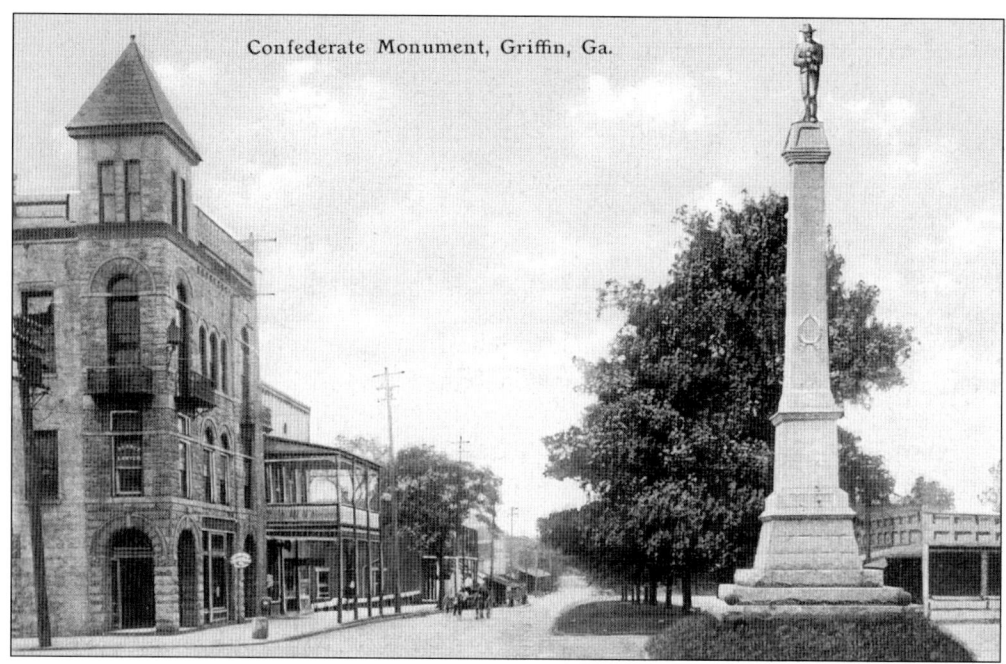

THE CONFEDERATE MONUMENT AT GRIFFIN, ERECTED IN NOVEMBER 1909 AT THE INTERSECTION OF HILL AND SOLOMAN STREETS. It was later moved to a park just outside Stonewall Cemetery.

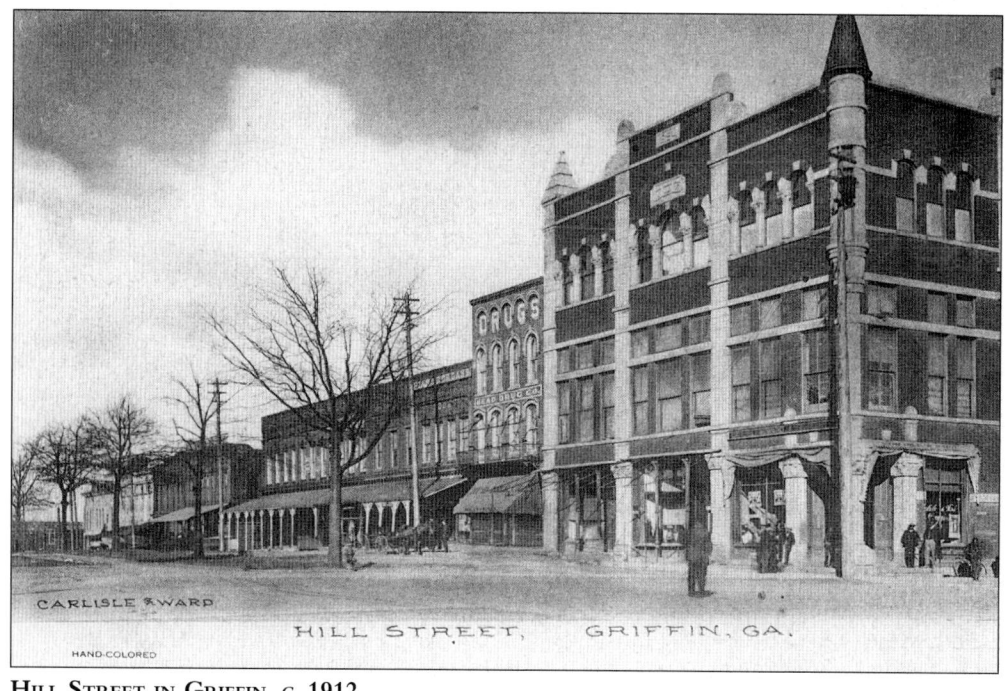

HILL STREET IN GRIFFIN, C. 1912.

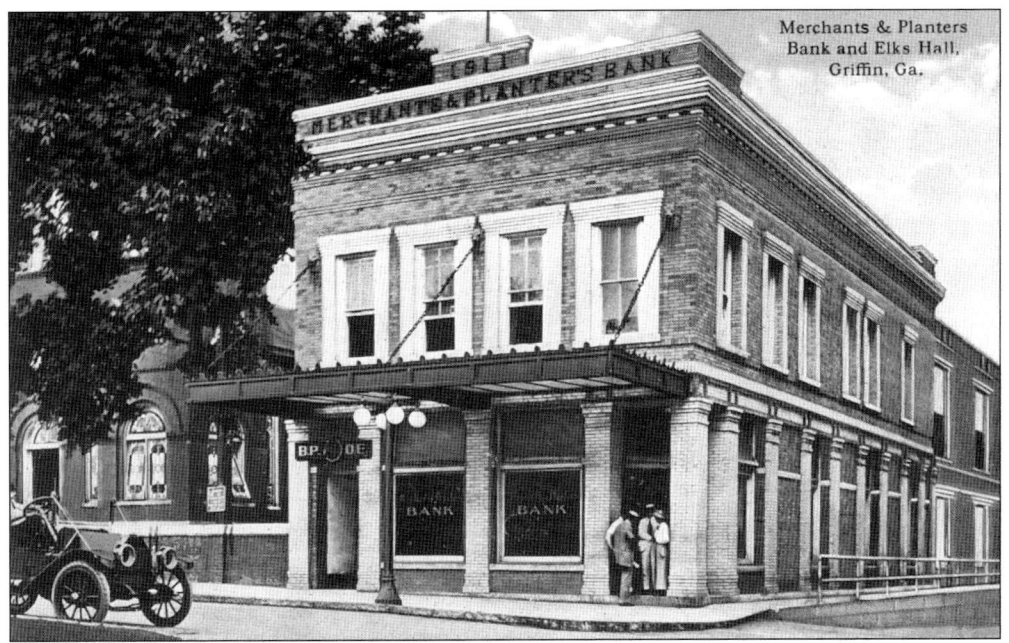

THE MERCHANTS AND PLANTERS BANK BUILDING AT 116 SOUTH HILL STREET IN GRIFFIN. The building also housed the Elks Club.

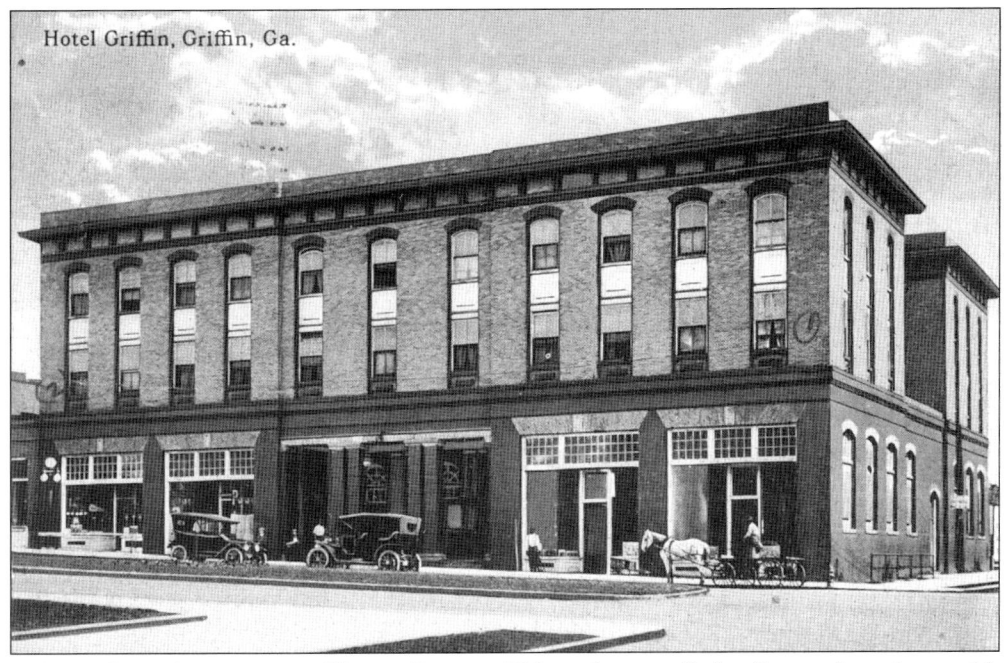

A POST CARD SHOWING THE HOTEL GRIFFIN. This card was mailed to Savannah on August 16, 1917. The message reads: "After very muddy slow trip, reached here in 3 hrs at 7 pm. If find I cannot reach Sav. tomorrow night will wire you from Statesboro. With love, W."

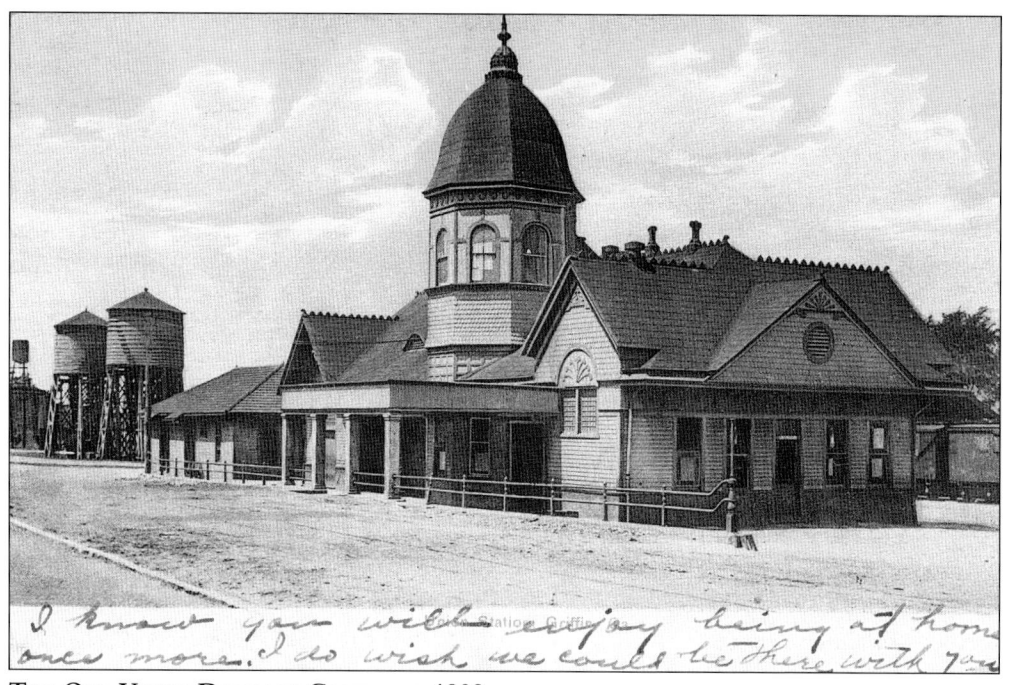
The Old Union Depot in Griffin, c. 1909.

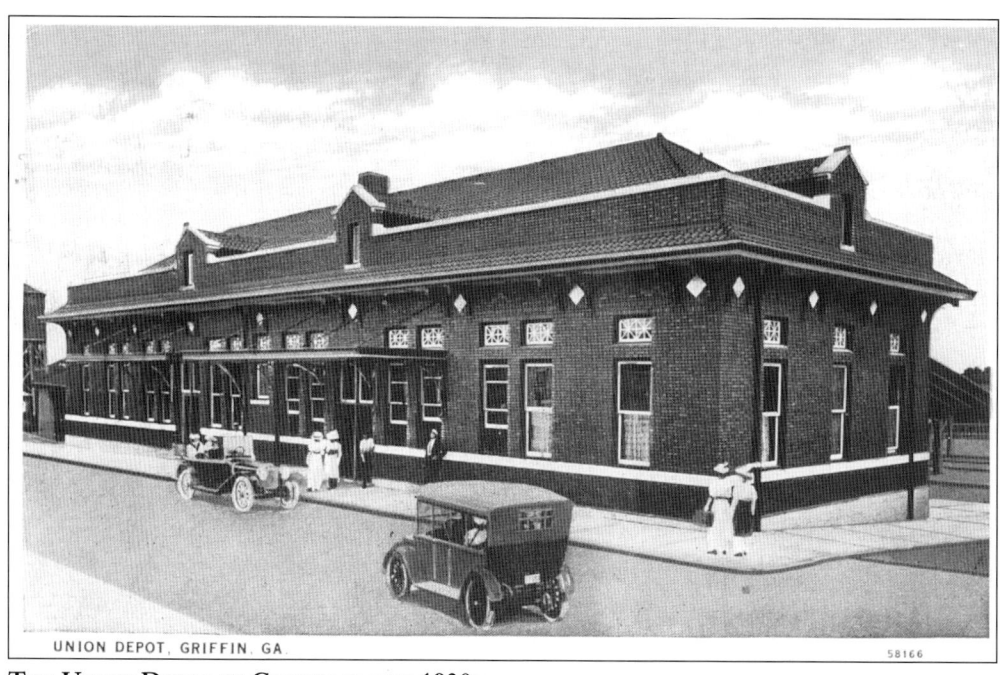
The Union Depot in Griffin in the 1930s.

BIBLIOGRAPHY

Anonymous. *1909–1910 Business and Professional Directory of the Cities and Towns of Georgia*. Atlanta, Georgia: Young and Company, 1910.

Jordan, Robert H. and J. Gregg Puster. *Courthouses in Georgia*. Editing and design by Patti Anderson and Mary Jackson. Norcross, Georgia: The Harrison Company, 1984.

Krackow, Kenneth K. *Georgia Place-Names*. Macon, Georgia: Winship Press, 1975.

McKenny, Frank M. *The Standing Army: History of Georgia's County Confederate Monuments*. Alpharetta, Georgia: W.H. Wolfe Associates, 1993.

Winn, Les R. *Ghost Trains & Depots of Georgia (1833–1933)*. Chamblee, Georgia: Big Shanty Publishing Company, 1995.

INDEX

Barnesville 105–107
Bullochville 86, 87
Butler 82
Chipley 83
Clinchfield 69
Columbus 9–22
Concord 108, 109
Durand 88
Ellaville 78
Flovilla 37, 43
Forsyth 118–121
Ft. Valley 74–77
Franklin 64
Grantville 52, 53
Greenville 88–90
Griffin 122–126
Hamilton 84–86
Hogansville 94
Indian Springs 37–42
Jackson 43–50
Jonesboro 51, 52
LaGrange 95–101
Leepope 67, 68
Locust Grove 64, 65
Macon 3–36

Manchester 91
Marshallville 71
McDonough 66
Molena 110
Montezuma 72, 73
Moreland 54
Newnan 54–61
Oglethorpe 73
Perry 69, 70
Senoia 62, 63
Talbotton 79–81
Thomaston 113–117
Warm Springs (see Bullochville)
West Point 102–104
White Sulphur Springs 92, 93
Woodland 81
Yatesville 117
Zebulon 111, 112